Move to Improve is a unique contribution to the sensory literature. It will be a great help to parents and teachers providing an understanding of the importance of movement to cognitive functioning. Most people do not understand the essential contribution that adequate neurological functioning plays in supporting higher level cognitive abilities. Society has become 2-dimentional: everything seems to be visual and auditory. Children who should be outside playing are inside on their phones, iPADs, iPODs or computers. By following some of the curricula presented in this little gem of a book, we can get kids moving again.

Lucy Jane Miller, Ph.D.,OTR
Director, Sensory Therapies and Research(STAR) Center, Denver. Colorado.

MOVE TO IMPROVE:

A SENSORY PROCESSING APPROACH TO TEACHING AND LEARNING

A guide for parents, teachers and other professionals aimed at providing a better understanding of the relationship between motor skills, sensory integration and teaching and learning.

About the Authors

Basil Howard Cert.Ed.; DASE; B.A; M.Sc.

Basil Howard is now retired after teaching in Primary Schools for 37 years, 20 years of which were as Headmaster. When he retired, he began working with his wife as an advisory consultant in Therapy Foundations for Education (a centre for children with learning difficulties) which specialises in the treatment of children with ASD, Dyslexia, DCD (Dyspraxia) and Dyscalculia. He has travelled with his wife to America - Denver, Salt Lake City and New York to extend his knowledge of various aspects of Sensory Integration by training with world experts in this field.

Amanda Howard Dip.O.T.;BSc.;MSc.; SIPT Cert.

Amanda Howard is a qualified O.T who has specialised in Sensory Integration, being one of a few Sensory Certified Therapists in Northern Ireland.

Having worked for 25 years in the NHS, she now has an independent practice which focuses on teaching and advising parents and professionals as to how to treat and manage children with developmental and motor issues who appear to be failing. She specialises in assessing and treating children with sensory problems, co-ordination and balance issues, handwriting and organisational difficulties, attachment and emotional challenges and recognised diagnoses such as Autism, Downs syndrome and Cerebral Palsy.

She works towards agreed, sustainable outcomes with parents and teachers, having raised the expectations and awareness of potential in children who are having difficulties and are perceived as failing.

She has worked with thousands of children, helping them to become happier, more sociable and more focused on learning so that they may enjoy school life better and become more independent.

Acknowledgements

We wish to thank our children and friends for their assistance and advice at various stages of production. A special thanks to Nancy Zeiders and Denise Fleming for their painstaking proof reading. Thank you all for your help and encouragement. We also wish to thank our grandchildren and other children who helped with the photographs. We wish to mention Kevin, our graphic designer, for his patience and long suffering in implementing the changes and help in getting the book published.

MOVE TO IMPROVE:

A SENSORY PROCESSING APPROACH TO TEACHING AND LEARNING

A guide for parents, teachers and other professionals aimed at providing a better understanding of the relationship between motor skills, sensory processing and teaching and learning.

Dedication

This book is dedicated to the numerous children and families, teachers and therapists from all over Ireland, England and the Isle of Man it has been our privilege to work with. We have learned much from the parents and professionals we have met and welcomed the opportunity to share intervention ideas and impart the 'what to do'.

Basil and Amanda Howard

Contents

Chapter 5

Chapter 6

Chapter 7

Chapter 8

Chapter 9

Chapter 10

Foreword

This book was initially written as a response to the early identification of motor (movement) issues in children at nursery schools, such as Dyspraxia or Developmental Coordination Delay (DCD). The underlying rationale was to give parents awareness of early interventions and make it easier for them to understand the types of therapeutic input that can make a major difference in their child's life.

We, at the Therapy Foundations for Education clinic, have used these treatments and interventions with positive outcomes in a wide variety of children, including those with Downs syndrome, Cerebral Palsy and many other varied syndromes. As you read this book you will discover we are not addressing "labels" which are commonly given to children, but instead the neurological difficulties with which these children present. Learning involves neural processing and is determined by the senses. We have come to the conclusion that all of us, regardless of any difficulty, learn in the same order and in the same way; we may be wired differently but we are constructed the same.

Our initial learning is based on the maturity of senses, and it is focused at the brain stem and limbic system level. Sensory learning is, therefore, the building blocks for our motor skills, postural mechanisms, regulation, emotional stability, perceptual skills, visual motor skills, auditory motor skills, problem solving, sequencing, reading, writing, spelling and number work. As myelination (a process that allows faster transmission of information and more complex brain processes to take place) occurs, we then begin to develop higher level skills until, about the age of 5 years, our higher order or cognitive processing skills develop. (See Developmental Building Blocks in appendices).

Higher order skills include reflection and prediction, the capacity to learn, remember and make implications, solve problems, communicate and develop socially and emotionally. These types of higher learning skills are identified in Bloom's Taxonomy of Learning Domains (1956).

Children themselves often know that they have difficulties. What they can't understand is that if they are clever in some aspects of school work, why do they find it so difficult to perform well in others? They are aware that they have equal or greater ability in some areas than other children and, while some children apparently find the tasks easy, they themselves have to struggle to keep up. They tend to focus on what they can't do rather on what they can do.

The main focus of the book was originally intended to be in the area of motor function. This was to include both gross and fine motor skills and the ways in which children might be assisted. However, we have decided to include body awareness, primitive reflexes and the senses, since all of these issues are so interrelated.

On the more technical side, there are significant publications addressing the correctness of the terms used to describe a child's motor difficulties. Some academics take the approach that defining the motor aspect of a child's performance is exclusive to motor-based diagnoses, whilst others prefer the comorbidity approach, i.e. conditions which can occur together.

As this book is focused on improved outcomes, any reference to motor challenges is addressed, not only to a DCD or dyspraxia diagnosis (European Academy of Childhood Disability 2011 does not recognise DCD and Dyspraxia as two separate entities but refers to all movement impairment as DCD) but also to include, Autistic

Spectrum Disorder (ASD), Attention Deficit Hyperactivity Disorder (ADHD) and other comorbid neurological difficulties.

We explore the impact of the five senses plus two more systems (the vestibular and proprioceptive), how these are linked together and the difficulties some children experience with the visual, auditory and tactile systems. Then we demonstrate the integration of these topics by specifically focusing on handwriting. Two additional chapters on eating and sleeping disorders are included because of the significant impact they have on family life. Finally, the Appendix includes helpful motor activities set out as lesson plans which nursery and "early years" primary school teachers may use to identify and treat children with early motor difficulties in a classroom situation.

It is our fervent wish that this book will enable and empower parents, teachers, and therapists to complement each other in the field of sensory processing. In addition, we trust that those parents who have some understanding of sensory issues will be aided in relating this information to the difficulties their children are experiencing.

Many of the children who come to the clinic for help have, what we might call, "locked–in behaviour patterns." These exhibit themselves in that the children can't speak or express themselves as freely as they would like, and they are imprisoned in an inner world where fear rules and the desire to flee dominates. Children on their own can sometimes find a way to push a hand through their prison bars, or maybe find a way to escape temporarily from this internal realm, but without help, they are destined to continually experience difficulty. An older child, when looking back on his early experience, described it like being in a cage and, when he wanted to do a particular activity said, "Something within me tells me I can't do it and people on the outside tell me not to do it."

These are the children who are trying extremely hard to keep up with the others in the educational journey to success, but find that they are hindered in some way. They are the way they are and it's not their fault – it's not anyone's fault! We don't feel the necessity to pigeonhole these children with labels. Rather we endeavour to understand their individual needs in order to provide the best solutions possible.

Our principal task as therapists and educators is to enter the child's world to discover what these difficulties are. Then we need to explain the difficulties to the children, parents and others. We also need to find ways to provide the keys to unlock access to a more level educational playing field so that the children may become happier within themselves.

Some people mistakenly categorise these children as: lazy, not trying, inattentive or unintelligent. Nothing could be further from the truth. They are invariably trying twice as hard as others in their year group and, even though they may have sensory processing problems, they somehow find strategies to enable them to cope at some level with the sensory issues and still learn something, in spite of their difficulties.

Every one of us has sensory issues of one kind or another. For example, do I prefer: spicy or salty foods, noisy or quiet environments, use or not use lifts and escalators, wear or not wear woollen clothing? The big difference for most of us is that we have learned how to handle our sensory drives and are able to make adjustments to avoid feeling apprehension or discomfort. Similarly, some children want to be continually on the go, while others don't move much. Some like crunchy foods while others can't bear them in their mouths. Some love rough and tumble games while still others can't even tolerate being touched

The significant issues are: how do we find the keys that will give these children a greater sense of freedom and what, if anything, can we do to make their lives, both academically and socially, more bearable?

Please note that we have used masculine as opposed to feminine pronouns throughout the text for the sake of brevity and also because there is a higher incidence of male children with these difficulties.

Parents and teachers reading this book will notice headings at the beginning of most of the chapters which are there to help you decide how relevant the chapter is to your particular child. Should the Red Flag issues be typical of your child's behaviour then that particular chapter will be of special interest to you. On the other hand, if the issues in the Green for Go section seem more appropriate and are more typical of your child's level of development, then the chapter will have less relevance and you may wish to proceed further. Of course, any of the chapters may be of general interest to you, especially if you are a teacher and have concerns about a number of children in your class.

To Begin With: Relationship and Engagement with Children

The importance of developing a good relationship and spontaneous engagement with the child you are working with cannot be over stressed. From a child's perspective, he may not know what is expected from him as he enters a new environment and comes for assessment. Such questions as, where is he going, what will the building be like, who is he going to meet, what will it be like and what will he be expected to do may be in his head. Obviously, he will go where his parents take him, but unless they have fully explained what is going to happen when he gets there, he will have little idea of what he is facing. It is helpful if the parent can discuss these issues with him before he comes in order to set his mind at rest and also ensure that the child is not hungry, ill, tired or overly anxious on coming for an assessment as these can have a big impact on the outcome.

On meeting the child for the first time the professional should be aiming to put the child at ease. The therapist's voice and facial expression should express welcome showing either enthusiasm or a calm approach depending on the initial reaction and observation of the child's responses.

Before launching into the theory, intervention and different models of practice employed when working with children, it is important to consider our own attitude to the child we are working with and our purpose for seeing or engaging with the child. The environment should capture the child's attention as being safe containing items or objects of interest, i.e. toys, swings, colourful equipment from which the child has the freedom to choose to engage with; opportunity driven rather than directed by an adult. The freedom to choose and not being adult led allows the child to feel in control. This will increase the child's intrinsic motivation and demonstrate his personal interests to the therapist. In so doing the child may feel free to develop his natural inquisitiveness and help establish his confidence. Frequently children will choose objects to play with that are familiar to them and they have the idea of what to do with them. The therapist should wait for the child to approach her rather than the therapist approach the child. It is then easier for the discerning therapist to tap into the child's interest and engage in the child's world in parallel play. This allows for reciprocal engagement and playing together working towards "the just right challenge".

The therapist should make the experience inviting and allay any fears the child may have. It may be necessary to take time to put the child at ease and not rush in to begin the session.

Initially you (teacher, psychologist, support worker, therapist or any one of an extensive range of professionals in a variety of Health Care or Educational roles whose sphere of activity is working with children) may be responding to a referral, providing an intervention in a clinic or school base or in the child's home on a community home visit.

The great comedian, W.C. Fields, is credited with the line, "Never work with children or animals." He probably had the fear of being upstaged. One can only surmise he just did not have the temperament, patience or appreciation of the fun of doing so.

When working with children in whatever capacity, you need to rely on your clinical skills and knowledge about development including motor, language, social, emotional and cognitive skills. It is also useful to have an understanding of culture, family dynamics and lifestyle, parental expectations and the natural environment of the child. We not only need to be aware of the child's needs, but also the goals of the family and their expectations of the outcomes of our interventions.

Just completing a formal assessment can all too often be the main focus or mission when working with referrals. Many have experienced the time constraints of formal assessment and ticking the boxes where the outcome is based on measurable performance. It is possible to become too focused on the tools in the assessment kit and getting through an assessment without fully engaging with the child or being sensitive to reducing his initial anxiety. For some children who may be extremely anxious we may need to be motivating them to enjoy the process.

We may become the "experts" and set goals and session schemes but as Occupational Therapists our intervention should be child led and focused on the needs we identify in the child we are engaging with. Where the child is engaged in play, the therapist gives the child the opportunity and the just-right challenge to learn through trial and error. They should feel safe in being either successful or unsuccessful and be supported in trying tasks a second, or even a third time, and encouraged to follow the modelling and instruction of the therapist.

The experienced therapist with sound clinical reasoning skills will intuitively recognise the need to establish a relationship with the child prior to launching into assessment or intervention. In doing so you allow the child to feel more comfortable and secure with you and with their performance.

The "Floortime" approach emphasises the necessity of establishing a relationship when working with children. Floortime was created by Dr. Stanley Greenspan for children on the autism spectrum and also those with developmental delays. It gives Therapists and Parents the skills to connect with children and encourage them to reach their potential. The goals of the Greenspan Floortime Approach are to Deepen Relationships, Develop Communications, Expand Thinking and Learning and Promote Positive Behaviour. It is known as "Floortime" because it is all about getting down to the child's level and working with them on the floor.

The Son Rise Programme, which is an American based programme, the principles of which are well documented on the internet, begins with the issue of relationship. They teach the importance of your attitude to the child and the desire to bond with the child, always remembering that children with Autism have difficult creating relationships with people and are challenged socially. They recommend the idea of using Energy, Excitement and Enthusiasm to engage the child and motivate them to observe, mirror and interact with the therapist/parent in the playroom.

Lucy Jane Miller at the STAR Institute in Denver, which is the premier treatment, research and education centre for children and adults with Sensory Processing Disorder (SPD), commends the value of having a sound Sensory Integration base and understanding the role of regulation and arousal whilst focusing on developing a relationship and engaging the child. The focus once more is not only the intervention method we employ but the way we go about getting the child to work with us and enjoy the Therapy experience. There is no better outcome from a therapy session than for a child to ask, "When can I come back?"

As therapists we are so often involved in hands on practice where we facilitate and promote patterns of movement, body adjustments and posture-directed challenges. We need to be energetic, facilitating and sensitive to the child's attitude, fears and personality to engage them initially. Engagement, regardless of the academic ability and skill of the therapist is essential to promoting positive therapy outcomes.

We all work better when we perceive positive attitudes and encouragement, feel valued and not judged and do not fear criticism or the possibility of being laughed at. Children are no different and will learn better when they feel safe, confident and encouraged. They learn better through trial and error whilst developing their exploratory skills and ability to question. Children need to use their bodies in the learning process and, as therapists, we are aware of the need to have established hierarchical motor skills, bilateral coordination and motor sequencing and good use of hand function.

Getting down and modelling the use of purpose- directed therapy equipment such as rollers, barrels, large therapy balls, suspended swings, zip lines and climbing apparatus allows us the opportunity to have fun and engage with the children we work with. As Occupational Therapists, working with children regardless of their challenges or needs, "we put the fun in function".

Chapter 1

The Link Between Motor Skills and Cognitive Ability

The Big Idea

There is a definite link between movement and learning.

Patterns of movement are essential to all learning. Whilst moving, we are learning how to learn.

The Academic Viewpoint

Movement is "the neurological process that organizes sensation from one's own body and from the environment and makes it possible to use the body effectively within the environment." (Sensory Integration and Learning Disorders, 1972)

Movement which is active:
Child climbing a fence
Child on roundabout
Child crawling

Movement which is passive:
Digestion of food
Circulation of the blood
Breathing

How could I have missed it? Was it because I was completely ignorant of the facts despite having spent almost forty years in education? Had I, consciously or otherwise underestimated, as I have now come to recognise, its very important place in education? Surely I must have come across it somewhere, or someone must have mentioned it during the many varied and in-depth studies I have taken over the years. Whatever the reason, I must hold up my hands and say, "Guilty as charged."

What AM I talking about? Simply this…. that movement is inseparably linked to cognitive development and learning.

Piaget, Rudolf Steiner, Montessori, Gardner and the like placed great emphasis on movement within their theories of education, but I tended to undervalue its importance. I did not view it seriously, but instead thought of these educators as being in the side waters rather than the mainstream of education. And yes, during initial teacher training we had courses in P.E. and Health Education, but I tended to see these subjects as a relatively unimportant part of the curriculum- a "fun for the children" subject, having little, or even worse, no bearing on the central issues of school activity, namely: English and Maths. What we then called the three R's (reading, writing and arithmetic). A real dinosaur or what? I can remember some thirty or so years ago hearing about what sounded like a crackpot idea propounding the notion that "crawling as a child" was of great significance to educational development. I can now say with all humility that my views have changed dramatically. This was in no small measure due to my affiliation with a paediatric occupational therapist, with qualifications and wide experience in the field of Sensory Integration and Sensory Processing and who, incidentally, has since become my wife and co-author of this book.

As we examine what might be called the elaborate interplay between the brain and the body, we come to one compelling notion: movement is essential to learning, to all learning.

Movement is taking place all the time within our bodies even when at rest; food is being digested, lungs are expanding and deflating, the heart is beating, blood is circulating and nerves are transmitting signals. Perhaps like me, you never thought of "movement" in this way before. You may have thought of movement as being more deliberate and less to do with the autonomic nervous system. However, it is movement nevertheless, whether active or passive, that initiates our mental capacities, integrating new experiences and information into our neural networks. It is vital to all our actions and the way we express our learning and come to an understanding of ourselves. Since movement is so important, I wonder if it is given the place it so rightly deserves in the rearing of children and, in particular, how they are taught?

Evidence for the Link

So you're still not fully convinced? Does it still seem like a hare-brained idea? Well, let me take you back to the first sensations of movement in the womb. It is in the womb that we experience the laws of gravity as our mothers rhythmically move about, walking, talking and breathing. Here are the beginnings of our understanding of language, maths and science. Our very first understanding of the physical world is linked to movement. After birth, as the baby's head begins to move, so the sensory organs of the eyes and ears are aligned to factors in the environment. Head movements allow an infant to pick up different scents, feel the wind blowing on his face, turn towards sounds which will form internal memories for protection or allow him to follow the movement of objects with his eyes. The eye muscles make small movements which enable him to focus on objects either near at hand or further away. Movements of the hands allow him to play with, touch and explore his world and, in turn, give expression to his emotions.

It is movement that permits our faces to express emotions such as anger, happiness, sadness, and allows us to be understood by others. At a later stage, facial muscles allow us to put words and thoughts into action. Through complex muscular activity, skills are built and therefore learning progresses. Our motor memory (this includes conceiving the idea, thinking of a plan and then using the idea to execute the task) allows us to follow a developmental sequence, i.e. lift the head, develop strength in the neck and back, roll over, sit with support, sit unsupported, crawl, kneel, stand with assistance, stand unsupported, walk with assistance, and finally, walk. These indeed are the major developmental milestones in movement for approximately the first eighteen months of life.

Learning may be thought of as movement which is integrated with our senses of seeing, feeling and hearing. Movement is crucial to so many aspects of higher order learning. For example, handling and feeling the shape of a 3D letter or number is essential to imprinting it on our perceptual motor memory so that it can be recognised in a variety of orientations and then represented in the movement of writing. Equally, speech requires the coordination of many fine motor skills – movements of face, tongue and eye. Memory is best stimulated by recalling the physical action or sequence of actions by means of a drawing or illustration, rather than just recalling spoken words.

By studying our earliest brain development we can come to a better understanding of how movement assists learning. As a baby develops and grows, going from lying passively in the womb to walking within the first eighteen months (which is a truly miraculous development), so the nerve networks undergo similar massive changes. The early movements of the neonate are primarily involuntary in nature and as such are beyond the control of the child. These reflex movements include the Moro or Startle Reflex for survival. This reflex is stimulated by sudden noise or movement, bright light, heat or pain. The arms thrust quickly away from the body, followed by a cry or sharp intake of breath when startled before the arms return back to the body. Another reflex is the Palmer Reflex which is exhibited when a child takes a firm hold of your finger when you apply a light touch to the palm of the hand. A third reflex is the Sucking or Rooting Reflex evident when a child will begin to suck on your finger if placed at the side of the mouth. Less well known reflexes, though still very important, are the Symmetrical Tonic Neck Reflex (STNR), the Tonic Labyrinthine Reflex (TLR), the Asymmetrical Tonic Neck Reflex (ATNR) the Landau Reflex, the Oculo and Labyrinthine Head Righting Reflexes and finally, the Amphibian Reflex.

These primitive reflexes are automatic and brain stem directed. They should have a limited lifespan (up to two and a half years with the exception of the head righting and amphibian reflexes which should emerge and are lifelong) and eventually be controlled by the higher brain centres. A voluntary, as opposed to an automatic response, gives the infant more control and allows the child to interact more effectively with his environment.

The emergence of primitive reflexes at different stages of early development allows for the maturation of head control, posture and the ability to move dynamically with control and stability. Some transitional reflexes play an important role in the move from primitive, survival instincts to postural control and motor development. Initially the STNR (developing at around six months) allows the baby to get up on hands and knees ready for crawling. This reflex allows for 4 point kneeling that is not dependant on the position of the head. If the STNR is not fully integrated the child will be a bottom shuffler. Children who have not actively crawled on all fours will most likely have an unintegrated STNR. The development of postural control is dependent on the inhibition and the integration of these primitive or early reflexes. These reflexes and their impact on development will be discussed in greater detail later.

A wider range of movement prolongs the opportunity for the sensory apparatus (ears, eyes, nose, mouth and skin) to take advantage of environmental factors. Opportunities to develop the repertoire, e.g. lift the head to see and hear, are very liberating. On the other hand, equipment which restricts movement does not encourage development. These include baby strollers and bucket-like car seats, particularly those where the infant is facing away from the parent. His ability to see far and near develops by about 6 months and so, in the early stages of childhood he is not actively developing his vision because he is looking away from, and not at the parent. Obviously car seats are essential for the child's safety while being driven around but many come as part of a buggy system which holds the child as though in a bucket and is restrictive of movement.

Key Points from Chapter 1

- Movement is essential to all learning.
- Movement takes place even when we are at rest.
- Movement begins in the womb.
- Facial movement allows us to express feelings.
- Motor memory and primitive reflexes are important for motor development.
- The survival reflexes need to be fully integrated to allow full development of the postural reflexes, which are necessary to allow further motor development.

Chapter 2

And so, to Crawling

The Big Idea

Crawling is one of the most important ways in which the two hemispheres of the brain learn to communicate with each other early on.

The Academic Viewpoint

Crawling is a unique experience in many ways. "It's a real step up for co-ordination because it's the first opportunity to practice bilateral coordination - using the arms and legs in reciprocal movements," says Jane Case-Smith who was director of the division of occupational therapy at Ohio State University's School of Allied Medical Professions in Columbus and an early-intervention specialist. "This skill is used in activities like getting dressed, self-feeding and sports. A child who sidesteps crawling may have more of a struggle catching up." *Do Babies Need to Crawl (2010)*

Red Flag Issues

- Bum shuffling
- Delayed sitting
- Commando crawling
- Use of baby walker
- Dislike of play park equipment: climbing frames, swings, roundabouts etc.

Green for Go

- Reciprocal crawling
- Exploratory hand play in sitting
- Prone extension
- Sitting with protective extension through arms
- Developing an amphibian pattern of weight bearing on the left side and then rolling to the right side or vice versa when in prone (as shown in the picture of the baby transferring weight across midline)

Crawling is an activity that I misunderstood a number of years ago, failing to see any connection there might be with learning. However, it is in fact a most important factor in the process of education. Now that I have a greater understanding of the underpinning neural processes, I am aware of the vital part it does play in a child's development. The question as to whether or not a child has crawled has great implications for his education across a wide spectrum of learning including Maths and Reading. By crawling I mean using an opposing limb pattern, as opposed to bum shuffling or even commando crawling which uses mainly the arms as a means of propulsion. Crawling will only become established when children are managed on their tummies and develop prone extension. This, in turn, promotes arm strength and shoulder girdle stability which are necessary later on for handwriting. Young babies can sometimes object to being placed on their tummies, but a rolled up towel placed under the chest, level with the armpits, will help get the child in the correct position of function with arms out in front. The child in the picture above, although not crawling, is crossing midline and transferring weight to adopt a crawling posture – a dynamic move and a precursor to crawling.

At first, when children are learning to crawl, the pattern may resemble a rabbit hopping. Both arms move forward, and then both legs. Then they may move on to a reptilian type of crawling where both left limbs move forward together then the right limbs. Cross-lateral movement in crawling is seen when the child moves the right leg and the left arm together and vice versa.

When babies crawl they learn how big they are in relation to things around them e.g. squeezing under a chair. They learn how to find and remember where things are, an essential skill for learning how to negotiate their physical environment.

A simplified explanation as to why this type of movement is so important is as follows. There are two hemispheres to the part of the brain known as the cerebrum. The left hemisphere is dominant in regard to language while the right hemisphere handles spatial perceptions and assists in new learning. The left hemisphere controls the right side of the body whilst the right hemisphere controls the left side of the body. Connected to both hemispheres is the corpus callosum, a thick band of nerve fibres which divides the brain into the left and right hemispheres. It enables communication between the right and left sides of the brain transferring motor, sensory and cognitive information between them. This is the neural link which ensures that movement takes place in an integrated way, i.e. both sides of the body move in relation to each other. The reference here is to the two eyes, the two arms and legs. Also included are the two ears which, although technically do not move, work as a pair and are significant when it comes to auditory processing. Equal stimulation of both sides of the body gives full access to the environment leading to more efficient action.

The more children explore a variety of movement and balance activities, such as may be found in a play park, the greater the access to learning. These early movements encourage adaptability and will prove valuable for future development. Identifying movement problems and providing early intervention can lead to the prevention of more pronounced difficulties at a later stage. Research in this area, mentioned in Hannaford (2005, p.109, 113), suggests two things. First, the chemicals which promote the growth of nerve cells and increase the number of new cells are stimulated by muscular activity. Also, higher levels of fitness are associated with higher academic achievement. On a more personal note, exercise was found not only to stimulate the brains of young children, but also prevent the deterioration of older brains.

Key Points from Chapter 2

- Crawling reciprocally, develops bilateral skills and functioning of the 'two's' ie.hands, feet, eyes, ears.
- Crawling develops from having "tummy time".
- Crawling is essential to develop arm and shoulder girdle strength which are crucial for fine motor skills and handwriting.
- Adaptability in early movement is valuable for future development.
- Early intervention can lead to the prevention of greater difficulties later.

Chapter 3

Five Senses or Seven

The Big Idea

You need to be organised on the outside (your body) before being organised on the inside (your brain).

The Academic Viewpoint

While it is generally accepted that during the process of maturation, higher centres in the brain should take control and direction over lower centres, the persistence of lower level dominance over certain functions will nevertheless have an effect on how a child functions, his ability to learn and his behaviour. (S. Goddard, 2002)

Red Flag Issues

- Wants to be upside down
- Excessive movement
- Seek/avoid touch
- Reverses letters
- Falls out of chairs
- Lacks routine
- Difficulty sleeping

Green for Go

- Calms when touched or cuddled
- Claps hands and waves bye bye
- Smiles and engages in social play from 8 months
- Can sit balanced in a chair
- Can hold a book steady
- Gets dizzy easily on roundabout
- Protects himself from falling over when loses balance or is pushed

So far we have discussed how movement makes an impact on our senses and on our learning. It is often assumed that we only gather information from outside our bodies through our senses (ears, eyes, smell, touch, taste) i.e. external input. However, of equal importance are the feelings or sensations that are internal to our bodies, so to speak, namely the vestibular and proprioceptive systems. Vestibular and proprioception were not words that I would have used in my active vocabulary. They had no connections for me in the educational context and seemed more like words out of a medical dictionary. Again, my association with the paediatric O.T, who is trained in Sensory Integration principles, allowed me the insight necessary to come to a clear understanding of the importance of these systems to movement, organisational skills and education.

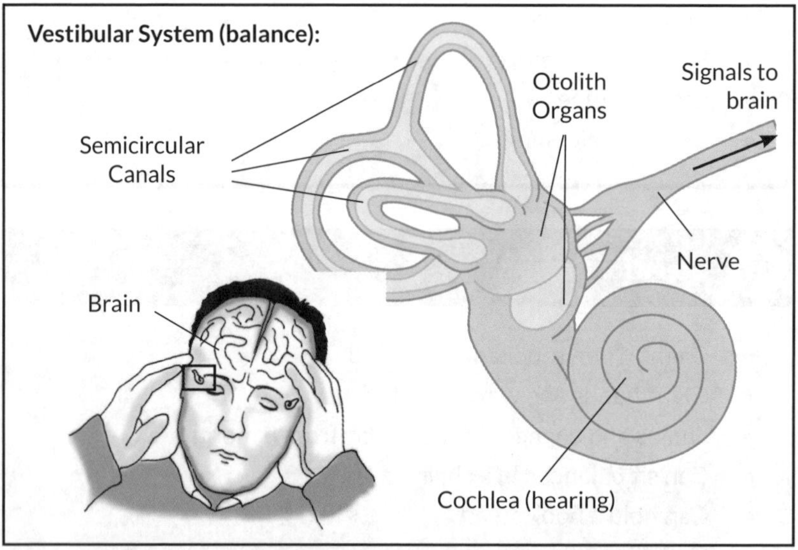

The Vestibular System

We detect external sensations of movement and gravity within the inner ear. These are transferred to the brain through the vestibular system. Within the inner ear is a system of three semi-circular canals set at right angles to each other and two vestibular sacs which contain a fluid. These canals are so placed as to be able to detect movement in any plane by the movement of the fluid through the canals as it touches and stimulates hair cells. The movement of the hair cells triggers nerve signals which send information to the brain about the direction and extent of the movement. Angular movement is detected by the semi-circular canals whilst linear movement is detected by the utricle, which is a linear accelerometer that detects linear head movements and head tilt. The responses for both the semi-circular canals and the utricle act on antigravity muscles to maintain our posture and balance when challenged by gravity. Utricle inputs produce more sustained postural responses and tonic (when static) postural extension, whilst semi-circular canal responses produce more phasic (during movement) equilibrium responses. It is important to highlight that movement responses can be in relation to rotatory movement or fear of over reaction to linear movement. Fear of, or over reaction to, linear movement, which can be either in a horizontal or vertical plane, is known as gravitational insecurity.

The vestibular system is the child's first sensory system and is fully developed by about 10-12 weeks post conception. However, it is only after birth that we experience more complex motions and develop mastery of movement in a gravitational world. The vestibular sense gives us our awareness of space and balance and is likened to our GPS system. The word vestibular comes from the word vestibule which means hallway. This sense is crucial to the development of the sensory system as it is the hallway to the brain. This system controls balance and movement and influences everything we do. In addition, it helps to maintain static balance, body orientation in relation to gravity, and dynamic balance (body position in response to sudden movements such as rotation, speeding up and slowing down as when walking). Through the vestibular system we gather information about the position of the head in relation to the ground. Each movement of the head from any static position or any change in speed or direction of movement will be registered by the brain through the vestibular system. Jean Ayres (2005) states that "the vestibular apparatus in each inner ear tells the brain we are moving, surrounded by something that is moving, on something that is moving or a combination of all three." "The vestibular sense plays a key role in helping us to develop efficient self-regulation of our arousal system and our ability to maintain a calm but alert state" (Brown D. 2007). As any Sensory Integration trained therapist will know, this is the key to Jean Ayres' Theory and Intervention on Sensory Integration.

This system also tells the brain where "down" is because it also registers the pull of gravity. According to Steve Cool, a neurologist, "One may have a well - developed sensory map of the external world and a well- developed motor map from one place to another, but if one does not know where they are with respect to that map they are virtually incapable of using that spatial mapping information. In addition, the vestibular system appears to be the system that gives information about the individual's location in the overall spatial map. (The "you are here.")" (S. J. Cool 1987)

The vestibular system is also necessary for postural control, especially when responding to a trip or a push. Furthermore, it includes the tone of the muscles and the muscle force or strength required to perform a task. We need sufficient muscle tone and strength to be able to sit in a chair, jump two feet together and ride a bicycle.

No attempt will be made to give a detailed medical explanation of the processes that take place. However, those interested will find a good explanation in Carla Hannaford's book "Smart Moves" (2005). Suffice it to say that vestibular stimulation is crucial to brain processing and its connection to the learning process is therefore very significant.

The vestibular system is considered to exert the greatest influence on all the other sensory systems. It is the unifying system in our brain which modifies and coordinates other information received from visual, auditory, tactile and proprioceptive systems. So, as a direct result of reflexive movements in the womb or in very early childhood, a child of approximately one to two years of age can learn to roll, crawl, sit, stand, walk, climb in a gravitational environment. There is much evidence, based on observations in Kindergartens on the Continent, that young children who climb rocks and ladders, hop, jump, skip, spin, walk on narrow surfaces like tree logs, train the muscles to work together and have bodies better prepared to learn when they enter school.

The Proprioceptive System

Holding a book steady to allow us to read, keeping our eyes level while we read, carrying an egg without breaking it, using clutch control in a car, applying just the correct amount of pressure on the brakes of a bicycle to slow down, moving and maintaining balance while walking, practising your golf swing just before striking the ball, the ability to sit in a chair without falling over, are all examples of the variety of the proprioception system in action. Every muscle has receptors which send messages to the brain providing the feedback necessary to perform any action. The system constantly aligns every part of the body and provides the necessary information to maintain muscle contraction and relaxation for every action. Should this system become faulty we would have difficulty maintaining our balance and the physical sense of where we are in space. This is one of our most important ways of being aware of where our bodies are, remaining balanced, moving our bodies adaptively in relation to the environment and allowing us to judge timing and distance, e.g. throwing and catching a ball. Both the proprioceptive and the vestibular systems are inextricably linked and are necessary to permit movement from one body position to another. Proprioception, in other words, means muscles, tendons and joints, skin and underlying tissue all working in harmony to allow us to move fluently without harming ourselves. When learning a new skill, the brain needs rehearsals of the minute muscle fluctuations that are required.

Waves of sensory information from the muscle to the brain strengthen the neural networks. The proprioceptive system, at any one time, sends information to the brain concerning the location of body parts, movement of muscles and joints, pressure on skin, pain and temperature felt in the tissue. It plays a key role in helping children maintain equilibrium and make progress through the stages of motor development while informing their body awareness.

Key Points from Chapter 3

- Movement affects both the external and internal world of the body.
- The vestibular system plays an important part in processing learning by informing us as to the direction and extent of movement and maintaining self- regulation.
- The vestibular system is necessary for postural control and helps us react to pushes and trips.
- The vestibular system is essential for us to do almost everything in life but few people are aware of this occurring.
- The proprioceptive system informs us as to the position of body parts in relation to each other, muscle movement, pressure and other sensations.
- The vestibular and proprioceptive systems together with vision are required for smooth coordinated movement e.g. ski walking.
- The proprioceptive system allows the hand to use tools with correct force and movement.

Chapter 4

Body Awareness

The Big Idea

I know that I have arms and legs which are equally important for movement and allow me to work and play.

The Academic Viewpoint

Learning sequences of movements or facts is an integral part of human behaviour. Sequencing our actions is important for everyday activities, from getting dressed in the morning, to playing sports or musical instruments. Robinson, E. et al. (2012).

Body awareness comes from our proprioceptive sense which informs the brain about our position and movement in space. Receptors are in our muscles and joints and activate with pressure and movement. When body awareness has developed, we automatically know where our body is in space and where our limbs are placed. For young children, this skill is less automatic and develops gradually over time.

Young children are still using a great deal of 'brain energy' to enable them to know about their body position, and when they are applying their concentration elsewhere, you often observe them fall, slide off a chair and be generally uncoordinated. (www.teachnursery.com)

Red Flag Issues

- Reluctance to weight bear on arms
- Trip and falls easily
- Drawings of himself showing limited body parts (usually no arms)
- Won't hold pencil/crayon and avoids tool use (scissors, cutlery)
- Poor trunk rotation
- Difficulty organising correct actions in a sequence
- Difficulty with dressing, cleaning teeth and self feeding using cutlery

Green for Go

- Likes colouring in
- Good letter formation
- Assists with dressing and feeding
- Good "b" and "d" discrimination
- Can use the number line left/right for addition and right/left for subtraction
- Early word spelling with no trouble
- Enjoys ball skills and motor activities e.g. bicycle riding, scooters, climbing
- Wants to become independent

In this chapter some issues are addressed which may, on the face of it, seem unrelated. However, they have significance, not only to movement, but to learning in general, including reading, writing and number work. The umbrella term of "Body Awareness" includes all of the following -

Body Image, Body Part Identification, Body Scheme, Laterality, Mid-line awareness and Directionality and each of these has a substantial bearing on movement, perceptual development, and learning in general.

Most therapists would have an understanding of the above terms but they may be novel to educators and parents. This is an area of development where teachers and therapists are now recognising the need for collaborative practice and a sharing of ideas for mutual benefit. Teachers may benefit from a greater knowledge of the hierarchy of motor skills, the impact of persistent reflexes and the insight this gives to a better understanding of a child who is having particular difficulties with numeracy and literacy, i.e. dyslexia and dyscalculia. A therapist may be able to better appreciate the impact of their work in promoting sequential motor development and its relationship to hierarchical perceptual and cognitive development.

All teachers have come across children who bump into things as they move around the classroom, knock things over, hit other children unintentionally, stumble or fall frequently, have difficulties moving their bodies over, under, between, in, out of objects in the environment. They cannot sit still or pay attention and constantly fidget. They have also met other children who dislike movement, are gravitationally insecure and do not like playground equipment, especially those involving movement. Some children's bodies do not seem to cooperate with them. Their movements are either jerky or rigid, or floppy and unstable. They may have difficulty with dressing or following the flight of a ball with their eyes. Some children resort quickly to a fight/ flight/ fright mode when faced with a situation which has an impact on their sensory system. In fight mode they may hit out, trip others, throw their bodies about and yell or scream. Alternatively, they may become extremely anxious and vigilant, over protecting themselves by not taking any risks or attempting novel things.

In flight mode they may want to go to the toilet continually, want to go home, feel tired, daydream, deliberately fall or forget gym clothes to avoid having to do activities involving movement. In fright mode they can experience the fright we would normally associate with extreme situations such as being attacked by an animal or walking near the edge of a high cliff.

A wide range of behaviours is deliberately covered here, all of which are motor based and may only occasionally be displayed. If children consistently refer to themselves negatively it may be an indication of a difficulty with some of the issues mentioned above. They may say, "I cannot master the number line or the concept of adding without using fingers, I am useless, I am no good at this, I can't do anything right." In this chapter reference will be made to these children and their behaviour embedded in a neurological basis with reference to the six areas already mentioned above.

Care should be taken to ensure that, while some of these children may have difficulty learning, their difficulty may be in integrating knowledge with motor skills or even slow processing of information and organising their bodies to carry out actions. This is called ideational praxis and will be discussed in greater detail later.

When children have reached school age there is often the assumption that they can process and integrate information well and produce appropriate responses. This is usually shown in their ability to listen to the teacher and carry out the instructions. Where children have processing difficulties, they have difficulty following the teacher's verbal instructions and only follow or imitate what other children around them are doing without fully learning from the situation. Others may be overdependent on visual information, distracting themselves in trying to decode auditory input and appearing slow, lazy or disinterested. Learning is about the ability to take in, process and absorb information in order to use it or reproduce it on demand within the environment. If a child is not functioning at this level we must question how the child is receiving the information in the first instance. This takes us back to exploring body systems like the vestibular, the tactile, proprioceptive, auditory and visual systems.

In a large number of children referred to the clinic by parents in response to teachers' concerns, assessment often confirms motor and coordination difficulties frequently associated with processing. These seem to present as the greatest barriers to learning in children who otherwise appear to have no other learning difficulty. Most parents, when asked about their concerns for their child's development, ability and progress, say their child has no motor problems. Children can mask core skill deficits by developing splinter skills, such as being a good footballer, swimmer or tennis player. However, they can still present with difficulty sequencing or carrying out unfamiliar actions. When, however, parents observe the child's performance on simple neurological- based challenges they can immediately see the motor difficulties observable in the child's functional ability to stand on one leg, copy body position, 4 point kneel and carry out reciprocal tasks.

Ideational Praxis

Before going on to talk about all the issues surrounding body awareness, it is important to understand the process of ideation which is closely linked to these matters. Imagine a child wandering into a room full of toys. He pauses briefly to push buttons, pick up and set down some toys, touch or look momentarily at others, but he never engages in constructive play with any of them. It might be expected that at least one toy will capture his attention, yet this does not seem to be the case. "What is going on?" you might well ask. The most probable explanation is that he has poor ideation skills.

Ideation is the ability to generate an idea of how to interact with an object, in this case a toy. A child who has no idea what to do with an object cannot interact with it apart from lifting it, holding it, looking at it and then setting it down or throwing it only to repeat the exercise with another toy. The purpose of the toy then becomes sensory rather than exploratory or constructive.

There are three processes involved in ideation :

1. Having an idea of what to do;
2. Organising and creating an internal plan of action;
3. Executing or carrying out the action. It is a cognitive process believed to be dependent largely upon the brain's ability to respond appropriately to sensory input.

Ideation is essential for praxis (movement skills) and the idea of moving the body forwards, backwards and sideways. Ideational praxis initially allows the child to develop more complex sequenced movements. This establishes the foundation for simple movement patterns involving relaxing and contracting alternate muscle groups as in clapping, rocking on hands and knees and using the therapy ball with the child starting in the prone position (lying on tummy over the ball) and coming back into tall kneeling.

Many children with autism lack ideation skills with both their bodies and objects. They get the idea to flap their hands when excited rather than clapping or doing a thumbs up. They line up toys and other items and they tend to "play" repetitively because they do not generate "new" ideas.

To understand the learning model of praxis and ideation it is necessary to explore the theory of Sensory Integration. Ayres (2005) states, " if praxis does not emerge the result is a sensory based motor disorder DCD (Dyspraxia) …… a brain dysfunction that hinders the organisation of sensory information and interferes with the ability to motor plan."

Sensory integration provides the body with a body schema or plan which is essentially a map of what the body can do. The map gives the brain all the information it needs to decide what to do with the sensory input it receives. However, if the body map is compromised (inaccurate, incomplete or non-existent), the brain cannot respond properly to sensory input and ideation becomes difficult or impossible. This is why it is vital to develop the child's body scheme awareness.

The organizational aspect of praxis, or the "how to do it" step, is the internal plan of action that bridges ideation and execution.

First, an individual decides what to do, and then a plan of action is determined. In most individuals, this process is automatic. An idea occurs followed rapidly by an action. There is no awareness of the organisational plan that was formed in that split second to orchestrate the action. Individuals with DCD however, tend to organize themselves cognitively. They must think through how to accomplish the desired action before they execute it. These individuals often require repeated exposure to an activity in order to master it. Essentially, they are organizing the action consciously and then committing it to memory because the body is less able to determine, automatically, the necessary steps for execution. Over time, these children need to learn to generalize their experiences to other situations.

Execution is the final, motor part of ideational praxis. It is the physical manifestation of the desired action. While it is not necessarily the major source of difficulty in DCD, it is the only part that can be observed. The DCD child in the room full of toys demonstrates difficulty implementing purposeful play, but it is likely that his true difficulty is in determining what to do (ideation) or how to do it (organization). Individuals with DCD have difficulty imitating actions, sequencing activities, and executing higher-level reasoning.

A simple test which may be used to determine if a child does have difficulty with ideation, is to give him a "howl" stick and ask him what he can do with it . If the problem is present, all the child will do is shake it back and forth or get it to howl. He can only see it for what it is – a stick. He has little idea of the affordances (object-specific qualities that invite interaction) of the stick. The howl stick might be construed as a walking stick, a bow for a violin, a golf club or a flute but he cannot initially visualise and demonstrate these uses. When, however, these possible uses are shown, he will gradually begin to see additional uses for the stick. Parents can further assist the development of ideation by getting the child to think about ideas for interaction with common objects around the house. For example, what might the lid of a box be used for, or a paper clip, or a brick, an envelope or a piece of string? May-Benson (2005) discusses the testing of ideational praxis in greater detail in a paper of the same title which is worth while investigating.

Effects of ideation difficulties

A child who has difficulties with ideation has trouble imitating or copying what other children do. This is one of the most important ways in which a child learns. Such children tend to be controlling and always want to do what they know they can do successfully. Children on the Autistic Spectrum tend to be rigid about the purpose of an object and they remain inflexible about deviating from original experiences. Children with ideation problems just don't know what to do with their bodies, so they engage in meaningless mannerisms. In its severest form, it manifests as a developmental motor praxis difficulty - pacing, hand-flapping when moving or engaging in apparently meaningless behaviours. Waving bye-bye, blowing kisses and knowing how to gesture thumbs up is beyond their practical ability as typically seen in some children with ASD. Others have difficulty with riding a bicycle, ball skills and handwriting. These difficulties cause them to give up easily and to isolate themselves from other children.

Body Image

By body image we mean a child's self-image or self-concept. This is directly related to how a child feels about himself either positively or negatively. These internal feelings develop from birth and are encouraged by positive affirmation. Negative attitudes may be picked up subconsciously from parents and others who, for what appears to them to be good reason, criticise the child. Statements are made, such as, "You're not trying hard enough, you're lazy, you're untidy, you never put your things away, and you're always tripping over yourself."

Sometimes parents want their children to develop at a faster pace than is best for the child. A wrong attitude may cause the child to feel a failure because he cannot live up to his parental expectations or if he does attempt the activity, failure is almost inevitable. At this stage, the child is lacking the ability to explain his difficulties or even know what his difficulties are. Some adults make unfair comparisons of a child to his peers or siblings, talking about how well another child was able to carry out the activity or the age at which an older sibling succeeded in doing it. "Your sister was able to do it when she was your age, so why can't you?" If a child feels secure, comfortable and content through his interactions with people and the environment, he builds up a positive body image which can be enhanced at a later stage through success in moving and controlling his body in the environment.

A child's self-esteem is a consequence of how much they feel they are worth, and how much they feel valued by others. The aim should be to encourage the child to feel good about him, build up self-esteem, self -confidence, self-acceptance, and independence and have the ability to develop good friendships. He will then be in a position where he is not afraid to try something new and learn to be resilient i.e. recognize mistakes and have the ability to bounce back and self-correct.

There are at least two ways of assessing whether or not children have a positive or negative self - image. One way is to listen to the things they say about themselves and it will immediately become clear as to how they see themselves. Children with negative self-image cannot identify anything good about them when asked to do so. They find it difficult to say the things they are good at and often belittle themselves. Another way to identify poor self -image/self-concept is to ask them to draw a person or themselves with other people in the picture. A child with poor self- image may draw himself with parts of the body missing, draw himself smaller than others in the picture or standing apart from others, or lack the motor skills necessary to draw the parts. A four year old should be able to draw a body with several body parts.

It is possible to eliminate poor body image by giving a child positive, emotional experiences through movement. A positive environment may be achieved by hugging and praising a child so that he feels good about himself. When he throws a ball, walks, runs, smiles, jumps on his own or plays well with other children, participates in group activities, or runs errands etc. there is ample opportunity for a parent or teacher to give positive reinforcement. Such support gives a child a sense of achievement both physically and mentally and so enhances body image.

Body Part Identification

Another term in the context of body awareness is body part identification ability. In this section, what will be discussed is how it develops, a means of evaluating a child's ability in this area, a description of how it may be taught and give some reasons why it is important.

Body part identification is simply knowledge of body parts, i.e. the ability to name and identify them. This is directly related to the amount of time family members spend at this activity. A baby of about eleven months begins to identify eyes and nose. By eighteen months he will have added hands, feet, ears and mouth. The progression is from recognising the parts first on himself, then on other family members, next on a toy (doll) and finally on a picture. By seven years of age other minor parts of the body are added until all parts can be identified by around age nine.

How well a child has developed this ability may be established by asking the child to point to his mouth, or nose, but a better way is to indicate a part of your own body and then ask the child to locate that part on his own body and name it without prompting.

Teaching this skill can be done very easily when a child is being dressed or is involved with games and activities which entail finding and naming body parts. "Put your sock on your foot, here is your hat, put it on your head, lift the hoop with your right hand, or kick the ball with your left foot." Another way is through singing the song, "Heads and shoulders knees and toes" with the actions. The ability to be able to name each part and know where each part is located on their bodies will assist them in the use of that body part in a controlled way.

Body Scheme

Body scheme follows closely upon an understanding of body image and body part identification. In the past some have used the terms body image and body scheme interchangeably, so for the sake of clarity, the following distinction will be made. If body image is about children's internal feelings about themselves, their perceptions and emotional responses to their bodies which, as we observed, may be either negative or positive, then body scheme is the internal awareness of where different parts of the body are in relation to each other. It has been likened to a body map. Body scheme is an internal representation of the body's position and shape as a three dimensional object in space. A coalition of sensory information is carried to the brain. This has been referred to earlier in the section on vestibular function as this is where we develop our G P S (global positioning system).

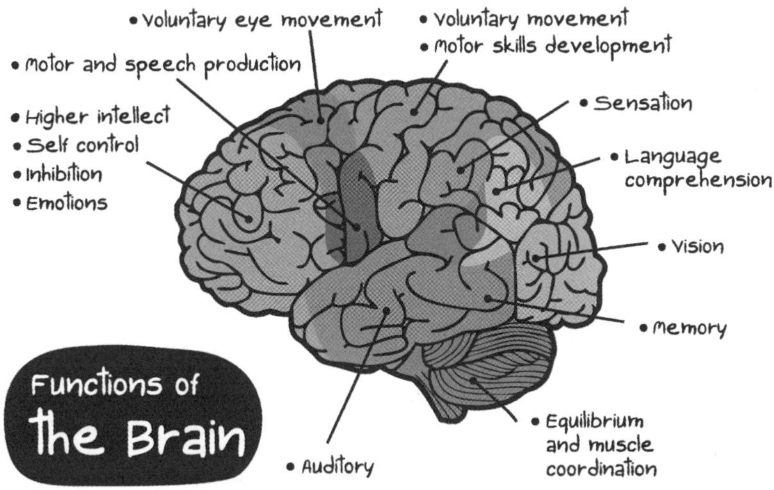

This sensory information, vestibular (movement), proprioceptive (muscles, tendons, joints) or tactile (touch), is then integrated continuously into a single entity to maintain the 3D representation or body shape. It is, for the most part, an automatic process which is continually being updated. It is used to bring spatial organisation to action (reaching out to catch a ball), but on occasions there may be a conscious perception of movement and position. For instance in rock climbing, a person may make a conscious decision as to where to place a hand or foot to obtain the best grip or think carefully about how far they can reach out without losing balance. It is a central representation of the body's spatial properties and any body representation which is used for action must continually track the body's position in whatever movement is taking place.

During about the tenth week of pregnancy the body scheme begins to develop in the child's brain. Later on, when a child moves during play, is touched or experiences the forces of gravity, information from soft tissue, skin, muscles tendons and joints is received. These sensations for each movement travel to the brain to be used and stored for later recall so that the movement may be repeated. This continues until such times as the movement becomes fluent, requiring little conscious thought. Pianists or ballet dancers for instance, practice a particular movement or action until they are satisfied they have perfected the action. We learn about the body first, then about how the body moves in space and finally about the body in relation to the environment.

Changes to body scheme are continuous and active. The body scheme is plastic (has the ability to change) as opposed to static and must be so to take account of the gradual changes that occur in growth during our lifetime. Relative sizes of arms, legs, feet and body all change and the development of the body scheme has to take all these changes into account including the effect these have on the centre of gravity. Also on a shorter time scale when using a tennis racket or a hammer, adjustments need to be made to allow differing points of contact. The hand may move to the tip of the tool and the changes may be gradual or rapid.

Difficulties with body scheme may be observed during movement and play activities and are seen as problems with coordination. The child may have difficulties getting in or out of a car, getting into a chair, or climbing on equipment in a play park. Other areas of difficulty may be in recognising touch on parts of the body out of sight, difficulty with back space (objects or things going on behind them), using parts of the body which are out of sight, hand movements when eyes are closed, perception of limbs in relation to the body (knock things over or hit others unintentionally), bump into things as they move around, stumble or fall frequently, getting low enough to crawl under an obstacle, moving in, out, over or under objects in the environment and difficulty with dressing or eating. A simple test, in addition to observing all the above difficulties, is to ask a child, with eyes closed, to raise the preferred arm to shoulder level and lower it three times. Then repeat with the other arm and finally, with both arms. It is best to demonstrate this activity beforehand. Any variation in height may indicate a difficulty. Another way is to get the younger child to clap. The hands should meet firmly in the central position.

There are many reasons as to why some children have poor body scheme. It may be that the primitive reflexes (discussed in detail later) necessary for survival have been retained. These need to become integrated so that the child can progress more smoothly to movement skills such as sitting, crawling, walking and running. Another reason may be that the child did not crawl properly using opposing limbs, and so did not build up efficient neural pathways between the right and left sides of the brain. The child may have low tone in the muscles allowing excessive flexibility and poor proprioception. A further possibility is that for some reason (possibly learning to walk in a baby walker) a walking pattern has developed that has encouraged an impulsive walking pattern without having gained good control of balance or motor attention. A final reason may be that the child is tactile defensive caused by an overreaction to touch or where he has experienced tactile deprivation. This results in an avoidance strategy rather than exploratory actions. If children are left alone for long periods they do not receive sufficient stimulation from touching and cuddling. This can lead to a disorganised tactile system and tactile defensiveness. Children with this condition frequently over react to normal touch and often display a painful reaction. Such children try to avoid contact with people or objects except on their terms.

Much can be done to help children with poor body scheme. If the underlying cause stems from body part identification then work should be carried out to assist the child's knowledge and awareness of body parts. Opportunities could be given for children to determine which body parts are needed for a given activity and how they can effectively move in/on/over /under /around /through various pieces of equipment, move through space, bear weight on arms, experience deep pressure, roll and crash. Crashing may be carried out on a thick bed of cushions when the child can be given the opportunity to crash forwards, backwards and sideways. Any activity involving deep pressure will prove helpful.

Laterality and Lateral Preference

Some people, when speaking about laterality combine this idea with that of lateral preference. The former is an internal awareness that two sides of the body exist and that they are different. Laterality is dependent upon gaining information through body part identification and body scheme. These are essential aspects of the development of body awareness. Lateral preference, on the other hand, is the favoured use of one side of the body over the other and may relate to one eye, one foot, one hand or one ear.

Awareness of laterality should be evident by about four years of age when a child develops the ability to use one or other or both sides of the body to make a desired movement. If a child is building a tower of bricks he may begin by using the left hand only to place the bricks on top of each other. Then he may switch to the right hand and finally bring both hands together in the centre to steady the blocks before continuing. Other examples are: one hand holding a pencil and the other holding paper to write on, catching a ball on the right side in the right hand and catching on the left side with the left hand or using one hand to hold the paper while the other hand uses scissors for cutting.

Development continues until, by about eight or nine years of age, a child is able, correctly and consistently, to identify body parts.

The development of laterality plays an important role in academic activities such as reading and writing which require left-right tracking. It is also important in numeracy for an understanding of sequencing and ordering of numbers and in P. E. for understanding instructions involving use of one side of the body or the other.

This internal awareness may be assisted by some of the following activities: climbing a frame in the playground, climbing up a slide, kicking a large ball, riding a bicycle, trunk rotation in both directions, juggling two bean bags, standing on a wobble board, using a reciprocal pattern for moving on a scooter board or twisting a nut on to a bolt.

Following on from this internal awareness that there are two sides to the body, the left and right, a child begins to favour using one side of the body over the other. This is in line with normal development and occurs naturally. As a child favours one side over the other he becomes more proficient at using that one side. An internal feeling develops which will be different in the favoured side until the child automatically uses the preferred hand/ arm/ leg /foot. The use of the non-preferred side will not feel natural.

At about four months old a child will automatically use the left hand for grasping. There then follows an "ambidextrous stage" for a few months. The preferred hand begins to emerge at around eight months and this is usually the right hand, but he may alternate between the use of hand depending on the proximity of the person or object. By the age of about three or four, lateral preference is normally established. This is usually the right side. Natural hand dominance can be observed when a child is given a ruler in each hand and asked to bang them together, one hand above the other. The dominant hand will always be on top.

Lateral preference in the hands allows the hands to work in opposition to each other as in cutting up food, using scissors or unscrewing a lid. It also allows other parts of the body to work in opposition, as in kicking or throwing a ball. If a child does not develop a dominant hand it can lead to difficulties in handwriting activities which require a consistent, dominant approach. Children who have mixed preference have a tendency to have difficulty identifying and forming letters, letter orientation and symmetry because they cannot identify the centre. They also do not have a sound knowledge of left and right. If an older child has mixed dominance in movement activities, but is not having trouble with handwriting or academic activity, there is no need for concern. If, however, the child is having difficulty, efforts should be made to establish a dominant side.

The dominant eye may be determined by asking the child to look at an object through a tube. The eye used is the dominant eye. The dominant ear is usually the one used to answer the telephone. The dominant hand may be established by posting coins in a post box using one hand whilst the other stabilaises the money box. Do this with the suspected dominant hand posting the coins followed by the non dominant hand posting . Time the activity as the dominant hand will emerge as the faster and observably more fluent. The non- functional hand does not assist but stabilises the box. Coins are posted one at a time. You will be able to observe the more fluent, dominant hand which will also be quicker in performing the task. It is common for children who are having motor difficulties to have problems related to poor motor control in vision and speech. It is our experience that if there is difficulty with laterality in the two hands and the two feet, there is likely to be difficulty with the two eyes as in reflexive eye movements in both horizontal and vertical tracking. Also difficulty with the two ears in auditory processing. These two issues will be referred to later.

Midline Awareness

The idea of midline awareness was a concept that was also novel to me as a teacher, but on close observation of children it immediately became apparent that some children have difficulty in this area. This awareness has ramifications not only for motor skills but also has a knock on effect in education. It is closely associated with laterality but takes this idea one step further. Children who have a midline awareness difficulty appear to have an imaginary line running from head to foot through the centre of the body and parts of the body on one side have difficulty communicating with parts of the body on the other. The left hand tends to be used when working on the left side of the body and the right hand on the right. There is little or no reaching across this imaginary line or bringing the two hands to work together as a pair in the centre. If a child with this difficulty is playing with a toy, he will tend to position himself in an asymmetrical position so that the toy is either on his left or his right side and he will be likely to use only one hand without reaching across the midline.

There is cause for concern if a child is not crossing midline by the age of five and a definite problem exists if he is not crossing midline by age seven. This inability causes problems with both physical and academic activities. On the physical side this manifests itself in a difficulty of reaching across his body to catch a ball on one side with both hands, in performing dance steps where one leg crosses over the other or arms cross each other, or in swimming when doing front crawl. He may use either side of his body when batting a ball, but neither have a relationship to each other. As you may have already deduced, in these instances, laterality or lateral preference may be delayed or non existent.

In so far as classroom activities are concerned, this midline difficulty affects not only arms and legs, but also vision and possibly auditory processing. When a child who has this difficulty is reading, the left eye may read the left side of the line to the centre and then the right eye will take over to complete the line. Sometimes the right eye does not know where to take over and the child loses the place. The same thing may happen when writing. The left hand writes to the middle of the page and then the right hand takes over. On occasions the child may develop a strategy to overcome this difficulty by placing the page on the right side and use only the right eye to avoid having to change hands. Any activity, such as cutting with scissors, fastening buttons or tying shoelaces, where both hands are used as a pair in the midline position, will cause difficulty, as will threading and screwing activities.

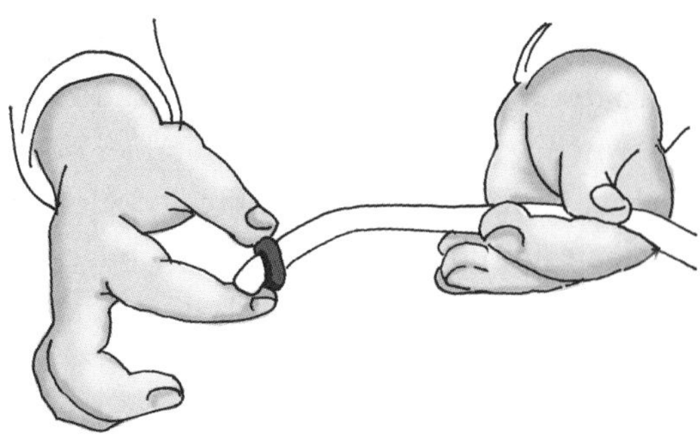

One quick way of assessing whether or not a child has these difficulties, apart from observing him at work, is to get him, when standing to touch his right ear with his left hand and vice versa using only a visual prompt. Also, get him to follow your visual demonstration of touching his left hand to his right knee and right hand to left knee with the instructions, "Do this. Do this." The difficulty will be immediately noticeable if the child puts his left hand to his left ear and does not cross midline for any one of these activities.

Another activity to confirm this difficulty is to ask the child to build a tower with wooden blocks. A child who uses only one hand or who switches to the other hand, but does not use both hands together may have a crossing midline difficulty. Such children tend to be ambidextrous. It is important to encourage one-hand dominance to allow the child to function with a dominant side.

The "Brain Gym" activity of drawing lazy eights in the air, first with one hand, then the other, and finally with both hands together is one way of increasing midline awareness. Another way is to have the child sit on a chair with objects placed on either side. The idea is for the child to retrieve one object at a time by reaching across his body with his left hand to the right side and vice versa. One further way is to get the child to stand on one side of a glass door, while you stand on the other and get him to mirror your actions as you move your hands in crossing midline movements.

Directionality and Directional Discrimination

Having worked through the issues of Body Image, Body Part Identification, Body Scheme, Laterality, and Midline Awareness, we now come to the concluding part of the whole issue of Body Awareness which is Directionality and Directional Discrimination. These ideas are closely linked to the idea of Laterality. Once knowledge has been gained of the left and right sides of the body, this information can then be transferred to the child's awareness of his body in space. This involves three reference points which are: left/right, up/down, behind/in front. These reference points are about objects in relation to the child's centre of his body when the child remains static.

. "The dog is to my left, my sister is behind me, and the light is above me on the ceiling." This learning is a gradual process and can begin at about five years of age. Following on from this, at about age seven, the objects may be referred to, not only in relation to the child, but in relation to each other." The dog is in front of the car, the book is under the table, the pencil is on the desk." It may take longer before a child recognises the right and left sides of people facing him and in front of him as commonly occurs in a game of cricket or football. "Kick the ball past his right side, throw the ball behind him."

Often in class pupils are given instructions involving the concept of directionality and it is important to ensure that the pupil has a firm grasp of this idea especially if giving instructions for getting from one classroom to another. Trying to teach simple origami with verbal instructions only can be very challenging and confusing but this can give some insight into the child's world and his difficulties.

Directional discrimination takes directionality a stage further and involves an internalisation of the concept of laterality. This is combined with the three points of reference, previously referred to, and also the idea of constancy – an object remains the same irrespective of its position. A doll is still a doll even if it is upside down, on its side, or pictured in a book.

From an educational perspective, this can become an issue for a child attempting to discriminate between the letters b, d, p, q, and words such as was and saw. Another area of importance, which has a connection with laterality and directionality, is the number line. In the early stages this consists of the numbers one to ten extending from left to right as the child looks at them. The processes of addition and subtraction are represented as movement from left to right for addition and right to left for subtraction. A child with directionality difficulty will find the process confusing. The teacher should also be aware that when facing the child to give a demonstration of these movements that the points of reference should be as the child sees it and not that of the adult, who will have the opposite perspective to that of the child.

In the early stage of directional discrimination of an object, a child may well orientate himself to the object before deciding which is left or right.

Hand Dominance

As previously discussed in the section on laterality it is important that the child knows he has a right and left side which remains constant. Children usually identify L/R by body dominance. "I write with my right hand, I kick the ball with my left foot." This is a more challenging concept for children with mixed or undecided dominance where they keep switching hands to write. These will be children who have difficulties with midline orientation. It is important for such children to be given activities like tool use which will reinforce dominance. Dominance may be identified by observing some of the following: finger feeding, scratching head, kicking a football, catching a ball or through using a standardised movement check like ABC Movement. However, it is not uncommon for children who have had dominance issues to score better results in time accuracy in the ABC Movement test when using their perceived non dominant hand.

The children will soon learn that they have a stronger or weaker side and will be more spontaneous to the dominant side. In older children, where dominance has been undecided and they present as awkward or clumsy children, there are usually associated academic difficulties. It is essential to work on these children's core motor skills first.

Once dominance has been established, it is important to encourage the child verbally to continue in the use of the dominant side.

Some of the following activities can create an awareness of dominance and reinforce it. Gross motor activities include hopping and jumping to instruction, jumping in sequence through an array of hoops placed on the floor to include jumping to the L/R, following arrows and route planning, throwing bean bags at different targets using different hands (targets may be placed to either side or behind the thrower), throwing or kicking a ball at skittles, following an obstacle course, using a scooter, riding a bicycle and using playground climbing frames. In fact any form of motor challenge involving adaptive motor skills on an unstable base (like a wobble board as in the picture, a see -saw, walking sideways, using a bat and ball) will serve to reinforce the dominant side.

Fine motor activities for children in the 3-5 age range include playing with play dough, cutting out shapes, building towers with blocks, copying block patterns, threading and lacing activities, grading stacking toys, matching puzzle pieces, orientating shape in space in a feely bag, self- dressing, drawing people and faces, dressing dolls and putting shoes on the correct feet (with red/ green dot prompts stuck on the shoes). In addition to these, older children can do various types of art work, use tweezers or tongs for picking up items, clay modelling, and construction toys (Lego), and transferring objects L/R using opposing hands. When teaching a child to name their body sides it is better to over teach the right side. This way they do not have to make a choice as whatever is left is **left**. This point is illustrated above.

Key Points from Chapter 4

- Body awareness is an umbrella term which covers an understanding of your own body parts and their capacity for movement.
- Self image is the image that a person has of himself and has to do with self-esteem.
- Body image is how you view your physical self.
- Body part identification is about the ability to identify and name body parts on oneself.
- Body scheme is the internal body awareness that allows you to know where body parts are in space in relation to each other.
- Laterality is an awareness that the body has two sides L/R which are different.
- Lateral dominance is a natural preference to use one side of the body instead of the other e.g. hand, foot, eye, ear.
- Some children have a difficulty crossing midline to perform activities using both hands.
- Children's awareness of space around them needs to be 3D.
- An object remains intrinsically the same. It may be perceived as unchanging regardless of its position or orientation.
- Use of the dominant side will make actions more spontaneous and should be encouraged.
- Over teach the right side, whatever is left is left.

Chapter 5

In Reflexive Mode

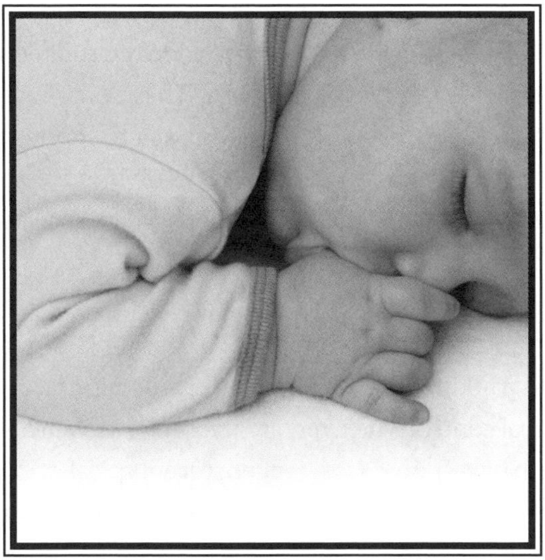

The Big Idea

The early survival systems in babies need to be integrated to promote motor development.

The Academic Viewpoint

"Primitive reflexes….are essential for the baby's survival in the first few weeks of life and they provide the rudimentary training for many later voluntary skills. They…only have a limited lifespan and, having helped the baby to survive the first hazardous months of life, they should be inhibited or controlled by the higher centres of the brain…which will then allow the infant control of the voluntary response." (S, Goddard.2002)

A reflex is a stereotyped response to a sensory stimilus. Reflex integration is the inhibition by higher centres of neurological control which modify the reflex in such a way that the pattern of response is no longer stereotypical.
Primitive reflexes and their impact on a child's function (Blog) Tools To Grow,
Inc. (2016)

Red Flag Issues

- Back managed avoiding tummy time
- Restricted flat lying as a new born due to reflux
- Has no protective extension
- Delayed in sitting
- No crawling
- Has no right/left awareness
- Poor posture
- Messy eater
- Has difficulty with handwriting
- Is highly aroused continually
- Needs to move constantly

Green for Go

- When rolling on floor head must be off floor , held in lateral tilt
- when moving from lying to curling into a ball the head moves first and does not remain on floor
- Prone extension
- Clapping hands and good early imitation skills
- Signs of assertiveness at 11 months (says no)
- Holding own bottle/spoon/cup (self feed)
- Reduced Startle reflex
- Can ski walk
- Learn to ride a bicycle
- Less anxious about novel sensations

No, reflexive isn't spelt wrongly. This is a deliberate attempt to consider the impact of reflexes on learning or reflect on the reflexes. In this chapter, five very important early reflexes will be considered. Everyone is familiar with the blinking reflex and the knee jerk reflex. We have no control over how we react when these are prompted. "So what," you may ask, "have reflexes to do with movement, education, and learning?" Speaking from an educational point of view, I would have been inclined to ask the same question. This is an area in which sensory trained OT's can assist teachers in understanding the impact of retained reflexes on learning. As an aside, we find an increasing number of children coming to the clinic with "retained" or active early reflexes, but more about that later.

The brain is the place where all learning occurs with the body acting as the means by which learning is acquired. The brain and the body work together through the central nervous system (CNS). This system is vital to the way we perceive the world around us including feeling, thinking, learning, communicating, playing, and, most importantly, surviving. The CNS is made up of the brain and the spinal cord. Although simplistic, it may be helpful to think of the brain as being comprised of three main parts which are all linked together. The **brain stem** is located at the back of the neck just above the spinal cord and is about the size of your thumb. A new born child functions at brain stem level which enables him to breathe, feed and move in response to stimuli. It is this part which controls what are called the survival or primitive reflexes. The **limbic system, including the cerebellum**, governs arousal, motivation, emotions and movement. This is the reactive brain. The third area, **the cerebral cortex**, is the part commonly called the brain. This region is involved in all the higher processes of thinking and the integration of all the other parts including the integration of the senses. This is sometimes referred to as the deliberate brain.

When children are born they come into the world with several survival reflexes. Most of the reflexes (Goddard 2002 lists ten p3) begin in utero and in normal development will, in some circumstances, persist for up to a year. Early reflexes have an initial function e.g. The The TLR (Tonic Labyrinthine Reflex) allows the baby's posture to adapt to its head position. On the tummy the body in line with the head will flex and on the back the head and body will extend.

If persistant the child will have difficulty raising the head against gravity when on his tummy to bear weight on his arms. On his back the child will have difficulty raising the head to look at his feet. The Landau reflex, essential to getting the head and shoulders off the floor in prone, and essential to early stages of crawling, (not discussed in detail here), continues for up to two and a half years. These reflexes integrate a few months after birth, having accomplished the purpose of getting the child's head off the floor allowing the emergence of the head extending and the arms coming forwards to bear weight. (Amphibian), arms weight bearing and legs alternately moving into external flexion, and the arms and legs maintaining the body in 4 point kneeling (STNR). The STNR (Symmetrical Tonic Neck Reflex) assists in allowing the child to move up against gravity and get into 4 point kneeling. The involuntary movements give place to voluntary movements (postural reflexes) and motor skills, enabling greater interaction with the environment. Should the survival reflexes be retained, they will interfere with a child's ability to self-regulate remaining in constant inner stress (Moro), roll over into crawling (non emergent amphibian), sit upright, difficulty holding head upright, (TLR), and crawl (STNR).

The emergence of the TLR backwards at birth is essential to the integration of the vestibular and then the proprioceptive systems.

Where the vestibular system has not integrated into early floor movements the child will not develop the ability to raise the head off the floor to move, but will develop an atypical pattern of moving limbs and body and then engaging the head. All movements when the child commences rising off the floor against gravity should be head led. This enables the visual system to develop the ability to stabilise images and for the body to move and adapt to balance against gravity ultimately to crawl and walk and dynamically move. It is easy to identify children who are not initially engaging their vestibular system. They tend to keep their heads in midline and do not invert their heads when going up or down steps, do not squat to play and when going into small spaces including tunnels and under chairs they lower the body by bending knees or getting unto their tummies or backs and not tipping or inverting the head to bend at the trunk.

From Goddard's (2002) list of ten reflexes, consideration will be given to the five primitive reflexes which, if retained, have arguably the greatest impact on learning. These consist of the Moro, the Palmar, the Rooting, the Asymmetrical Tonic Neck Reflex (ATNR) and the Symmetrical Tonic Neck Reflex (STNR). All of these, with the exception of the STNR, begin in utero and are fully present at birth.

The Moro Reflex

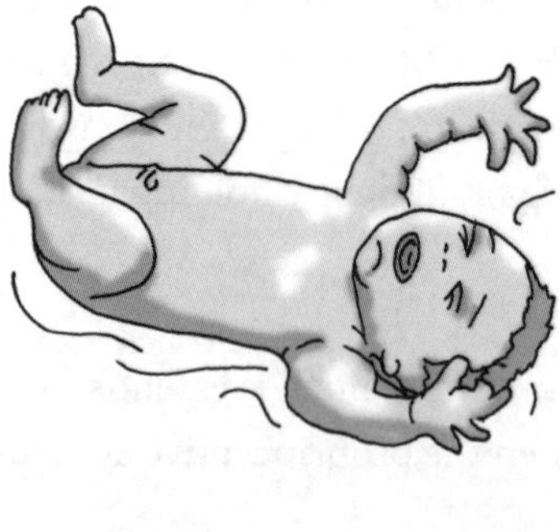

The Moro reflex is triggered by sudden, unexpected stimuli such as noise, light, temperature, movement or pain. In response, the arms move suddenly upwards away from the body, hands open, and there is a sharp intake of breath or possibly a cry and a pause before the arms return back across the body. It produces a fear/flight/fright response to a perceived threat and is used to alert the parent to a need and to summon help. Later in life this Moro reflex is replaced with a startle response which remains with us for the rest of our lives, but we exercise more control over it and recover more quickly when startled.

Should the Moro reflex remain uninhibited, it may well result in hypersensitivity to sound, light, touch and movement with the child remaining in a heightened state of alertness when it is triggered. The child will find it difficult to filter out stimuli of a sensory nature. As Goddard (2002) says, "The eyes will be drawn toward changes in light and to every movement within his visual field. His ears may receive too much auditory information……so he becomes easily overloaded." (p6) His reaction to this sensory information will be initially fright, followed by flight/fight. If the response is fight, then he may display aggressive, overactive, excitable, manipulative behaviour. In flight response, he may display fearful, withdrawn, sensitive and difficult socialising behaviour. Other difficulties the child may experience are poor balance, car sickness, tiring easily, poor stamina, and dislike of change, mood swings, feeling anxious all the time, poor self esteem and feeling a need to control events. No other reflex has such wide-ranging implications for all the senses.

The Palmar Reflex

Pressure in the palm of the hand will result in the palmar or grasping reflex. If a finger or object is placed in a child's hand, he can exert a surprisingly strong grasp on the object using only three fingers, sufficient at times to enable the child to "pull to sit" lifting the head. The thumb is scarcely used at first, but the child will progress to the pincer grip using the thumb and forefinger in opposition. Before using this pincer grip the child must learn to release an object which may take quite a bit of practice. A further refinement of the pincer grip is an awareness of the pressure required for the weight of the object.

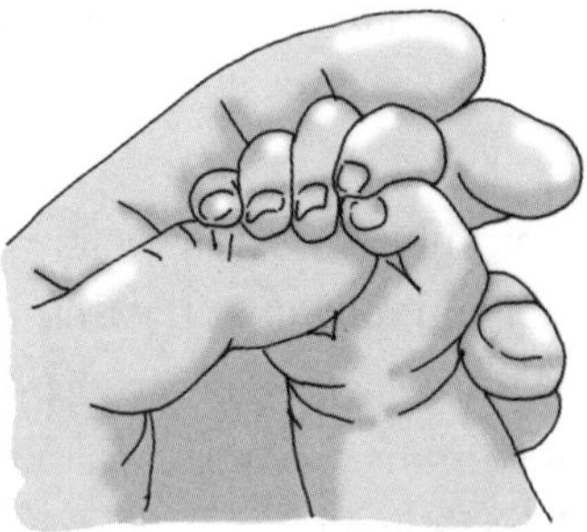

The Palmar reflex should be inhibited by the age of six months. If it is retained, it will have an impact on manual dexterity, may well affect pencil grip, and cause sensitivity to touch in the palm of the hand. An unexpected side effect may be poor articulation and independent muscle control at the front of the mouth due to the Babkin Response. (Babkin showed the relationship of the hand to the mouth in a sensory motor way so that when pressure in the palms of both hands of an infant was exerted it resulted in the infant opening his mouth). You may have noted that when a child is breastfeeding the hands may knead in time to the sucking. There is a relationship between hand movements and activity around the mouth. This may be seen in later years if the tongue is extended through the lips when concentrating on a manual task.

The ATNR

The Asymmetrical Tonic Neck Reflex (ATNR) begins to emerge about halfway through pregnancy. Mothers will be aware of fluttering or kicks as the baby moves around inside the womb, but they are unlikely to be aware that if a baby's head turns to the left the arms and legs on the left follow the direction of the head and vice versa. This type of motion increases neural connections in the brain and

facilitates the development of balance. During the actual birthing process the ATNR (arms following the side to which the head is turned) assists with the passage of air when the baby is in the prone position. In the early months of life the ATNR allows the baby to train one side of the body at a time and assists with eye/hand co ordination for reaching movements and gaining awareness of distance. There may well be a protective mechanism associated with the ATNR, so that when a baby is lying face down the reflex will encourage the turning of the head to the side of the extended arm to prevent suffocation.

The ATNR should be inhibited by about six months of age to allow the child to progress to more complex skills such as creeping and crawling which demand a cross-patterning skill (left knee/right hand extended).

Should the ATNR be retained, the development of eye/hand coordination may be compromised. This may also have an impact on further development. If cross-patterning does not develop in crawling, this may well lead to bilateral difficulties such as manipulating an object with both hands and delay in the development of a preferred hand. Later on, when learning to walk, the child may walk with the left hand and left leg moving forward at the same time giving rise to an odd appearance. (These difficulties of crossing midline are discussed in the chapters on midline awareness - Chapter 4 and eye tracking, Chapter 13). There will also be a tendency for vision to be more fixed to objects at arm's length rather than in the distance. Eye tracking, in both the vertical and horizontal axis, can also be impaired and scanning a line of print or copying from a white board challenging. Integrating the ATNR is essential for school readiness.

When this reflex is retained, the head and arms will want to move in the same direction. Handwriting may become difficult because, as the head and arms move to the right, the fingers will want to open. Great concentration will be required to overcome this tendency and, because more pressure is required to keep hold of the pencil, the writing hand will tire quickly. The child may compensate for this either by adopting a weak pencil grip or by rotating the page. If the latter is the case, the writing will slope in different directions. The child will thus have poor fine motor skills, delayed dominance, difficulty with putting ideas down on paper, difficulty using utensils, confusion for direction of letters and numbers and a tendency for DCD, Dyslexia or Dyscalculia. This difficulty associated with a retained ATNR, may also be observed when children are learning to ride a bicycle. If a child turns his head to look to one side, the arms will also tend to move in that direction, causing the bicycle to swerve. It is also causal to a difficulty when learning to swim, especially the front crawl.

The Rooting Reflex

The Rooting Reflex involves three separate reflexes: searching for, sucking and swallowing. As with the previous reflexes already mentioned, it develops in utero at about six months into the pregnancy. It is present at birth when it is at its strongest. A light touch around the mouth will subsequently cause a turning of the head towards the stimulus. The mouth will open wide and the tongue

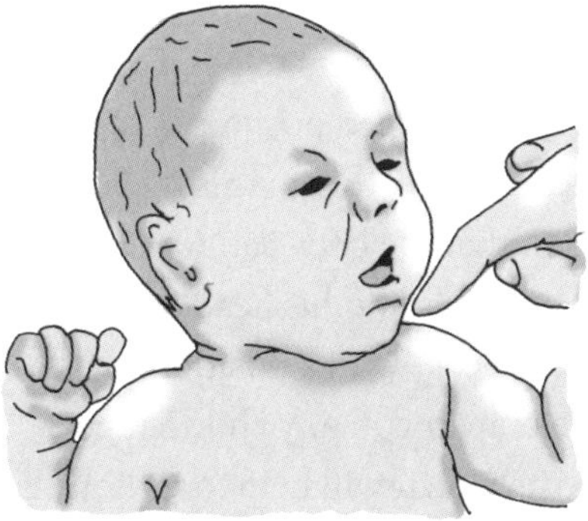

will extend in readiness for sucking and swallowing. This reflex develops from being tactile stimulated to being visually stimulated. The sight of the nipple or of a teat on a bottle will trigger the Rooting Reflex. The Rooting Reflex will be present while breast or bottle feeding but should normally be inhibited by about four months. If it is not inhibited, the tongue will remain too far forward in the mouth and may cause dribbling, chewing and speech problems later on. Also, since the hand and mouth are closely connected (Babkin Response), this can lead to poor manual dexterity.

The STNR

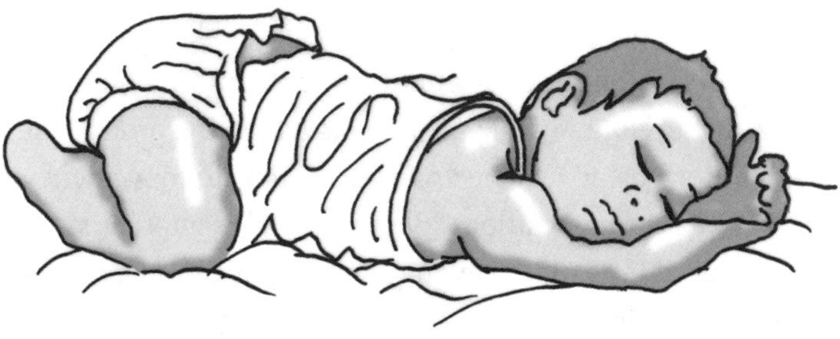

The final reflex in this section which has implications for learning is the Symmetrical Tonic Neck Reflex (STNR). This reflex persists for a short time from about six to eleven months of age by which time it should be inhibited. The purpose of this reflex is to enable the child to progress from lying on his tummy to getting on his hands and knees in readiness for crawling. The reflex first causes head **flexion** (curling the head in towards the chest), which causes the legs to bend and the arms to extend when the baby is in the quadruped position. Then there is head **extension** (lifting the head back). This causes the legs to curl up and the arms to straighten so that the baby can now come into a position where he is seated on his heels and his head and trunk are supported by straight arms. The child is now in a position from which crawling may begin, but before crawling, many children go through a period of rocking movements which will help to inhibit the STNR.

While the ATNR tends to divide the body into a left and right side, the STNR divides the body at the pelvis giving an upper half and lower half. When the head extends the upper part of the body extends and the lower part bends, whilst the reverse occurs when the head bends.

The retention of the STNR tends to prevent children moving in a good crawling pattern with opposing arms and legs extended at the same time. Children get around this problem by "commando crawling", using elbows while the body is flat on the ground, or by "bum shuffling", using feet, heels and arms to gain movement while remaining in a sitting position. "Bear walking" is another strategy sometimes used instead of crawling. In this position the child's bottom is in the air, with arms straight out to support the head and trunk while the feet remain on the ground with legs straight supporting the bum. Children may go through a bear walking stage when learning to walk. This is because they fall over so often and may use it as a protective mechanism when moving across a room which is not carpeted. When creeping, children develop eye/hand coordination, the ability to look ahead, a sense of balance, space and depth perception and bilateral skills. These skills are essential to reading and writing.

Children who retain an STNR slump over the school desk, have poor hand/eye coordination, are messy eaters, have difficulty learning to do the breaststroke and tend to be slow at copying from the board because of having to relocate eye position; they sit on the ground with their legs in a W position (not sitting on the backs of their legs but with their legs out to the side). furthermore they exhibit poor muscle tone and limited ability to concentrate and sit still. They also have difficulty playing with balls.

A significant number of the children we see present with reflex retention. This is characterised by low muscle tone, poor balance and vestibular difficulties including gravitational insecurity, as well as by an absence of smooth coordinated movements that lack rhythm, by increased anxiety and inner stress and an absence of postural reflexes. Early primitive reflexes are arousing and protective. It is necessary that these become integrated thereby allowing motor- based, postural reflexes to develop. Reflex integration is hierarchical and the developing reflexes allow for efficient connections between the brain stem, cerebellum, temporal lobe and the frontal lobe of the brain. The pre frontal cortex allows children to think about what they are doing, become organised, control impulses and develop reasoning. Where children have not integrated early reflexes they present with high arousal. Moreover, they have emotional and anxiety issues as well as motor based difficulties, including coordination and handwriting problems.

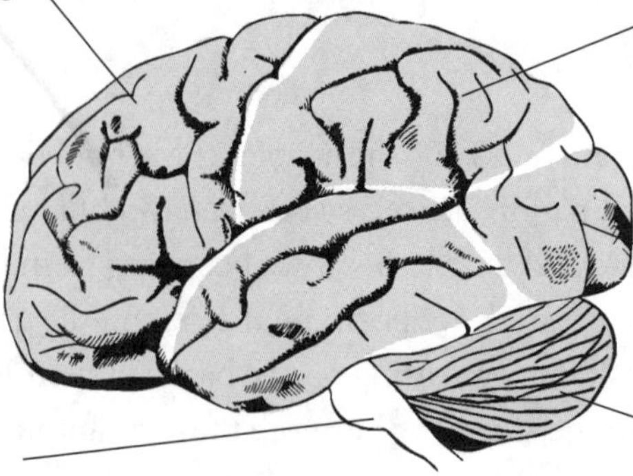

Intervention to Encourage the Transition from Primitive Reflexes to Postural Reflexes in Young Children

Active or retained reflexes that present in children with motor-based difficulties may be improved by implementing a programme of physical activity both at home and in school. The exercises are designed to promote the postural reflexes and encourage transition from the primitive to the postural reflexes. This will be a gradual process in line with normal growth and development. Programmes such as Primary Movement and Brain Gym should prove helpful. The integration of retained reflexes is crucial to the Occupational Therapist when implementing therapy using a sensory integration framework, as sensory development is based on mature reflexes and associated neuro development.

A programme of motor activities for this purpose is included in the appendices and is specially designed with young children in mind. Since the equipment required is minimal and all instructions are included, parents and early years teachers wishing to make a start may find this programme useful.

Key Points from Chapter 5

- The TLR backwards reflex must be developed at the time of delivery to develop the integration of the vestibular and then the proprioceptive senses.
- The TLR helps the infant to adapt to moving against gravity and become spatially aware.
- The primitive reflexes develop in the womb and are present at birth, but most should be inhibited by about one year old.
- The Moro or Startle reflex may be prompted by sudden movement, pain or abrupt changes in temperature, light or noise.
- A child will have a strong grasp of an object placed in his hand using three fingers which will develop into the pincer grip.
- The ATNR assists with eye/hand coordination and prepares a child to develop a cross lateral crawling pattern.
- A Rooting reflex which persists beyond a few months can lead to feeding and speech problems.
- The STNR prepares a baby for crawling, but its retention prevents the establishment of a good crawling pattern and can lead to problems with reading and writing.
- Where early reflexes persist, arousal and regulation difficulties are evident.
- Handwriting, eye tracking and reading, poor coordination and motor difficulties can occur as a result of retained reflexes.

Key Points from Chapter 5

- Sensory over reactions to sound and light may be present
- Concentration and attention may be impacted by sensory distraction
- Age appropriate reflex integration is essential for all later aspects of brain development, including integration of the sensory systems, vestibular, proprioception, vision and auditory

Chapter 6

Gross Motor Skills

The Big Idea

You make the football team

The Academic Viewpoint

Movement is at the very centre of young children's lives. It is an important aspect of all development, whether in the motor, cognitive, or affective domains of human behaviour. To deny children the opportunity to reap the many benefits of regular, vigorous physical activity is to deny them the opportunity to experience the joy of efficient movement, the health effects of movement, and a lifetime as confident, competent movers. Gallahue, (1993), p24

Red Flag Issues

- Inability to jump two feet together
- Lack of crawling and delayed early motor skills
- Can't kick a ball
- Can't think and do at the same time
- Difficulty forming letters, particularly "x"
- Cannot draw a man

Green for Go

- Reads and writes well
- Claps hands and initiates gesture
- Enjoys using all playground equipment
- Can stand on one leg for 5 seconds and jump two feet together
- Can cross midline
- Can dress and undress by 5 years

Gross motor skills not only enable a child to be good at sports and various types of physical challenges, but they have a much wider influence impacting on a child's ability to read and write well, to develop good foundation skills for maths, and to be able to concentrate effectively in the classroom. They will also increase a child's confidence and improve his self-esteem.

Basically these skills are jumping, walking, running and any activity which involves using the body's large muscles. Control of these muscles starts to develop from birth, beginning with the head and torso. This continues until he has mastered a wide range of activities that an adult can do without thinking: sitting, crawling, standing, walking, running and jumping, balancing, kicking, throwing and catching, usually in that order. A child will continue practising a new skill until it is mastered and becomes automatic, or until the child is happy with the way he is doing it. This may take several weeks. Outdoor play will give many opportunities for the development of these skills and will be greatly enhanced when playground equipment is available. A climbing frame is a particularly good piece of equipment when used in a safe environment and within the child's limits.

The word "basically" was purposely used at the beginning of this chapter because these skills involve much more than the act of moving. They rely on the body's sense of touch, vestibular and proprioceptive processing, good muscle strength and tone, control of the trunk and a good understanding of the physical environment. It is important to understand that movement is dependent on an intact sensory system, and also that the quality of the movement requires continuous sensory feedback. It can be static, as in remaining balanced while sitting in a chair, or dynamic, as in regaining balance after running and kicking a ball.

Praxis

Any movement has three parts to it which we call "praxis," i.e. the process of **conceiving** an action, **organising** the body for the action and the **execution** of the action. It is not intended here to discuss in any great detail what happens within the brain to facilitate movement, i.e. how the various lobes of the brain, limbic system and cerebellum all interact and work together. It is sufficient to say that the child needs to be sufficiently aroused and able to detect a sensory input in the environment, usually a voice, to produce an intention to act. The organising of the body brings together the issues discussed in the chapter on Body Awareness, namely Body Image, Body Part Identification, Body Scheme, Laterality, Midline Awareness and issues surrounding Directionality, all of which are needed to produce a motor plan. The motor plan includes the intention of the action, the motor image, the motor preparation of which muscles will be used, and finally, the execution of the plan, which is the movement itself.

For gross motor activity to be adequate, a child must deal with various types of incoming information and respond quickly and accurately with appropriate movements. At the same time he must make use of on-going sensory feedback to tell him how well he is doing, and to prepare him to feed forward into the next movement sequence.

As the child carries out the movement he begins to build up a "motor memory" which allows him to recall the muscle groups to be engaged quickly and properly, in the right order and at the right time to improve the activity. Some children will do this instinctively, while others may need further training and practice.

A child who is unable to follow the verbal command to hop, skip and step, an action sequence taking them across the room, is displaying a sequencing problem. Sequencing commences as a motor skill but develops as a perceptual and cognitive ability, i.e. matching patterns and organising letters for spelling. This sequencing difficulty, alongside an absence of midline awareness, is frequently seen in children with Dyspraxia (DCD).

Gross Motor Skills: Developmental Milestones (birth-6 years)

Included here is a developmental checklist to outline the skills which may be expected in children up to the age of six years old. Since all children are different, some will reach these milestones sooner than others, but the milestones will provide a range of indicators of what may be expected at each stage.

By 3 months

- Follows a moving object or person with eyes
- Turns head from side to side when lying on his stomach
- Lifts head when held at shoulder, with only slight head lag
- Grasps a toy when given one
- Wriggles and kicks arms and legs
- Turns head towards bright light or colours or the sound of a human voice
- Rounded back in sitting

3 months to 6 months

- Holds head steady while sitting
- Good sitting posture with enough stability to reach for objects with both hands
- Lifts head and chest while lying on the floor
- Reaches out, picks up an object and brings it to midline
- Transfers objects from hand to hand, starting to use thumb in opposition to radial finger
- Moro reflex and asymmetric tonic neck reflex are integrated
- In prone, the chest is all the way off the floor and weight is supported on hands

6 months to 12 months

- Crawls on hands and knees
- Rotates on trunk when sitting
- Pulls to stand
- Takes steps while holding onto furniture
- Stands alone momentarily
- Places small blocks in/out of box
- Sits alone
- Finger feeds
- Drinks with help from a cup
- Uses index finger to point or poke
- Puts blocks in and out of a container
- Copies sounds and actions
- Sees then crawls towards an object
- Responds to music
- Raises arms to be picked up
- Says first word

One year old

- Pushes or pulls toys
- Kicks a ball while holding on
- Walks alone
- Climbs onto low furniture
- Climbs stairs with assistance
- Feeds himself finger foods
- Fine pincer grasp is developed
- Places small beads in a cup
- Can stoop over and recover a toy

Two years old

- Walks with smooth heel/toe motion
- Runs fairly well, but lacks control over turns and stops
- Climbs onto furniture
- Kicks a ball
- Stacks four blocks
- Walks upstairs holding bannister
- Hangs from a bar
- Names 4-6 body parts

Three years old

- Runs smoothly and stops suddenly
- Jumps from a low step
- Goes up and down stairs with alternating feet, holding rail
- Throws and catches a ball
- Pumps a swing
- Undresses self
- Stacks nine blocks
- Can walk backwards
- Can throw a ball overhead
- Verbal instructions are understood

Four years old

- Runs fast
- Jumps well
- Hops forward on one foot
- Balances on one foot for five seconds
- Catches a ball from five feet
- Jumps over a rope

- Dresses and undresses
- Draws simple shapes
- Copies block designs
- Cuts with scissors
- Walks upstairs using alternate feet
- Bounces a ball
- Catches a beanbag in hands
- Can count to ten
- Knows days of week and seasons
- Begins to show empathy and avoids conflict

Five years old

- Hops on one foot for seven steps or more
- Does star jumps
- Carries objects up/down stairs
- Catches a ball from five feet with two hands
- Bounces a ball in place
- Skips with a rope
- Rides a bicycle with supports, with help from an adult
- Dresses self
- Can attend to own toileting needs
- Can vary speed when walking and running
- Aware of upper and lower case letters

Six years old

- Rides a bicycle with supports
- Walks along a balance beam
- Kicks a rolling ball
- Jumps over low objects
- Tries to stand on head

- Throws a beanbag accurately into a tub
- Speaks in complex sentences
- Commences independent reading

These milestones are just guidelines because each child is different and develops at differing rates. However, if your child is displaying an absence of some of the age appropriate milestones, this may indicate signs of a possible delay in motor function for these age ranges.

Postural Motor Function

Just as gross motor skills are directly related to posture, so effective movement control depends on the development of the following postural motor functions:

- Reflex integration: the ability to inhibit primitive reflexes and to develop postural motor control;
- Muscle tone: adequate muscle strength to provide stable posture against gravity and to allow movement;
- Girdle stability: core stability at pelvic and shoulder girdles to allow effective changing of body positions. (Needed especially for handwriting);
- Body balance: ability to maintain static and dynamic balance is essential for all coordinated movements.

If a child has problems in the above postural motor functions, he will have difficulties in motor coordination and organisation in both gross and fine motor activities. Where a child has poor midline crossing, usually as a result of not crawling, early walking, use of a baby walker, and lack of tummy time, he will generally have difficulties in left/right awareness. Consequently, this will include problems in finding the centre of themselves, (essential for knowledge of the direction and rotation of objects outside the body), and poor body awareness and spatial orientation. Ultimately, this difficulty may result in letter reversal and poor sequencing for maths skills.

Motor development is therefore significant as an early foundational skill for academic and higher brain functions.

Posture Based Motor Difficulties

From the issues mentioned above, here is an indication of the type of trouble which may result.

Difficulty with :

- Sense of body in space- problem with balance and location of the body in a steady position;
- Kinaesthetic–difficulty tracking body movement in the middle of an activity;
- Motor planning- problem choosing a strategy or planning to meet a motor challenge. This is particularly evident in "novel" challenges;
- Coordinating muscle groups- problem in deciding which muscles to use for a specific task and synchronizing them during activities;
- Motor memory- difficulty in quickly remembering a sequence of muscles necessary to complete the task;
- Monitoring- problem getting feedback from the proprioceptive system to give information as to how well muscles are performing during an activity;
- Muscle tone- has insufficient strength for completing the activity and tires quickly;

- Verbal/motor input- difficulty achieving desired responses from verbal instructions;
- Visual/spatial input- difficulty timing and judging flight of balls.

Many children with posture based motor challenges tend to have poor vestibular and proprioceptive function resulting in motor challenges and poor core stability. They tend to have omitted the crawling stage and walked too early or struggled to get onto their feet. Ultimately, such children have very poor upper limb strength, cannot weight bear on straight arms over a therapy ball and are challenged to do a wheelbarrow even when legs are supported. These children grow up to dislike physical activity and sport; they also have difficulty with fine motor skills including tool use and handwriting.

The SIPT (Sensory Integration and Praxis Test) allows specific standardised assessment of such postural motor based difficulties.

There are several environmental reasons which may contribute to these difficulties that stem from lifestyles in the twenty-first century. Many children spend much time watching television or playing computer games, so that both gross and fine motor skills do not develop as they should. Another reason is that many children grow up in an overly protected environment, with the result that outside play, walking and cycling activities are restricted, but, in attempting to keep children safe, motor skills are affected. Children spend quite a considerable amount of time in a baby transporter car seat or in a baby walker so that active play is restricted, and that may be another factor.

It is interesting to note the research carried out by Richardson and Wilmer (2001) into the remedial effects of Omega-3 fats on

DCD. Stordy (1997) also demonstrated that children in her dyslexic/dyspraxic study group, who were initially assessed as being in the first percentile, showed significant improvement in manual dexterity, balance and ball skills within twelve weeks of taking a course of fatty acid supplements. The anecdotal evidence of some parents would lead us to believe that this might well be the case. One other general point to make is that DCD children were often found to be unsettled as babies, were difficult to soothe and had sleeping issues.

May's Story:

A Case Study of Gross Motor Difficulty and Ensuing Action Programme

May, a five year old, came to the clinic at her mother's request because the mother was concerned about some problems she had noticed in her child's development. She was concerned about May's balance, frequent falls, her posture, letter and number recognition, processing of speech and the loudness of her voice. The mother, an Occupational Therapist, had some awareness of the consequences of sensory processing difficulties.

When May arrived at the clinic she was cautious while climbing the stairs, taking them one step at a time and at each step placed one foot beside the other. She kept hold of the handrail all the while. She presented as a happy child who was anxious to please.

May was initially asked to sit on the suspended bolster swing (a covered tube of about twenty centimetres in diameter and a metre long) as though it was a horse. She looked at her mum for guidance but, when she received no help, sat on it in the conventional way as on a swing with feet forward. When shown how to do it, she had no difficulty in sitting astride the swing. It soon became apparent that she responded immediately in the correct way when shown what to do, but had much greater difficulty when just given verbal instructions. She depended more on her visual sense and had difficulty processing auditory instructions. Her mother confirmed her own awareness of May's difficulty in responding to relatively simple tasks when given mainly verbal instructions.

The focus of May's visit was to determine her muscle tone, core stability and bilateral skills, and then to identify any retained reflexes, midline awareness difficulties and body and spatial awareness issues. An Auditory Processing Check was also administered because of the loudness of her voice and her apparent difficulties processing speech. A Clinical Observations check, a Sensory Processing Tool, The Scan C (auditory processing check) a handwriting check, and Developmental Age Observations were used.

The assessment began with motor challenges. May was asked to crash on to the piled-up duvets which she was unable to do until it was demonstrated. Her motor skills were observed, including her ability to use both sides of her body separately, alternately, or acting together to move her body through space efficiently and automatically in a physical environment.

May struggled with the majority of the tasks and was unable to stand on either leg without vision. Furthermore, she was not able to cross midline as in touching the opposite ear with her hand, also having poor core stability in maintaining balance in tall kneeling or 4 point kneeling. May was additionally unable to counterbalance quickly enough to prevent herself from falling over. There was evidence of a retained ATNR which should have been integrated at infancy. This reflex will cause her to lack trunk rotation, to dissociate arm and head movements when rotating her head (head, shoulders and trunk turn as a block movement) and impede her ability to assume anti-gravity positions. All of this will impact on her left/right awareness, body dominance, and ability to work to midline, as well as her fine motor skills and her ability to integrate a series of motor moves that incorporate sequences of movement.

May further showed evidence of poor body awareness and poor body scheme. She needed to see her limbs in order to be aware of their position in space. Her proprioception (information from muscles, tendons and joints) was also was poor. Proprioception is needed for success in self-care skills such as getting dressed, self-feeding and tool use. In addition, it is required for balance reactions and negotiating obstacles without falling.

When May was building a tower of blocks, she sat in an asymmetrical position and built the blocks with one hand without using touch feedback to inform her building skills. This emphasised her lack of bilateral skills. She had difficulty identifying known letters in a feely bag and difficulty touching each finger with her thumb fluently. May was slow in determining hand dominance and a posting coins test showed that she was quicker and better at manipulating items with her left hand. This would lead to the conclusion that she was left hand dominant and would suggest that this should be encouraged. May had difficulty multitasking on the wobble board, which shows that her ability to think and do is impaired by poor motor skills. Her mother described May as an on-the-go child. A vestibular processing check showed her to have an under-responsive vestibular system. This will cause her to seek movement and to have a need to fidget. An auditory processing check, using the Scan C, indicated a score on the first percentile, showing a significant auditory processing difficulty.

Overall, May presented with difficulties involving most of the major sensory pathways, including the proprioceptive, tactile, vestibular and auditory systems.

An action programme will include the following:

- A reflex integration exercise programme
- Increase concentration and attention through self-regulation skills and fine motor skills focusing on hand dominance and tool use
- Using a listening programme for auditory intervention
- Promoting the identification of letters and numbers through touch
- Extending and encouraging a wider range of play skills, especially pencil work and construction skills
- A sensory integration programme with sensory diet to enable self-regulation and fluent processing of both intrinsic and extrinsic input
- Bilateral and sequencing activities
- Mat work and core stability activities
- Use of suspended equipment for motor planning and body awareness challenges
- Visualising/verbalising programme for numeracy and literacy

John's Story:

A Case Study of Gravitational Insecurity

John is a 17 year old who attends a special school for children aged 11-18. He travels to school every day on the school bus. He is a heavily built child weighing about 16 stone. Furthermore, it takes several adults to get him on/off the bus due to his fear of heights. When walking to town for social skills training, he has to follow the same route to get there because he needs to use the footpath ramping to help him get from the road on to the footpath. John will only use the ramping to mount the footpath and will not take the step up. He also has problems with escalators or stairs and will walk around an obstacle in his path rather than step over it. Besides this, he does not like playground equipment. He is a highly anxious child who likes routine and who is reluctant to try anything new or different. His overall behaviour is affected by his perceived threat of movement.

This young man is displaying classic symptoms of gravitational insecurity, an area which has never been explored or remedied with him. He will not grow out of this difficulty, but as movement is such an essential part of daily living, he has developed a series of avoidance strategies. In the absence of language skills, the frustration of movement will be demonstrated in his increasingly challenging behaviour. Understanding the sensory reaction to movement, and possibly other areas such as auditory or tactile difficulties, is the key to managing this young man and increasing his ability to remain regulated in everyday situations. The closest we can come to understanding his fear is the fear many experience when going near the edge of a high cliff.

John's tolerance for having his feet lifted off the ground one at a time needs to be increased by using a suspended glider swing. The stages are as follows: John shows interest in the swing and accepts it, subsequently engaging with it while it is stable on the floor. Then he touches it, steps over it, sits on it, swings it, and kneels at it. The swing is then ramped while he is kneeling on the ground. He sits on it while it is ramped with feet on the ground. The range of movement is then extended until the swing is swinging free at minimal height while John's feet are on the ground, then increasing the height and his tolerance to the swing. The ultimate aim is to have him swinging freely while sitting and then standing on the swing. It is important to remember that all these activities are child-led. He should be encouraged to engage with the equipment but must never be forced. To this end, positive reinforcements may be used initially, such as objects or healthy snacks. In John's case, after a week's intervention, he was first of all sitting on the swing and then standing on it while allowing himself to be swung. This made a great difference to his ability to get on/off the bus, his lifestyle in general and home management.

Key Points from Chapter 6

- Motor skills have an extensive bearing on cognitive skills.
- Praxis is the ability to decide upon, organise and carry out a series of actions and complex body movements.
- Postural motor functions include reflex integration, muscle tone, shoulder and girdle stability and body balance.
- Many problems both motor-based and academic may result from poor postural motor function.
- Midline crossing difficulties will have a cumulative effect on academic achievement.
- A passive life style can contribute to existing postural motor difficulties.

Chapter 7

Fine Motor Skills

The Big Idea

Have I got hands that work as a pair, or do I have a right hand and a left hand working separately?

The Academic Viewpoint

Recent research has demonstrated a clear connection between the development of fine motor skills in early life and later success in math, science and reading. Such skills – those as simple as how an infant can use her eyes to track her mother's face and then reach her hand out and touch her mother's nose – may just help us understand how ready that child will be for Kindergarten, as well as what kind of achiever she'll be over the next few years. (The motor–cognitive connection, The Science of Learning Blog)

Red Flag Issues

- Avoids or is destructive when block building
- Can't use scissors
- Has difficulty reading from the whiteboard (ocular motor)
- Does not cross midline when doing tasks
- Switches objects from hand to hand
- Can't stay within the lines for colouring in

Green for Go

- Uses non-dominant hand for support and when block building
- Is constructive
- Can feed self
- Can rotate body
- Can copy from the white board accurately
- Can write own name
- Enjoys colouring in
- Has good gross and fine motor skills which help inhibit early reflexes
- Is not impulsive
- Forms good social relationships

Gross and fine motor skills do not develop separately, but they come together when a child does things for himself. If the gross motor skills are about using the large muscle groups in the body, then the fine motor skills are about using the small muscles for such activities as writing, grasping, fastening clothes and doing or undoing a button. These activities involve strength, control and dexterity. The main parts of the body in use are the hands, wrists, fingers, feet, toes, lips and tongue, or some of these in combination.

Prior to engaging a child in fine motor repetitions, it is essential to establish the foundations for fine motor development. These include core stability at the pelvis and shoulder girdle, ability to weight bear on either foot, stability in 4 point kneeling with opposing arm/leg extended and copying a demonstrated body pattern with right arm touching left ear and vice versa. It is also necessary to be able to assume the pattern of prone extension when lying on the tummy.

There are two approaches to intervention for fine motor difficulties. In the top-down approach, the deficient skill is taught in isolation, e.g. shoelace tying. The bottom-up approach is where the core or foundation skills are worked on and improved to allow skill attainment. (see Developmental Building Blocks and Approaches to Treatment in the appendices). In shoelace tying, this includes core stability in shoulder and pelvic girdles. Dynamic postural ability and midline awareness, balance and coordination fluency with bilateral integration are also required. In addition, it is necessary for the child to have the idea of what to do to successfully tie a shoelace.

Included here are some activities to illustrate the end product of visual and fine motor skills.

- Hand/eye coordination: the hands guided by the eye for accuracy in placement, direction and speed as in placing pegs in a pegboard.
- Ocular motor: this is the ability for the eyes to follow, track and focus on an object, like the flight of a ball.
- Eye/foot coordination: doing actions with the feet which are guided by the eye like kicking a rolling ball.
- Manual dexterity: the ability to manipulate hands and fingers when handwriting
- Stereognosis: the ability to recognise objects in a bag with vision occluded using touch alone.
- Tactile perception: interpreting information using touch to send messages directly to the brain as in using Braille.

At each stage it is important to use positive reinforcement to encourage the child, and while we all want to see children reach their potential, it is not necessary to overstimulated them in an attempt to develop super babies. However, weakness in this area will have a big impact, not only on life in general, but particularly in the school environment and also, weakness here can shape how a child feels about himself.

There are **four** main skills which a child must learn before he can move on to more complicated tasks. Prior to engaging in these tasks, a child needs to have developed internal body awareness and have a sense of where his limbs are in space, a general direction for targeting and the ideation of what to do. These skills are:

- grasping an object
- reaching out to an object
- deliberately releasing objects
- turn the wrist in various directions

(The appendix includes two tables, one for the Learning Sequence for Skillful Play and the other for Hand Function and Fine Motor Skills)

Weight bearing through the arms is very important as it is this which gives proprioceptive feedback to make a baby aware of his arms and hands and enables him to use them efficiently. Weight bearing also causes a baby to open his hands, straighten his arms and raise his head and trunk.

Bilateral Hand Use

Bilateral use of both hands to manipulate objects in midline is also essential. While a child's hands are busy, he is absorbing information and learning about his environment. Hands that are busy in purposeful activity will not adopt sensory mannerisms such as biting, sucking, flicking or flapping. Before listing fine motor developmental milestones, here are some bilateral activities to be promoted in younger children.

- Clapping hands
- Holding a toy in each hand for a period of time
- Banging toys together

Developmental Fine Motor Milestones from Birth to 6 years

0 to 6 months

- Reflex grasp, hand mostly closed
- Reaches out for objects but not accurately
- Clasps hands together
- Reaches out, visually and purposefully directed
- Begins to hold small objects

6 to 12 months

- Transfers objects from hand to hand
- Picks up larger objects more easily
- Reaches forward and sideways accurately
- Can rake or scoop up small objects
- Picks up items using finger and thumb
- Points with index finger
- Attempts to help with dressing

Up to 18 months

- Holds crayon in fist, scribbles
- Stacks 2 blocks
- Helps put toys away
- Removes socks and shoes
- Points at pictures in a book
- Uses pincer grip to pick up small toys
- Holds a toy in the middle of his body with both hands
- Gets frustrated easily when playing

Up to 2 years

- Scribbles
- Turns knobs
- Pulls zipper up and down
- Wants to help with household tasks
- Turns forearm so thumb is pointing down
- Attempts to take off and put on socks and shoes
- Uses a spoon
- Can draw a vertical line
- Can build a tower with 3 blocks

Up to 3 years

- Strings large beads on a stick
- Cuts paper with scissors
- Can manage large buttons
- Rolls out a snake in play dough
- Draws a horizontal line

Up to 4 years

- Copies a circle
- Pours own drink from a small container
- Puts pegs in a pegboard
- Strings small beads
- Can hold a pencil or crayon in a tripod grip

Up to 5 years

- Dresses himself, may tie laces
- Cuts out shapes and pictures with scissors
- Prints some capital letters
- Holds a fork
- Puts key in a lock and opens it
- Draws diagonal lines

Up to 6 years

- Cuts out complex pictures with scissors
- Does more complex jigsaws
- Copies a sequence of letters and numbers

Signs of Delay

The above milestones will act as a guide in determining whether or not a child is delayed in developing fine motor skills. Early indicators of delay include being unable to wave bye-bye, not engaging with early posting or threading, inability to build blocks, not holding an object in either hand, or holding two objects but not reaching for a third. Recognition, however, should first be made of what a child has already achieved and also of the child's neurological status by means of a physical examination. This may be carried out only if it is not possible to determine other underlying factors.

Fine Motor Skills Suitable for P1 Children

The following is by no means a comprehensive list, but it will serve to give some indication of the range of activities a child in P1 may be doing. There should be a variety of tasks which include an element of fun. Suggested activities include the following:

- Taking a pencil/crayon/chalk for a walk and see how long you can keep it going;
- Sorting small objects into containers according to size/ shape/ colour;
- Cliping things together using pegs/paper clips;
- Dressing up activities;
- Posting shapes;
- Threading small beads on a lace;

- Cutting, pasting;
- Tracing lines/shapes/colours;
- Tracing pictures;
- Copying writing patterns using coloured sand/chalk;
- Dot-to-dot pictures, drawing lines (mouse to cheese);
- Modelling in clay, plasticine or play dough, painting;
- Painting using different sizes of brushes;
- Jigsaws (building up the number of pieces used);
- Using pegboards;
- Block building;
- Construction toys (using screws, plastic nuts and bolts);
- Pouring sand/water from cup to cup or to make various toys spin around.

Skills for Various Parts of the Hand

There are many activities which will improve manipulative skills in various parts of the hand. The parts of the hand include the wrist, the thumb side of the hand, in- hand and fingers.

Wrist Stability

The wrist joint should be straight in line with the hand or slightly extended during hand skills. The child should be discouraged from flexing his wrist during manipulative activities.

Activities for Encouraging Wrist Stability

- While on all fours, shift weight onto the palm, rock backwards and forwards and donkey kick
- Two children face each other with palms together and push against each other
- Draw on a vertical plane above eye level
- In a vertical orientation, carry out lacing activities, stamping with an ink pad, using a pegboard, using a "Magnadoodle"
- Use rolling pin to roll clay or dough whilst keeping hands open as opposed to using the handle
- Use Louie Lobster Claw Catcher to pick up objects

Activities to Encourage Development and Control of the Skilled Side of the Hand (thumb side)

- Roll small pieces of play dough into small balls using finger movements to make a bird's nest with eggs in it
- Play tug of war with objects of small diameter,e.g. straws/ laces
- Pinch and seal zip lock bags with fingers and thumb in opposition
- Roll small pieces of tissue paper using thumb and first two fingers to make a collage
- Turn a row of coins over from heads to tails
- Encourage child to cut using scissors, making sure the last two fingers touch the palm of hand
- Squeeze trigger of a spray bottle to spray
- Pick up small objects using tweezers

Pushing down on the buttons of the "Rock 'Em Sock 'Em ROBOTS" game from Mattel really strengthens the muscles of the thumb and allows for more stability, leading to an open web space.

In-hand Manipulation

In-hand manipulation refers to the ability to reposition objects within one hand without having to use the other. This is a most complex fine motor skill and there are three aspects to this type of manipulation. The first is **translation**, i.e. moving a small object from the palm to the fingertips. The second is **shift**, i.e. moving an object between fingers. The third is **rotation**, i.e. turning an object using only the finger pads. Magicians are masters at using these skills, and while we do not expect children to have anything like this level of expertise, a child who does not have a basic ability in these skills will be slow to complete jobs, appear clumsy, have to use two hands when only one is required and will have to stabilise an object against his body. These skills are required for positioning a pencil for writing, adjusting grip on the paper when cutting out and when using a screwdriver or tightening nuts and bolts.

Activities which will help to improve these skills

- Turn a coin in hand from heads to tails
- Move a coin from the palm of the hand to the fingertips to pay for an item

- Play with construction toys
- Turn a dice in hand to see different faces
- Hold several small objects in one hand for posting activities
- Hold a pencil between fingertips and walk fingers along the pencil from one end to the other and back again.

Separating the Motor Function of the Two Sides of the Hand

The functioning of the two sides of the hand may be seen if you pretend to wind up the small knob on the side of a watch or thread a needle. The two little fingers either curl into the palm of the hand or extend away from the other fingers. This gives us best control when using the middle, the index and the thumb for precise movement. It demonstrates that when the two small fingers on the outside of the hand (one side) are stabilised, refinement of skill with the thumb side of the hand (the other side) is best achieved. Where children have difficulty bending or closing the outside of the hand, you may try getting them to hold a small object under these two outside fingers when posting coins or doing peg board activities.

Separation of these two sides of the hand begins from birth and develops when a child crawls and bears weight on the outside of the hand while carrying toys using the thumb side. This separation is important for writing and cutting with scissors. In writing, the outside of the hand stabilises the hand and allows the hand to slide along the page and keep the writing on the line. In cutting, the outside of the hand steers while the thumb side opens and closes the scissors.

Activities to Improve In-Hand Manipulation

- Tear paper when holding a coin to the palm with outside three fingers
- Use eye droppers, tongs or tweezers
- Snap fingers
- Use a squirt guns with one or two fingers whilst other fingers grip the neck of the toy
- Use small beads to make things
- Roll play dough into a small ball with fingertips

Readiness for P1 Checklist

Included here is a list of what every P1 teacher would like your child to be able to do on entry to her class. Some activities are already mentioned in the Fine and Gross Motor Section so there may be some degree of overlap.

1. One leg standing on either leg without wobbling and then blindfolded
2. Walk upstairs putting only one foot at a time on each step
3. Draw the letter “x”
4. Carry out (a) 1 instruction (b) 2 instructions
5. Hop
6. Jump 2 feet together
7. Say the numbers 1 - 10
8. Communicate needs
9. Retell a well-known story
10. Self-toilet
11. Remain quiet to listen
12. Sit still for a few minutes
13. Can make friends
14. Understand rules
15. Self-feed and drink
16. Identify own belongings
17. Share toys
18. Transition well (goes from one activity to another)
19. Clap hands
20. Throw/catch/kick a ball
21. Crosses midline
22. If pushed, can protect himself from falling
23. Name the letters of the alphabet
24. Take turns and wait for his turn

Key Points from Chapter 7

- Gross and fine motor skills are interdependent.
- Fine motor skills include eye/hand and eye/foot coordination, manual dexterity, stereognosis, ocular motor skill and tactile perception.
- Prerequisites to fine motor development are internal body awareness, body in space awareness, direction awareness and ideation.
- Success with fine motor skills is essential for handwriting and self esteem.

Chapter 8

DCD

The Big Idea

Am I awkward and disorganised in movement?

The Academic Viewpoint

Dyspraxia is an immaturity in the way that the brain processes information, which results in messages not being properly or fully transmitted. It affects the planning of what to do and how to do it, and is associated with problems of perception, language and thought. (NAS Dyspraxia)

Red Flag Issues

- Wants to control play
- Doesn't play in the playground with other children
- Spelling is impossible, also comprehension
- Doesn't know right from left
- Doesn't imitate other children
- Non-determined hand dominance
- Has difficulty self-feeding
- Has difficulty with new learning
- Lacks emotional assertiveness, always seeking help with physical activities such as dressing, self feeding, handwriting, riding a bicycle and ball games

Green for Go

- Can be reasonable
- Is a good team player
- Learns in different ways
- Can follow a verbal motor instruction
- Can do a star jump
- Can wobble on a wobble board and throw and catch
- Can organise school belongings and remember to relay information home
- Can dress, do buttons and tie laces

Following on from the discussion of gross and fine motor skills, we now come to a condition which greatly affects fluency in both types of skills. DCD (Dyspraxia) is sometimes referred to as Clumsy Child Syndrome, Perceptuo-motor Dysfunction or Motor Learning Difficulty. It is a condition more often found in males (up to 1 in 12) than females, and is thought to affect 6% of the population (Dyspraxia Association of Ireland) or about two children in the average sized classroom. It is a difficulty associated with coordination and the brain's struggle or inability to organise the person for movement. The reason for this is because the neural messages are not being properly or fully transmitted. DCD (Dyspraxia) hereafter referred to as DCD, affects the planning of not only what to do, but also how to do it in smooth, coordinated movements. As such, it has a great impact on both gross and fine motor skills. These skills never become automatic and, for the child with DCD, they have to be learned. This, in turn, affects the ability or ease with which a person learns, but it does not affect a person's intelligence. DCD often occurs alongside other conditions such as ADHD, ASD, Dyslexia or dyscalculia and is associated with problems of thought, perception and language. As a person grows older, he may find ways of dealing with the effects of DCD, but it often continues to have adverse consequences on into adulthood.

The associated difficulties are not restricted to just motor skills, but often include problems with expressive language (the ability to form words correctly and put thoughts into words and sentences that make sense), and also with perception and emotional difficulties. Children with DCD frequently struggle with comprehension and putting their thoughts on paper. Furthermore, they find it difficult to explain their needs and to express their feelings and emotions.

They are unable to give sequential instructions for others to carry out tasks and frequently struggle during sessions to verbally recall the motor plan for a dynamic action they have just completed.

Indicators of DCD

The following is a list of indicators of DCD in each of these five areas- gross and fine motor, perceptual skills, expressive language, emotional and behavioural indicators, and academic and performance indicators. The difficulties may be observed in one or several areas. Children do occasionally trip and fall and bump into things but this does not necessarily mean that they have DCD. However, persistent difficulties, a cluster of difficulties in a particular region, or some difficulties in more than one area should be investigated.

Indicators of DCD in Gross Motor Skills Include the Following:

Poor posture, clumsy gait, poor balance, easily fatigued, weak/low toned muscles, difficulty in learning new motor skills which require motor planning and the memory of movement, difficulty in playing games involving running, jumping, hopping, throwing, catching, playing ball, stopping, starting, changing direction; falling, tripping, bumping into things; poor eye/hand, eye/foot coordination; arms flapping when running, lacking rhythm, difficulty chewing solid food, under achieving, over avoiding, difficulty engaging in new activities, poor bilateral integration, difficulty riding a bicycle or walking up and down stairs, poor at dressing, poorly organised, inability in crossing midline, consequently a 2s difficulty- two feet, two hands, two eyes, two ears, working across body planes, i.e. right/left, top/bottom and backwards/forwards.

A typical observation at initial assessment of a child with motor difficulties is an over use of vision. When a child gets to three year of age they begin to depend on vision less and automatically become aware of the internal sense of body awareness and becoming able to do novel movement challenges without hesitation. This intrinsic body sense also enables the development of fine motor skills , in hand manipulation, posting small objects and threading beads.

Children beyond 3 years old who are dependent on vision skills do not have a good sense of body awareness, lack vestibular engagement and tend to be impulsive. They appear impetuous, lack thinking and doing simultaneously and move before thinking. Additionally, they present with poor handwriting skills, difficulty dressing and have sequencing problems both with motor skills and academically.

Indicators of Difficulty with Fine Motor Skills

Poor manual dexterity with a difficulty crossing midline; difficulty using cutlery, buttoning, tying shoe laces, using keys, staying still, handwriting; poor compressibility, poor grasp, limited manipulative skills, and or keyboard skills; undecided hand dominance, lack of interest in pencil skills or drawing and colouring in and a lack of motivation to self feed or develop use of cutlery or hold a cup to drink, inability to put on coat, shoes or attend to toileting needs.

Indicators of Difficulties with Perceptual Skills

Over/under sensitivity to touch, taste, smell, heat, light, pain or tight or loose clothing; poor sense of time, speed, weight, distance, direction, body awareness in space, poor recognition of left/right, visual tracking and relocation of place from one object to another, poor concentration and attention; slowness to pick up new skills; difficulty with auditory processing especially with background noise; tendency to spill or drop things frequently; difficulty with jigsaws and shape sorting, poor understanding of such concepts of location as in/on/in front of/above/below/behind.

Indicators of difficulty with expressive language

Including delay in speaking, slow to learn how to speak, speech often incoherent, parts of words omitted, inability to make certain sounds, tendency to talk slowly/quickly, loudly/quietly, high/low pitch; difficulty communicating thoughts, needs, wants, recalling appropriate words and putting sentences together coherently.

Emotional and Behavioural Indicators

A child may present with some of the following behaviours and emotional responses: tactless, difficulty in picking up nonverbal signals, interrupts frequently, emotional outbursts, impulsive, easily frustrated, gets stressed, low self-esteem, may be timid and submissive and prefers to play with younger children. Children with DCD tend to become withdrawn and solitary with few real friends, or act like the "class clown", becoming witty and sociable thereby distracting others from their challenges and motor limitations.

In our experience, the most prevalent concerns for parents are children "having no friends, being emotionally immature," becoming "controlling and inflexible," and having "negative feelings of self-worth and low self-esteem." These children are sensitive to all criticism and frequently call themselves "stupid." Giving these children insight into the cause of their difficulties greatly improves their attitude towards themselves.

Academic and Performance Indicators

Literacy: Handwriting tends to be slow and illegible; poor spelling, punctuation and sentence structure; poor sequencing of sentences. Story writing is kept to a minimum with a reluctance to self correct. Comprehension is a significant challenge and children fail to visualise the sequence of the story tending to make word associations and distract themselves.

Reading: Mispronounces new words, speaks indistinctly, problems in tracking for reading on screen and in books also displaying poor comprehension skills. When younger, memorises text and does not learn to think in pictures to enable comprehension, which is generally a struggle.

Maths: Difficulty memorising table facts, muddles numbers. i.e. number reversals and omissions; difficulty in sequencing the order in which processes should be carried out, not understanding complex processes, learning and applying rules; difficulty with mental maths and following instructions; poor memory and attention span; counts on fingers; not visualising the number line or basic maths processes.

Children who have difficulty grasping spatial awareness using the number line have trouble knowing the direction of increase and decrease. When they turn around they do not change the direction of the number line not realising number one is always at the left hand. This causes number and directional confusion. These children have difficulty seeing more/less, bigger/smaller and cannot get the idea of number sequencing. They need to learn to visualise the order of numbers by side stepping the number line, going up and down adding on steps and taking steps away. This will improve maths confidence and enables the child to "see" rather than guess the answer.

General Difficulties: Organising and sequencing skills, fidgets, poor pencil grip and manual dexterity, a difficulty with handwriting including letter formation, spacing, sizing, orientation of letters and legibility when writing at length or speed, increased compressibility on pencil where writing is impressed on next page and work is messy and frequently excessively scored through, homework is a battle and exhaustively long, poor sense of direction and spatial skills, personal grooming issues, cannot sit still on a chair, desk very disorganised, socially withdrawn and difficulty making friends.

Lisa: A Case Study in DCD

Lisa is a four and a half year old who was referred for assessment due to parental concerns about slowness to reach developmental milestones; she displays poor attention, listening skills, gross and fine motor skills; difficulties with balance and coordination, expressive language, self-care and sleeping. Teachers reported that Lisa struggled with jigsaws, shape sorters and needed more one-to-one assistance than others. She tended to avoid activities that involved fine motor skills. On the plus side, she is a loving, friendly, enthusiastic young girl who enjoys playtime with friends and family and also enjoys reading and being read to.

During the assessment, Lisa was sociable, cooperative and spontaneous in her actions. She found difficulty crossing midline, was overly dependent on vision to keep her balance and could not do reciprocal tapping of a pattern with her hands. She had a strong ATNR which has a big impact on her gross motor development and ability to cross midline. Lisa had difficulty following verbal instructions and organising herself to do dynamic motor tasks. She was clearly confused and bewildered by the demands of the activities. Furthermore, Lisa exhibited high arousal overall and was easily distracted by other sensory input.

Other challenges for her were trunk rotation, ideation, and protective extension, one or both feet leaving the ground, visual tracking, motor planning, bilateral and sequencing skills, and not thinking in pictures to assist recall.

On observation, Lisa had a desire to walk on her toes and had difficulty negotiating obstacles in the room. On the Scan 3 C auditory processing test (she was five years old when she did this test) she scored on the fifth percentile which indicates difficulty in processing auditory information. This means she will only get part of what was said or read but not get the whole idea.

Interventions

- Motor based exercise programme to develop bilateral skills
- Work on prone extension and mat work to increase muscle tone
- Use of suspended equipment to engage the proprioceptive system and improve core stability
- Develop ideation skills in relation to body awareness
- Develop body awareness skills using both static and dynamic challenges
- Work on reflex integration
- Use visualising/verbalising programme to promote thinking in pictures
- Commence a handwriting programme focusing on shoulder girdle stability and fine motor development
- Use a therapeutic listening programme to improve auditory processing

Conclusion

Lisa is presenting with many indicators of DCD. She was slow to reach developmental milestones, had sleeping issues and avoided activities involving fine motor skills. In addition, she has coordination difficulties, poor core stability, body awareness, ideation and motor planning skills and is lacking in rhythm. She evidenced gravitational insecurity, i.e. increased anxiety when both feet leave the ground and sensory difficulties causing increased anxiety and fear when challenged by an activity. Her cognitive ability was good, but it was possible to see the impact which these difficulties were having on her overall performance, self-esteem, confidence and assertiveness as well as her concentration and attention. She will require additional support to help keep her on task, especially when learning something new.

Key Points from Chapter 8

- DCD or coordination difficulty is about the brain's ability to organise a person for movement
- It is not about intelligence or cognitive ability but is easily confused as such
- While DCD does not affect intelligence it may affect the ease with which learning takes place or the development of novel motor skills
- Indicators of DCD, in addition to fine and gross motor skills, may be found in perceptual skills, expressive language, and emotional, behavioural and academic issues.

Chapter 9

Autism

The Big Idea

I am differently wired.

I search for what I think is the only one right answer when asked an open ended question.

Don't look at my symptoms; look at the fundamentals that control me.

The Academic Viewpoint

By definition, people with ASDs have difficulties with social interactions and communication, and with adapting to changes in their environment or daily routine. Some people with ASD have little or no language, while others have perfectly good language skills but struggle to engage in conversations and make use of body language. Many people with ASDs also have motor coordination difficulties, while sensory- perceptual problems are common. (A, Bereton; Australasia Autism Research Collaboration)

Red Flag Issues

- Avoids eye contact and touch
- Displays sensory mannerisms
- Has poor reciprocal skills
- Searches for the one right answer when there are several possible answers
- Has a poor idea of what to do
- Lacks the idea of how to use language out of context
- Dislikes new situations and is fearful and anxious
- Tend to need to control peer games and home activities with a difficulty seeing the perspective of others

Green for Go

- Good social interaction
- Good regulation
- Takes turns when playing with others
- Displays reasonableness
- Has the ability to wait
- Tolerates not winning all the time

Autism, or now more correctly called Autistic Spectrum Disorder (ASD), is a condition that appears to have become more prevalent in recent years, possibly affecting as many as one in five hundred of the population. It is four times more likely to be found in boys than in girls. It is designated a spectrum disorder because of the wide range of ways in which it may affect people who, nevertheless, share certain common difficulties. Autism has been described as a lifelong developmental difficulty affecting how people communicate with and relate to others, and how they make sense of their world. The difficulties arising from Autism range from lacking in empathy and poor social skills in its mildest form, to profound difficulty in dealing with sensory issues and social and emotional isolation in its severest form.

Increasingly professionals other than Occupational Therapists are becoming aware of implications of sensory overload in Autism. There is an acknowledgement of a lack of adequate sensory processing with underdeveloped neural pathways connecting the limbic system with the frontal cortex. This results in a maintaining of survival mode with hyper vigilance, increased fear and overwhelming anxiety. On assessment these children tend to present with a retained MORO and FPR reflex and a number of retained postural reflexes.

Consequently they present with poor frustration tolerance, heightened sensory awareness of visual and auditory input, poor impulse control and a tendency to react to sensory input without thinking rather than respond with thought.

No one is quite sure as to the cause of Autism. It has been variously attributed to trauma, genetic, and/or environmental issues. Leo Kanner in 1943 was the first to identify the condition which he called Autism (literally selfism), but most people only became acquainted with the disorder in the 1990's. On a personal level, as principal of a mainstream primary school, I first came into contact with an autistic child around the year 2000. My knowledge of the condition was rather limited. In fact, the parent of the child was better briefed on the disorder, having lived with the consequences for a number of years and having read up on the condition herself.

Now, having worked with a large number of such children and travelled widely in pursuit of knowledge and professional skills, (including a mentorship at the STAR Institute in Denver with Lucy Jane Miller – a highly recommended experience), my understanding of the condition has changed immensely. Engagement, relationship and motivation are the most powerful means of intervention. With these children, who may develop exclusive behaviours such as lining up toys, flapping hands, pacing the room or visual preoccupation with spinning and movement, the aim is to join them in their activities and make sure the behaviour is **inclusive**.

Engaging with and imitating a child's mannerism allowing them to observe the behaviour renders it no longer exclusive but inclusive. Rather than encouraging behaviour, the mannerism or exclusive, meaningless behaviour, this allows the child to then engage in the behaviour as a shared or joined activity.

Wearing a variety of novelty glasses, face masks and funny hats will attract the child's attention to the facial area and assist in engaging eye contact. Initially in these sessions, the emphasis is on participation and enjoyment regardless of the toy or gross motor play that is involved. Also, the activities in which both adult and child share are entirely child led; in effect, the child becomes the teacher.

The initial aim when we work with children with ASD is to facilitate interaction and engage in relationship. The focus is on sensory development and play. The therapist must enable the child to engage in silly play and have fun, acknowledging the person when playing with the object of preference.

In typical child development, a baby will spend months responding to facial gestures and then attempt to imitate them.

Communication face to face with children on the Spectrum should always be with the intent of registering imitation of facial expression, and the spoken word. Engagement in speech should always follow engagement in eye contact. This is most important and, in our experience, can be learned.

Children who lack this fundamental communication skill become the centre of their own world and tend to live parallel lives with other family members.

Broadly speaking, the signs and symptoms of ASD may be divided into four categories:

1. Sensory motor
2. Language
3. Social
4. Emotional

Sensory Motor

Difficulties in this area include the absence of eye contact, lack of imitation of facial expression and movements, pointing or gestures like waving bye-bye, inability to follow objects visually. In addition, there may be rigid routines (lines up toys), inflexible behaviour, repetitive behaviour, lacks ideation, dislikes or avoids cuddling, clumsiness, abnormal posture, pacing the room, stimming (hands flapping, raking, twirling) and preoccupation with strange objects.

Language

Language concerns include: not responding to name, making noises to gain attention, speech and language difficulties in general, no babbling, no spoken words by 16 months, using gestures for communication, no meaningful two word phrases; may repeat words/ phrases from TV programmes, speak with a polite/American accent, be literal in his use of language, a tendency to use nouns and a lack of reference to self either by name or "I".

Social

Social worries take in the child referring to himself in the third person, not initiating human interaction, not asking for help or making basic requests, an absence of: using toys creatively, playing with others, empathy, reaching out to be picked up; engages in exclusive behaviours, uses social experiences for social gain and exclusive behaviour.

Emotional

Emotional problems embrace absence of smiling, poor sleep pattern, emotional outbursts, temper tantrums, aggressive behaviour, attachment to unusual items or objects, distancing himself from loved ones, over/under sensitive to sensory stimuli - taste, smell, noise, light, touch also including vestibular and proprioceptive stimuli.

Should you have any concerns about your child after reading through the list of signs and symptoms, you may visit the National Autistic Society's website to view their checklist for autism in toddlers (CHAT). The list is divided into two sections. Section A has nine yes/ no type questions for the parent to answer and section B includes four observations to be made by either the GP or a health visitor. It is straightforward to administer, easy to score and is part of the 18 month developmental check-up. Its aims are to identify children who are at risk for social and communication disorders and, as such, may well point to whether or not a child requires investigation regarding ASD.

Ryan:

A Case Study of a Child Diagnosed with ASD

At the age of two years and nine months Ryan was diagnosed with severe scale ASD, moderate learning difficulties and Global Developmental Delay (GDD).

Ryan was born by c section due to a breech birth at 38 weeks. He had no difficulty until he was 12 weeks old when he suffered bilateral reflux of the kidneys and had to be treated with antibiotics. This continued until he was five years old. Ryan did not crawl and couldn't bear to be touched at any time or to be held for feeding. He lacked self-regulation and was a poor sleeper (approx. 2 hours/night). Also, he made no eye contact, had no play skills, no ideation, cried constantly and at 18 months had only one word, "ook." Ryan had major issues with bathing, washing hair, cleaning teeth and cutting nails. These were all a constant battle. His parents could not take him out because he would scream, throw himself back in his car seat and be sick. This happened so frequently that they had to change the car seat five times over the period of a few years because of the vomiting. On the occasions that Ryan was in the car, he would never fall asleep, as some children do, and, if the car stopped at traffic lights, he screeched and screeched until the car moved on again.

His mother and father were so distressed by the situation that Ryan's mother gave up work. He was in ABA therapy for a period of about two months during which time it was concluded that he did have perceptual skills. His mother and father attended an introductory lecture in the Queen's University, Belfast on the Son-Rise Programme given by Raun K. Kaufman. As they listened to him, the simplicity of the programme seemed to make sense. They then read the book, "A Miracle to Believe in", by Barry Neil Kaufman and decided that, although they could not afford the training involved, they would embrace the principles of the programme and begin working with their son.

The family's moving house to the mother's home district brought them a different mindset to Ryan's condition. They felt more in control, were more positive, had hope for the first time and were very determined to see it through, whatever they might have to face. Both father and mother were like minded in this and had the full support of the extended family living in the district.

They purchased a mobile shed measuring about 6m by 3.5m and set it up in the back garden. It was painted cream on the inside, had a vinyl floor covering and some shelves placed high up to hold the toys and keep them organised.

For a period of two and a half years the mother worked every day with Ryan from 9.00 am to 2.00 pm. They spent the whole time in this room and the food was brought in with them every morning so that there would be no interruptions. Ryan, at first, kicked up a fuss when taken to the shed. The toys Ryan played with were limited to a small number, with his mother having exact replicas of his "exclusive" toys for herself. These toys were rotated when Ryan was able to cope. Those not in use were placed on the high shelf. Initially, the toys they played with were cause and effect toys of a predictable nature, e.g. a ball falling through a tube. His mother insisted on Ryan giving her eye contact and, when he did so, celebrated this event. She also pretended not to know what toys Ryan wanted and made him take her to the toys on the high shelf, which he could not reach and "ask" for them by making some sort of noise. The noises eventually became more recognisable.

From 6.30 pm to about 9.00 pm the father took over from the mother. His play with Ryan was more "rough and tumble" adventurous play which was different from the mother's, but the play always had a common goal, i.e. to save the princess, to rescue the dog, etc.

At nursery school age, the Educational Psychologist carried out various assessments and it was concluded that Ryan had very low ability. The Education Board agreed to Ryan being home schooled. When the parents felt that Ryan had reached the stage where he could cope with the school environment, he went to mainstream nursery. From age five he was home schooled from 9.00 am to 12.30 pm and then from 1.00 pm to 3.00 pm he went to the nursery school, which was quite a distance from the family home. The father continued to work with him in the evenings after tea. In P1 he went to school from 9.00 am to 2.00 pm. Following this, he went home to do homework and then in the evening had 2-3 hours of role play during which the parents had time to sort out any issues resulting from being in school. Role play was a pivotal part of Ryan's education at home because he had great difficulty with any new outings with the family such as going to the beach, going to the shop, playing in the park and waiting in queues to name but a few. Sand, for instance, was brought into the mobile classroom and spread on the floor to simulate the beach. This continued until the issues became less numerous, approximately in P.3. When waiting in the car or elsewhere, the mother found that reading to the child helped keep him engaged and keep him self- regulated, so she always took a good supply of books wherever she went.

Initially, all the activities in the mobile classroom were child-led and child centred until eye contact was gained based on engagement, relationship and motivation. Although Son-Rise principles were used, the mother and father combined this with an integrated approach including Greenspan's Floor Time, The Hannon Programme of Speech and Language and an SI approach.

Built upon these approaches, communication came on well so that by eight months into the programme Ryan had a vocabulary of about 200 words and good eye contact was gained after 5-6 months. The mother and father built complexity into the commands so that eventually he was able to sequence the order of events to carry out the activities. Although, at times, they felt like hamsters on a wheel, the mother, who incidentally is an OT, and the father showed great belief and unconditional positive regard for their own child. Interwoven with this they provided a secure foundation (drawn from Maslow's Hierarchy of needs) and remembered the importance of encouraging flexibility and boundaries within their play.

At age ten there followed a rigorous six months of assessment, both school based and clinical, by an Autism Intervention

Team. This team, comprising of a Paediatrician, an Educational Psychologist, a Speech and Language therapist and some Early Intervention Team Members, concluded that Ryan's diagnosis should be removed. However, they found it difficult to obtain the forms to do so, having never done it before.

Asperger's Syndrome

In the 1940's the Austrian child psychiatrist Hans Asperger began to identify a personality disorder which was a strand of Autism. Asperger's Syndrome (AS), as it became known, is a form of autism. People with AS usually have average or above average intelligence. The character "Sheldon" in the TV series "The Big Bang Theory" springs to mind as one example of a person with AS. Children with AS tend to have special interests or hobbies which may be obsessional. Dinosaurs and Thomas the Tank Engine usually fall into this category. Because of their predictability, Maths, Science subjects, Computers and Music are often found to be areas of special interest. These children can be exceptionally gifted and knowledgeable in such areas and tend to have a great memory.

Asperger's Syndrome is not always observable in people except in social situations where it is more noticeable. In the past this caused it to be more difficult and time consuming to obtain a diagnosis. The three main areas of difficulty in this domain are:

1. Social imagination
2. Social interactions
3. Social communications

The difficulties which these children have with **social imagination** include problems in relation to trying to guess what other people are thinking, ideation difficulties and predicting what will happen next. These children lack insight and are frequently brutally honest to the detriment of themselves, frequently getting into trouble in school as they lack cunning, streetwise, behaviour and cannot reason discretion. The problems associated with **social interaction** are imitating and maintaining social relationships despite wanting to be sociable. Consequently, making and maintaining friendships and interest in other people, understanding social rules, predicting how people will act and behaving in an appropriate manner, all present as difficulties. Issues with **social communication** include: understanding tone of voice, gestures and facial expression, choosing what to talk about and being very literal. Being literal means they will have difficulty in understanding metaphors, sarcasm, rhetorical questions, and idioms and understanding jokes.

Apart from these three areas, children with AS can have difficulty processing and retaining oral information simultaneously, even if they have good oral skills themselves. Parents and teachers may help with this by following a few simple strategies:

1. Always use the child's name to gain attention
2. Do not always insist on eye contact initially as this may be intimidating
3. Recognise that they have a difficulty interpreting facial expression and processing oral language at the same time
4. Give extra time for processing
5. List important instructions on a page for them to follow in their own systematic way.

In order to make the world less confusing, people with AS develop rituals and rules which are inflexible. They like the sameness and routine of everything. Accordingly, it is important for parents and teachers to get it right first time because the tendency will be that this will be the way they will always want to do it. Any change, or delay, to the expected routine can lead to anxiety and upset or even "melt down". In these contexts two very important objectives which should be promoted, both at home and in school, are flexibility and reasonableness. Flexibility will help the child see that there is more than one way of doing something, and reasonableness will assist in the understanding of other people's perspectives.

There are many sensory issues associated with AS. Children may be either over/under responsive to: sound, light, smell and touch, food texture and the feel of certain materials. This over/under sensitivity can cause anxiety or even pain. Body awareness may also be an issue, and to help deal with the problems of balance and posture, they may well need to rock or spin to inform themselves of their body's position in space.

Since 2013, because of new criteria in the DSM-V, children who formerly had a diagnosis of Asperger's syndrome have been incorporated into the more general classification of ASD.

Angela's Story:

A Case Study of a Child with Asperger's Syndrome

Angela, a very bright 11 year old, who at the time of the first assessment was a first year student at a very prestigious grammar school, was referred to the clinic by her mother. The mother was at her witsend having received thirteen phone calls of complaint from the school about Angela in the first week of term and there was talk of expelling her. It all came to a head in the French class when Angela found it difficult to keep up with the female teacher (who was also a Nun). She said in a rather loud voice, "Will you slow down you old hag, I can't keep up with you!"

Angela has a diagnosis of AS and has been seen by a variety of professionals. Her mother's concerns were that Angela lacked social insight, appropriate social skills, and the ability to formulate social inferences. She also had difficulty with emotional understanding, needed routine and viewed things in a very literal way. Prior to her visit to the clinic her mother completed a Sensory Profile and a pre-assessment questionnaire. These were used to guide the assessment which consisted of clinical observation and auditory processing checks.

It soon became apparent that Angela had poor eye contact and was somewhat exasperated by the proceedings. She tended to speak in a low voice with her head averted. When motivated, she tried hard at the activity; otherwise she expressed boredom or even a slight intolerance. Angela was extremely impulsive and tended to do everything in a hurry. She thought quickly, but her body had difficulty in keeping up with her thinking, which caused her some frustration.

She had difficulty with: motor challenges, crossing midline, directionality, proprioception, motor planning and completing new motor tasks. Angela lacked tactile and body awareness which caused her to appear awkward and hesitant in new motor demands. A reflex integration check evidenced a retained ATNR and associated eye tracking problems which made taking notes from a whiteboard challenging.

Other clinical observations showed that Angela had low tone, poor pelvic and shoulder girdle stability, a difficulty with bilateral activities and poor use of kinaesthetic touch. She did not like being told how to do the things she thought she should be able to do but which she found taxing.

Analysis of the Sensory Profile indicated difficulty with auditory and tactile processing, modulation of visual input affecting emotional responses, and difficulty with emotional, social and behavioural outcomes of sensory processing. All of these are problems of sensory integration causing Angela to feel anxious and threatened in many circumstances, ideally requiring understanding from others as opposed to criticism.

An auditory processing check revealed significant auditory processing difficulties. The consequences are that she will find it problematic to follow conversations or instructions; in fact, any kind of auditory learning will cause great frustration, hence the outburst in the French class.

Significantly, since Angela lacks emotional awareness and empathy, she will express her thoughts without reference to the feelings of those around her. The impact of her poor motor skills will cause her to focus on these at the expense of other skills. She is very impulsive and has high expectations of her own ability. Consequently, she is easily frustrated when she gets things wrong. Angela is very factual in her approach to life and takes things literally. This makes her world very rigid, causing her great difficulty in anticipating change.

Remedial action will include exercises in reflex integration, adaptive motor skills, bilateral and reciprocal tasks, social skills, emotional and self regulation exercises to reduce anxiety, balance and equilibrium exercises, exercises to strengthen core and shoulder girdle stability and finally, the use of a therapeutic listening programme to assist with auditory processing demands.

As a postscript, when the assessment report was made available to the school, the teachers took on board the therapist's recommendations, apologised to Angela for not recognising her difficulties and made special arrangements for her when she was feeling overwhelmed. She received the "Pupil of the Year Award" at the end of her first year!

The next chapter on Sensory Integration explores in detail the sensory motor difficulties of children who over/under respond to sensory stimuli referred to in the section above, dealing with the emotional indicators of autism.

Key Points from Chapter 9

- Autism or ASD is considered to be a lifelong condition affecting how individuals communicate with and relate to others and how they make sense of their environment.
- Intervention involves issues to do with engagement with others, relationships and motivation.
- Signs of ASD are to be found in four areas: sensory motor, language, social and emotional.
- A strand of ASD, identified in the 1940's by Hans Asperger, is Asperger's Syndrome (AS).
- The three main areas of difficulty for people with AS are social imagination, social interaction and social communication.
- The development of praxis, ideation skills for language, perspective thinking, flexibility and reasonableness will greatly assist a person with AS.

Chapter 10

Sensory Processing Understood

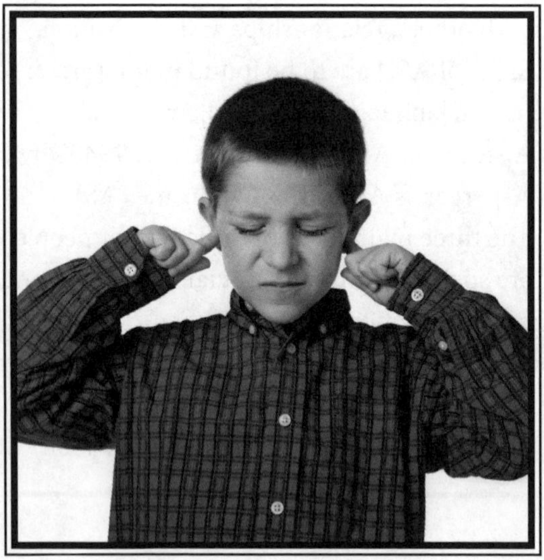

The Big Idea

Can you produce all the appropriate responses to a given sensation?
Can you self regulate your emotions and return to a calm, alert state in a reasonable time ?

The Academic Viewpoint

Sensory Processing Disorder (SPD, formerly known as "sensory integration dysfunction") is a condition that exists when sensory signals *don't* get organized into appropriate responses. Pioneering occupational therapist and neuroscientist A. Jean Ayres, PhD, likened SPD to a neurological "traffic jam" that prevents certain parts of the brain from receiving the information needed to interpret sensory information correctly.

Sensory Processing Disorder, in simple terms, is difficulty taking in and interpreting sensory information so that the appropriate response can be generated. (Bailer & Miller, 2011, p20).
Lucy Jane Miller, a student of the pioneering Occupational Therapist Jean Ayres, gives a practical definition of sensory processing in her book, Sensational Kids: "We are constantly managing sensory messages, sight sound touch taste and smell - the five familiar senses that let us hear the clock ticking in the background, feel the breeze blowing in the window, smell the cookies baking in the oven - come instantly to mind, but we are also constantly managing sensory messages from two less familiar sources. It is your sense of vision enabling you to see the words on the page, your vestibular sense signalling that you know how much resistance is needed to hold up the book". Miller, (2006), p5

There are a number of Sensory Processing Difficulties within three broad categories Sensory Modulation Problems, Sensory Discrimination Problems and Sensory-based motor Challenges.

Red Flag Issues

- Displays unusual behaviour or patterns of play
- Avoids getting dirty
- Has poor sleeping patterns and was difficult to settle as a baby
- Over/under reacts to "normal" situations
- Has behavioural/academic difficulty
- Is irritable when getting dressed

- Shows a reluctance to play with toys
- Is in constant motion, needing to be on the go constantly
- Problems with executing movements and motor planning
- Avoids motor tasks when they are perceived as challenging
- Distracting behaviour in acting as the class clown or engaging in humour to divert from own failings
- Problems with discriminating force when playing, writing or talking too loudly
- Distressed or overly anxious when both feet are lifted off the ground ie. stairs, swinging, over a large therapy ball
- Impulsive and regularly acts without thinking

Green for Go

- Has good sleep/wake patterns
- Displays good regulated reaction and reasonableness
- Has no obvious difficulty with literacy and numeracy
- Has good constructive and play skill
- Good attention and concentration for tabletop skills
- Good personal care skills, dressing, eating and tool use
- Able to think and do simultaneously
- Copes well with rules and authority
- Can organise thinking and converse fluently when recalling a sequenced story
- Transitions easily, even when absorbed in an activity
- No difficulty with self regulation, calms self down quickly

In the chapter entitled "Five Senses or Seven" two particular systems, namely, the vestibular and proprioceptive systems, and how their related senses enable us to gather information and thereby assist with learning were discussed. The emphasis thus far, has been on movement, including the physical functioning and development of the body, as well as what happens when things go wrong and how to provide answers.

Other issues are not so obvious, and it is more difficult to get to the core of the problem. Some children are slower learners and they require more time to absorb and process certain types of information to help them arrive at solutions. Others behave in a manner which is often described as "badly behaved", but the reasons for their bad behaviour are not always clear. Is it that these children are wilful and always want their own way, or do they have other issues that they find difficult to deal with? Behavioural problems often stem from the senses working inefficiently. When working well together, the senses give us information about our physical bodies as well as the environment around us. A mass of information is constantly flowing to the brain from every part of the body - the eyes, ears, skin, nose, taste buds, etc.

As this information reaches the brain, the sensation is located according to its source, then sorted and ordered to form perceptions. If the information is well ordered and directed, it enables the sensory impulses to flow to the brain easily and reach the destination quickly enabling us to behave in an expected, productive manner. However, should a person's sensations be disorganised, jumbled or mixed up, life for that individual can become difficult and he cannot cope with the ordinary demands of living. It is this inability to cope with these jumbled up or inadequately received sensations that leads to the behaviour which has a neurological basis and, if not properly understood, may be classified as "bad". Some children tend to present as chaotic, needing a lot of sensory input and creating a sensory filled environment. The teacher knows they are in the class because they have difficulty sitting still, are impulsive and need to make noise or talk. They are disorganised both in the environment and internally. Such children are poor problem solvers, and struggle to think and plan sequenced actions in novel challenges. Their behaviour is usually controlling, since they need to control play and manipulate others to ensure their world is less challenging for them. Other children may present as very quiet, maintaining a low profile, being reluctant to answer class questions, slumping over the desk and becoming easily fatigued. They are slower to register information and generally appear as though they need to wake up. They are often mistaken for being lazy or not trying when in fact they are really struggling to cope with the demands of the school day. These children are under responding to, or slow to process sensory information.

Processing information

Most often the brain deals easily with sensations coming from more than one source at a time. For example, when a child is in a shopping mall there is the movement and noise of people coming and going, the smell of cooking in the various food kiosks, the bright lights in the shop windows and the need for him to watch where he is going, possibly on an escalator, and to keep his parents in view. The brain takes in all these sensations and integrates them into the whole experience of shopping.

This integration of the senses, or 'Sensory Processing' as it is known, is a neurological approach to intervention, as opposed to a behavioural approach. It is focused on identifying, not just the behaviour itself, but the underlying neurological causes for the patterns of behaviour. It looks at thresholds for all sensory input and works on either increasing tolerances for certain sensations or reducing the threshold to increase awareness of the experience; in sum, it is the organising of the senses.

Dysfunction at any stage during the brain's processing of this sensory information, can occur either because (a) the information is not received efficiently or (b) once received, the neural connections are poorly modulated as to the 'how much' sensation was being received. These difficulties can readily be overlooked because they may not be recognised as such by those closest to them including parents or teachers. They may realise a problem exists but, unless they have a knowledge of the nervous system and neurology in particular, they may not understand fully what is going on. A scientific work group suggested that, "… as many as 1 in 6 children experience sensory symptoms which are significant enough to affect functional aspects of everyday life." Ben-Sasson, Carter, Briggs-Gowan (2009) (in Journal of Abnormal Child Psychology p713)

Sensory Processing training enables the practitioner to look at how the senses are processed, and how the body is enabled to produce acceptable and appropriate responses to stimuli from the environment at any given time, e.g. filtering out extraneous noise whilst listening to a teacher in a classroom, tolerating clothing (usually woollen) when this is first put on, coping with the invasiveness of a dental procedure, remaining seated in an aeroplane for an extended period of time and having nails manicured or hair washed and cut. All of the responses to these activities are usually carried out at a subconscious level and can usually be managed quite easily. For some children however, experiences such as these are almost unbearable and can cause them to go into sensory overload resulting in meltdown.

How Sensory Processing Typically Develops

Sensory processing begins as the foetus in the womb senses movement, sound and touch. Later, it is further refined through the demands of living and continues throughout life as we learn to crawl, stand and walk and later as we learn to read and write. These latter responses require complex integration of eye/hand movements and neck and shoulder muscles. Sensory experiences such as these give rise to purposeful responses which help the brain develop further, produce better organisation, and make more complex skills possible.

We live through our senses, and every aspect of what we do, the choices we make,the pleasures we gain or the experiences which repel us, are in direct relationship to our sensory experiences. Our senses not only give us pleasure but guide and direct our interests, the activities we engage in and the reactions we have. The impact of the senses on our everyday experiences is often overlooked or not acknowledged.

If a person has an obvious sensory impairment such as deafness or blindness, society makes allowances for such in the provision of special schooling, the supply of equipment and environmental adaptations in support of the health and safety of these individuals. Other more subtle issues of a sensory nature can cause extremes in behaviour, irrationality, anxiety, depression, inattention and under achievement, but these can be misunderstood and thought to be "behavioural" issues.

Children with sensory issues do not develop these problems as they progress through school, rather these have been present from birth. For children with Sensory Processing dysfunction the sensory signals do not get organised into appropriate responses and the child's daily functioning and social relationships are disordered. Classic symptoms include poor feeding, difficulties with sleeping, not calming to soothing touch, startling to sound, issues with bright lights, problems when lifted off the ground or when feet leave the ground and difficulty with certain types of movement. Children with sensory processing issues are usually described by parents as having been restless, difficult to settle babies. Additionally, a number of children we now see, who are referred for sensory based difficulties, have a history of reflux, consequently presenting with poor early head control, delayed sitting and non crawling.

Until about the age of seven, most of what the child does involves processing sensations and moving the body in relation to these sensations; they are more physical than cognitive. Later these sensory-motor activities, as they are known, are replaced with cognitive and social functions which have a foundation in these processes. When a child is able to respond in a way which satisfies and pleases him, he has fun. In other words he can integrate his senses efficiently and with purpose. The movement that children enjoy, such as running, jumping and playing in a playground, give sensations that feed the brain and promote further development.

You may notice difficulties in preschool children when a child does not respond as quickly as others or does not understand as other children do. He may appear awkward or clumsy and trip and fall frequently because, although he has no physical difficulty or impairment, his brain has difficulty putting it all together. He is not responding adaptively to what he sees, hears or feels.

When a child goes to school, complex activities such as reading and writing require good sensory processing. So, if a child cannot eye-track, cross midline, has difficulty filtering out extraneous sounds, cannot bear others in his personal space for whatever reason, or can only process information slowly, then he will feel anxious. He may not be able to express his needs and may even believe other children are having similar difficulties. The net result is that what was a minor issue for the preschool age child becomes a major deficit once he begins attending school. In some cases these children are described by the teacher as having special educational needs, having severe learning impairment or challenging behaviour. The inference is that these children are of low intelligence, need to be streamed into special classes or special education and will have poor outcomes in relation to achievement. This is not always the case. Sensory processing and integration of information can be so challenging for children that they develop school based anxiety. They may develop an avoidance of going to school, fearing failure and dreading the challenge of learning. This can occur to such an extent that they feign illness and it can significantly affect their daily lives.

Sensory Processing Disorder

When the brain does not appropriately process the information it receives from the senses the child will experience "Sensory Integration Dysfunction" or Sensory Processing Difficulties and such dysfunction may not show up on formal assessment or standardised test other than SIPT. SPD is not a disease. There are cultural differences in the acceptance of this terminology. Most parents who refer their children to us speak in terms of a Sensory Processing Disorder and some children have had a diagnosis of such. In the UK SPD (Sensory Processing Disorder) is not acknowledged as a discrete disorder and is recognised and referred to as Sensory Processing Issues. It is not a disease and, although it may not get worse, its effects on a child's life may at times be more apparent. It should not be confused with learning disability because some of these children have a high IQ, but their development progresses in an uneven way and may only affect some areas. Although a child may not outgrow his difficulties, he may well find ways to compensate for them. One child had auditory processing difficulties (discussed later) and had difficulty making out what the teacher was saying. His compensating strategy was to sit beside a student who could process well and copy from his friend's diary what the homework should be for the next day. Such children are, as we describe them, "bright but not right". This simply means that their progress is being held up by some issue or other and this, when detected, can sometimes be dealt with quite easily. On the plus side, this difficulty may best be seen as a dysfunction, and the good news is that the process may be reversed or its impact reduced.

Sensory Modulation

Information coming in through the senses must be identified and registered by sight, smell, touch, sound, taste or by the vestibular or proprioceptive systems. If a child is not registering this information he cannot react to it. Such children appear tired, uninterested, do not engage in tasks, are passive and tend to want to be by themselves. The child without difficulties will be able to modulate all this information easily. The ability to modulate information is a bit like having a receptionist on duty, in that only the important information gets through to the director through a selective process. The important information produces a whole picture of who we are, where we are and what is going on around us. This ability to filter out or ignore some aspects of the environment demonstrates the brain's ability to prioritise sensory information. It is seen when we ignore the sound of traffic outside while working, the ticking of a clock when we are in bed and trying to sleep, or the feel of the clothes on our bodies. When a child does not have this ability, the lights may appear too bright to him. He may think people are talking too loudly when in reality they are speaking normally. He may find it difficult to bear others touching him or being too close to him. The scent of perfume may be overpowering to him. Such a child will not like his routines changed because he knows that if they are, he may not be able to cope. He will find it difficult to move from one activity to another. In the wider picture, he will have attention deficits, be impulsive and become easily frustrated, being unable to cope with the amount of input the brain is receiving.

Sensory Processing Understood

There is a growing awareness of children having Sensory Processing Difficulties. An increasing number of our referrals come from parents due to concerns raised by teachers. Typically these children cannot pay attention and focus, are too distractible, need to excessively move and keep on the go or cannot keep up with their peers in learning. They may struggle with handwriting or sequencing activities, have difficulty with comprehension, cannot understand maths processes or impulsively answer without thinking.

Both parents and professionals need insight into understanding differing Sensory experiences and the impact these can have on learning and life in general for children.

Children can often experience sensory input differently and find unusual ways of meeting or responding to their sensory needs. If a child moves excessively and wants to continually be on the go, needs to touch others, but objects excessively when he himself is touched, wants deep pressure by throwing himself forcefully at surfaces, wants to chew his clothing, excessively pulls on clothing, bites on objects, continually needs to mouth items, or seeks to hug and be hugged, then all of these can be signs of a Sensory Dysfunction.

Other Signs of Sensory Difficulties

- Over sensitive to touch, avoiding touch from teacher or peers
- Selective about clothing, sometimes wanting to wear familiar clothing
- Irritable when touched or not wanting to be in close contact with others
- Sensitive to shoes and other clothing
- Chews or sucks hands, pencils or other objects
- Fearful of movement, avoiding swings and being lifted
- Seeks out body spinning or forceful bouncing on ball or trampoline
- Sensitive to or oblivious to pain
- Fidgets constantly
- Avoids changes in head position, especially tipping backwards
- Distressed by loud noises
- Complains that everything is too loud
- Does not seem to hear you
- Complains about smells or does not seem to notice strong odours
- Avoids eye contact
- Difficulty judging space in the environment
- May be a thrill seeker
- Likes sudden, quick movements and will take movement risks
- Overly sensitive to hair brushing and washing
- Picky eater, only eating certain food textures and tastes
- Tends to overheat and can appear flushed and clammy

The above list reflects parental concerns and, although not exhaustive, is fairly typical of the challenges children with Sensory Processing Difficulties may display.

A detailed Sensory Processing Checklist completed by the parent allows the Occupational Therapist to understand the system or systems in which the child is not adequately processing information.

Of the eight sensory systems, five detect information from the external world, i.e. touch, vision, sound, smell and taste, which are known as Discriminatory Senses. There are also three internal detectors or body senses that integrate with the Discriminatory Senses enabling us to function or produce the adaptive response to all sensory stimuli.

The brain receives constant information from all the sensory systems. Two of the internal senses, or power sensory systems, are the vestibular and proprioceptive systems. They provide information on direction and velocity of movement, body position, muscle tone and posture. When all systems are balanced and integrated, information from the vestibular, proprioceptive, visual, auditory and tactile systems is essential to forming judgement regarding discrimination and grading of precise motor actions.

A further internal sense is the interoceptive sense which detects regulation responses, such as heart rate, respiration, temperature, hunger, thirst and bowel and bladder sensations.

When senses integrate, this synchronisation allows us to engage in the following: athletic and dynamic sports, ride a bicycle, pick up a drink, open a crisp packet, step over an obstacle, use scissors, tie shoelaces, develop handwriting, hop, read a line of text and notice details in a picture, crack an egg, pour liquid into a glass, peel an orange, put toothpaste on a toothbrush, allow hair brushing and teeth cleaning, or move efficiently on an unstable base.

Any difficulty in sensory processing is categorised by the presenting behaviour or response. When children present with sensory processing problems, the Occupational Therapist uses observation, analysis of the Sensory Checklist and clinical reasoning to identify the dysfunctional system. The next stage is to determine whether the child is seeking increased input or avoiding input within that system. When a child is seeking increased input, he may need additional sensation or increased input to process efficiently through that system. Alternatively, when a child is avoiding sensation he may be processing with increased intensity and require less input.

Within any of the sensory systems, a child may have responses that are disproportionate, and may under register or over register that sensation. The regulated response is a calm alert response. Modulation difficulties can result in the presentation of specific stereotype behaviours. The presenting behaviour determines both the sensory system and the complexity of the sensory response. Over responders respond too much, or for too long to be able to naturally tolerate sensory input. Under responders show a reduced awareness of sensation and respond slower, with reduced responses.

It is important to note that a child can be an under responder in one system and an over responder in another. He may be over responsive or defensive to touch, whilst simultaneously seeking increased input from the proprioceptive sense. Alternatively, a child may be under responding in the vestibular sense, whilst being auditory defensive or over responding to sound. There is no standard pattern for sensory dysfunction or a sensory processing disorder.

The vestibular, tactile and proprioceptive systems are those in which a child will noticeably over or under respond. (See the table below for categorised behaviours.)

In children with sensory processing issues it is important also to establish both auditory and visual processing. Where there is auditory and visual system modulation dysfunction, the response is usually over responding to stimulus, resulting in sensitivity.

Sensory Processing Observations of the Vestibular, Proprioceptive and Tactile Systems (Modulation Difficulties)

Over Responding	Under Responding
• **Vestibular**	
Cautious of all movement and dislikes head moving into backward space	Does not seem to notice head or body movement, seeking out novel movement experiences
May be Gravitationally Insecure, preferring sedentary play	Loves excessive fast movement
Extreme response to feet leaving the ground	No fear or awareness of heights
Dislikes swings, having a preference for slides	Needs to be on the move and on the go more than peers
Fear of using trikes or motion toys	Seeks out crashing and forceful activities
Poor eye/foot coordination with little observational head tilt	
• **Proprioceptive**	
Does not tolerate hugs	Poor body awareness, seeks out increased body sensation, jumping and hopping
Tense rigid body posture	Poor spatial awareness - gets lost easily
Avoids contact sports	

Difficulty dressing Poor drawing of a man Excessive difficulty in pencil skills, grasp and judging force through a pencil	Low stamina and poor postural support Low tone and increased flexibility Difficulty one leg standing Over dependent on vision to inform body position
• **Tactile** Does not notice temperature changes High threshold for pain Not bothered by dirty hands, face or wet body; tolerates dishevelled clothing Difficulty with sensory discrimination and identifying numbers, letters and objects through touch which impacts on perceptual skill	Avoids bathing and showering Distressed by light touch, bothered by clothing, fabric and labels Overreacts to light or accidental touch Cannot cope with lining up or sitting too near other children Hates dirty or messy hands Intolerant of grooming

Auditory Over Responding Observations

Startled by loud noises and distracted by environmental sounds, including awareness of white noise

Intolerant of some appliance sounds, difficulty filtering out background sounds and may struggle to determine what the teacher is saying

Avoids shopping or noisy environments and tends to act out at birthday parties or social events

Frequently covers ears and will say that there is too much noise or that you are talking too loudly without being aware of the volume of their own voice

Visual Over Responding Observations

Bothered by bright lights and busy environments with excessive wall decoration and surrounding clutter

Frequently blinks and presents with a MORO response to movement in the visual field

May struggle with proximity of eye contact and tends to avert eyes

Children can over respond in the visual and auditory responses due to a modulation difficulty or due to a primitive unintegrated MORO reflex response. This may be observed in a sudden change of arousal state where the child presents with excessive blinking or is distracted and alarmed by a sudden noise. Where the overresponse is alerting in nature, the child may present as anxious, questioning and in need of reassurance. However, when a response is due to sensory intolerance that may not be predictable, the child may present as withdrawn or avoiding.

Sensory Craving is another aspect of Sensory Modulation Difficulties. This is observable in children who constantly need to move. They continually move and keep on the go, seek out intense movement feedback and crash and fall without reacting to being thrown to the ground forcefully or being hurt. These children do everything quickly and appear impulsive, showing poor spatial awareness. They do not predict consequences and put themselves at risk from throwing themselves heedlessly on and over equipment. When jumping on the trampoline, they need to incorporate excessive movement, including arm swinging and rotating.

This type of child can often be acknowledged as having Attention or Hyperactivity Disorders as he acts impulsively and is so driven at a sensory level that he appears to have poor attention skills.

Children who are sensory cravers often seek so much input that they actually become more disorganised. When working with such children the aim should be to create organised movement experiences for them, e.g. obstacle courses. By increasing frequency, varying speed and incorporating heavy work in the experiences the children are encouraged to think more and therefore register the input they are receiving, whilst becoming more aware of changing their own movement intensity.

Sensory Based Motor Difficulties

A number of children who present with Sensory Based Motor Difficulties are identified in Occupational Therapy literature as having a difficulty in planning and performing a novel motor act or series of motor actions that a medical diagnosis or developmental difficulty cannot explain. Dyspraxia, now known as DCD, refers to a sensory processing difficulty in praxis and motor planning. Children with DCD have difficulty planning or carrying out a motor challenge. This means that they have problems following verbal instructions to complete a motor challenge. These children cannot process the auditory instruction whilst simultaneously processing the sequence of the movements. In other words, they cannot think and do. Consequently, they are dependent on visual instruction and once they are shown what to do and get the idea, they then can attempt the task.

Sensory Processing Disorder (SPD)

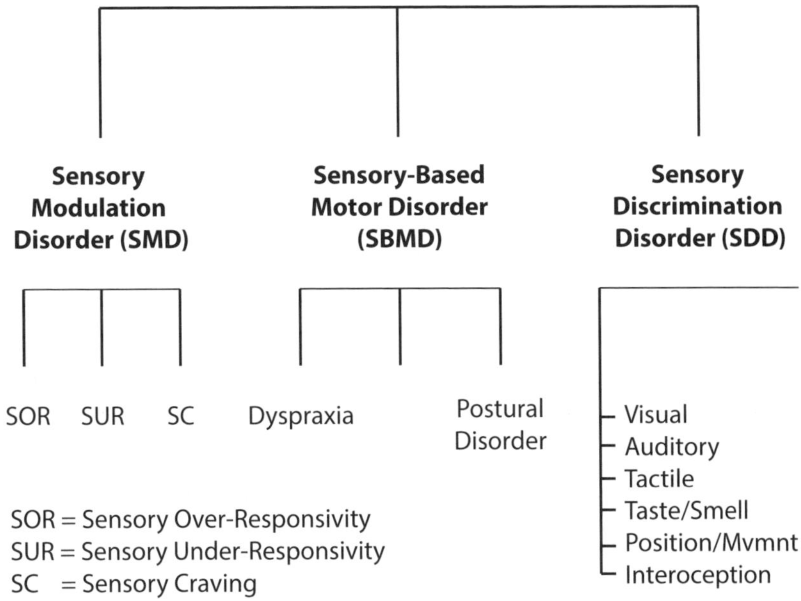

Miller LI et al., 2012

Children like this have difficulty motor sequencing and consequently struggle with cognitive sequencing. They are disorganised externally and have difficulty with organising body planes (upper/lower limbs, right/left side, backwards/forwards) to copy body challenges. Furthermore, they are disorganised cognitively and struggle with problem solving, organised verbal responses and expressing what they are thinking.

Typical DCD indicators include difficulty with core stability, crossing midline, one leg standing, riding a bicycle, poor ball skills in throwing, catching and kicking with accuracy, difficulty solving mathematical problems, analysing and evaluating and multitasking.

Sensory Discrimination Difficulties

Difficulties in this area include a problem in recognising/interpreting differences or similarities in the qualities of stimuli. It is commonly seen with problems in processing sensations from touch, muscles and joints (proprioception) and head movements (vestibular or inner ear sensations). Children who have poor discrimination abilities are poorly informed about the position of their bodies in space. They have difficulty discriminating force, having a poor ability to discriminate touch. In addition, they have poor central processing as opposed to a modulation difficulty. Unlike modulation difficulties where the degree of difficulty differs from day to day, discrimination difficulties are constant and are causal to other sensory processing disorders such as bilateral integration, sensory motor based difficulties, sequencing problems, handwriting difficulties and poor fine motor skills and tool use.

Common Signs:

- bumps or pushes others;
- grasps objects too tightly or uses too much force;
- frequently drops things or knocks things over;
- mouths, licks, chews or sucks on non-food items;
- craves movement, e.g. likes to spin self around;
- afraid of heights/swings/slides;
- has poor balance.

(Ref: May-Benson, Teasdale & Koomar, 2006)

Other presentations of sensory discrimination difficulties can be visual and auditory discrimination.

Visual processing difficulties are complex and not only have an impact on learning but on everyday living. (See Chapter 13.)

Discrimination difficulties cause letter and number confusion. Spatial problems result in difficulty judging distance, poor ball skills, fear of crossing the road due to the speed and proximity of traffic. There is also difficulty with reading, maths and learning about time where accurate perception and understanding spatial relationships are very important.

Auditory processing difficulty interferes with the ability to make sense of information through the ears. (See Chapter 14.) This can interfere with the capacity to recognise differences in sounds, store and recall verbal information, sequence sounds in a word or blend or put sounds together to make words.

For some children this can make Phonics, and therefore reading and spelling, a very difficult challenge. They may struggle to listen, follow verbal instruction and "do" or write simultaneously.

Interventions and Treatment

Sensory Processing Difficulties have a neurological as opposed to a behavioural basis. Intervention is based on the principles of Sensory Integration, well defined by Fisher & Murray (1991) "where the therapist incorporates meaningful activities that provide specific sensory stimuli to elicit an adaptive response, thereby assisting the child in his or her overall motor and conceptual learning. Therapy is Praxis based and was developed to help children improve self-awareness, self-confidence and self-esteem through the medium of play, which is the occupation of childhood." (p.252)

Movement is the key to early learning, and sound vestibular and proprioceptive systems are fundamental in the development of sitting up, crawling and walking. The first stage of motor development is established during tummy time and subsequently develops into whole body movements. The child then learns neurologically and establishes a basis for gross motor development, integrating reflexes and cognitive development. Development continues in a hierarchical way based on efficient sensory processing. Where a child has problems with tummy time and maintaining the head in extension when placed on his tummy, or when he reacts anxiously to changes in head position, this can be an indicator of vestibular dysfunction. Consequently, this may lead to other areas of sensory processing difficulty.

Accordingly, all intervention must commence with the power senses and a sound analysis of vestibular and proprioceptive functioning.

Vestibular dysfunction is observed when the child cannot heel/toe walk beside a rope and keep the head tilted down, observing the feet and alignment to the rope. This child is evidencing poor vestibular engagement. When asked to move from a star position on the floor to a curled ball, he does so without lifting his head off the ground. Alternatively, a lack of vestibular engagement may be observed when a child is skipping using a hoop and not maintaining or displaying a need to look down at his feet.

In much younger children, vestibular dysfunction can be identified by a difficulty sitting up, a dislike of being lifted, an extreme dislike of being upside down and a need to maintain the head in an upright position.

The child with poor vestibular function is driven visually and tends to be impulsive in his environment, not planning or anticipating movement adaptations and thereby appearing clumsy and lacking coordination.

Proprioceptive function can be observed in one leg standing, 4 point kneeling and when the child is using a wobble board. In younger children, proprioceptive dysfunction is identified by an absence of hopping, walking and running forcefully, difficulty with fine motor skills, using cutlery and pencils or playing with increased force.

Children, who present with sensory challenges, on entering a therapy room, look to see what they may be interested in. The under responders or sensory cravers will instantly seek out a motor driven activity. They usually throw themselves on top of the large therapy ball. They tend to be impulsive, have no idea of force or danger or of being on an unstable base and inevitably crash to the floor. Parents struggle to restrain the child from taking movement risks either backwards or forwards and especially climbing. They generally confirm that the child is on the go continually.

Alternatively, the over responding child may remain close to the parents and appear cautious or anxious. He usually watches the therapist suspiciously and the task the latter is organising for for him to carry out. Over responders prefer to do activities on the floor, usually lying down with as a lot of body/floor contact, rather than use the dynamic motor equipment. These children are challenged by head tilt and anti-gravity postures. They are over responding to vestibular input and may well be Gravitationally Insecure. When children are Gravitationally Insecure their first response, when moved off the ground unexpectedly over a large therapy ball, is increased anxiety with an exaggerated emotional response, a pronounced Moro reaction and visible fear in their facial expressions because the child is experiencing primal fear.

Another observable sensory processing difficulty is with auditory processing. Children who are too sensitive to processing sound hold their whole hands over their ears to block out sound or reduce the sensation. They tend to hear white sound or environmental sounds that others filter out or do not notice. Examples include sounds such as those produced by a fluorescent light, whiteboard when switched on, and pens writing on the whiteboard or the sound of a fridge running. These may all be overwhelming.

These sensory processing difficulties can be observed by the parent or teacher and understanding the cause of the behaviour can support the management of both the child's environment and understanding his needs.

Intervention is based on the outcomes of assessment which identify the child's sensory challenges and therefore give insight into sensory solutions. It is helpful for both the child and parents to understand his sensory makeup and be given reasons for the odd or unusual behaviour, e.g. the difficulty with PE or motor skills, the need to be shown things rather than have verbal instruction when learning a novel task and why he craves movement or feels more comfortable in familiar surroundings.

Vestibular Intervention

Movement is the key to a healthy vestibular system, i.e. swinging and using a variety of suspended equipment including hammock swings, bolster swings, glider swings, disc swings and platform swings. This is used primarily to develop tolerance of front/back, side/side and spinning motions with movement graded through frequency, intensity and duration of the activity.

Proprioceptive Intervention

Registering pressure input to tendons and joints is the key to optimal functioning of the proprioceptive sense. This is done in therapy through activities which involve pushing and pulling, carrying weight or moving weighted objects and using body resistance. It is also developed through jumping and bouncing on trampolines, bouncing on therapy balls and peanut balls and in wearing body weights or pressure garments.

Tactile Interventions

Tolerance of touch and normalising the way in which the nervous system registers how we become aware of the variety of tactile sensations which we experience every day is the key to the intervention. The touch system is discriminative and responds to light touch. Intervention must come through the proprioceptive system using heavy or more forceful input. Experience has shown that one of the best interventions for this is the Brushing Programme designed by Patricia Wilbarger. (See Chapter 15.)

Having the child with Sensory Processing Issues assessed by a Sensory Certified Occupational Therapist will determine the difficulties and problems the child faces as well as provide effective solutions with positive outcomes.

Effective intervention can produce immediate outcomes by providing strategies for helping the child to cope better, become calm, and improve motor skills and develop effective multiprocessing, allowing tolerance of sensations and situations that were previously challenging.

Expected Outcomes:

- regulate emotions, alertness and increase attention span;
- reduce unwanted sensory seeking and sensory avoiding behaviours;
- handle transitions with less stress;
- reduce anxiety and regulate impulsiveness or hesitation and
- improve self-confidence and social skills.

The Sensory Diet

The phrase "sensory diet" was coined by Patricia Wilbarger (2002). Therapists now tend to refer to it as a "sensory break" to avoid confusion. A term which we find to be more reflective of the purpose is "brain boost". Wilbarger's idea was that, just as a child needs food at different times during the day, so he needs sensory input to help him stay focused, regulated and organised throughout the day. There is some misunderstanding about sensory diets in that they are seen by some as a method of treatment, whereas they are really just a means of regulating a child **before** treatment can begin. There is nothing adaptive or novel in a sensory break, therefore it does not add to the child's existing skills, but it does change a child's regulation. The input needs to be synchronised with recommended treatment approaches.

Each child is unique and has exclusive sensory requirements. A qualified paediatric occupational therapist (preferably SIPT certified) needs to evaluate a child's needs and develop a sensory break specific to the individual. Such a break takes into account all the senses that are impacted by the sensory processing disorder, and should be modified frequently to take note of the changing needs. The effects of a sensory break are often immediate and cumulative. It helps to make connections between the cerebellum and the prefrontal cortex within the nervous system so that a child can tolerate situations and sensations he would normally find challenging. Engaging the Basal Ganglia by doing slow rhythmic movements regulates the early brain (Basal Ganglia) with the thinking brain (prefrontal cortex). Working on these connections increases attention span, facilitates thinking and doing simultaneously and helps him handle transitions whilst also limiting sensory seeking/avoiding behaviour.

The completion of a Sensory Profile and having the scored results explained by an SI Certified O.T. will determine which sensory input a child is seeking or avoiding, whether the sensory systems themselves are seeking or avoiding and therefore which activities are appropriate. Children with sensory processing difficulties can be seeking in one sensory system and avoiding in another, exclusively seeking or exclusively avoiding, or alternating between the two states depending on tiredness and anxiety levels.

Feedback from a sensory profile or sensory questionnaire will help answer such questions as: "What are his food preferences, how does he transition from one activity to another, what are his gross/fine motor difficulties, has he tactile sensitivities such as nail/hair cutting, washing and bathing? Also, is he over reactive to noise and does he prefer roughhousing or being alone?"

After finding the answers to these and similar questions, the therapist should involve the child, parents and teachers in planning activities that the child likes, and that are feasible as part of a daily schedule in either the home or school environment.

With the understanding that every child is unique and requires personalised activities appropriate to him, the following is a sample sensory break or brain boost for an imaginary child with proprioceptive difficulties.

	Key Events In the Day	Brushing	Sensory Break	Comments
Time (To suit family routine)	Wake-Up	Begin with brushing	Rolling on bed, wrapped in blanket. Passive linear rocking.	
			Bounce x20 on bed holding hands with Parent.	
			Come down stairs on tummy head first. (supervised).	
	Breakfast		Crunchy Food –apple, dried fruit to bite on and chew.	
			Trampoline x 50, jumping, wall presses,wearing heavy schoolbag.	
	School Day		Bilateral exercise and primitive reflex integration movements x10 mins.	Activities which the teacher should incorporate to some degree into brain boosts to support regulation.
	School day Ends - Home	Begin with Brushing	Trampoline, jumping x50 on the therapy ball. Prone extension (aeroplane landing/taking off), wheelbarrow over the ball slow linear movements, weight through your head over the ball x5.	

	Key Events In the Day	Brushing	Sensory Break	Comments
Time (To suit family routine)	Outside Play - Park		Swings, roundabouts, wall climbing, scooter board on tummy slow, trainer bicycle.	Outdoor activities to include throwing and catching. Jumping and hop-scotch Targeting with a ball and a net Beanbag throwing Playing with hoops.
	Pre-Dinner	Begin with Brushing	Lying on tummy on floor- watching television, colouring in reading books – whilst using the Listening Programme. (15min block)	
	Dinner		Remaining seated at table with weighed cushion and ankle weights. Eat a variety of food textures and temperatures. Drinking using a straw.	
	Bedtime Routine	Drink using a straw, Story time (in hammock with linear movement) Brushing in bed with Mozart in the background	Wind down activities. Slow linear rocking/ rolling and jellyfish/ starfish It is preferable to use the listening programme at this time and have the child complete the daily requirement.	

Positive Outcomes

Of the academically successful adolescents who are referred with sensory processing difficulties, one such young man aged 17 stands out. He was unable to get off the floor from sitting unaided and had no medical motor based issues. Another 18 year old could not tolerate lining up or being touched, even if it happened accidentally, by other pupils. The major consequences for older children with sensory processing challenges are poor self-esteem, difficulty in daily living skills at school, challenges with social skills and difficulty making friends and sustaining friendships. This can then result in anxiety, social fear and depression.

Key Points from Chapter 9

- Behavioural problems often stem from and may be confused with sensory processing issues.
- Sensory processing is promoted through the right type of physical activity.
- Engaging in slow linear passive movements will support neural connections between the early reactive brain and the deliberate or thinking brain supporting the integration of early reflexes.
- Children with sensory issues are not necessarily slow learners, but may be affected in some distinct motor areas, especially the cerebellum, with an absence of rhythmic movements.
- Sensory modulation is about the ability to screen out and select pertinent sensory information.
- There are three types of reaction to sensory stimuli: over responder sensory craving, over responder sensory avoiding and sensory under responders.

- For children to be in the learning zone they need to be in calm, alert state
- To reach this state, sensory needs must be attended to first.
- Avoiders experience systems overload to nearly everything in the environment and need strategies for calming.
- Over responsive sensory cravers are hyperactive and desire more sensory information. They need to move and fidget to concentrate and self-regulate.
- Sensory under responders pay scant attention to their bodies or their environment and require alerting activities.
- A sensory break or brain boost is not a treatment but a means of regulation before treatment begins. It is unique to every child's requirements and will change as the child changes

Chapter 11

Sensory Based Feeding

The Big Idea

You have no difficulty eating anything, but have normal food preferences

The Academic Viewpoint

The vast majority of children with a feeding disorder have a medical condition, an oral motor skills problem, a sensory processing disorder, a behavioural issue or some combination thereof that is affecting their ability to eat. (C.Fraker, M.Fishbein, S.Cox, L.Walbert, 2007)

Red Flag Issues

- Difficulty sucking and early feeding
- Poor transitioning to solid food
- Over picky eater
- Over reacts to the smell of food
- Limited range of food intake
- Won't try new foods

Green for Go

- Healthy response to early feeding
- Willingness to tolerate solids
- Normal, acceptable food preferences
- Finger feeding
- Tolerating touch and smell of different foods

You may have come across a family whom you were visiting or who or was visiting you, and noticed how selective the children were about their food choices. They are usually in the two to eight - year - old bracket. No matter how appealing the food seemed to you, no amount of persuading would get them to eat it. This is in contrast to what we would call children with "normal" appetites who have no difficulty in eating virtually everything that is set before them, though they still may have perfectly normal preferences.

In today's terms we might call the former group of children "picky" eaters. When, however, does this become problematic or a sign of a physiological feeding disorder? Physiological disorders may include food allergies, low muscle tone, problems with oral mechanism structure (mouth, lips, tongue and jaw) and gastric, cardiac, metabolic or genetic disorders. It is important to check the tongue elevation and the ability of the child to touch the roof of the mouth with the tongue. Several children who attended the clinic and had been referred for suspected sensory based feeding difficulties actually needed tongue release as they had 'Ankyloglossia' or tongue tie. Added to these conditions is neurological sensory-based dysfunction. To understand feeding disorders better, we need to compare them to the natural order of feeding patterns.

The Normal Development of Feeding Patterns

When a child is in the womb, feeding is mainly through the umbilical cord and is passive in nature, but he will also, from the fifth month, drink amniotic fluid at a rate of about 400mls/day. The child is not even aware that the feeding process is taking place. From the moment of birth all of that changes and the child begins the process of becoming more assertive in his actions. This includes feeding. As the child becomes aware of his needs, he signals them to his carer who recognises these signals and responds accordingly. With the young infant, a calm, alert state is required for a good feeding pattern. Should the child be sleepy or irritable, the act of feeding can become demanding for both carer and infant. At this stage two people are involved, but the parent is just supporting the child's emergent skills in preparation for self-feeding. As the child becomes more independent and more assertive, it can become a battle of wills as to who is going to put the food in his mouth.

The table below shows the expected feeding development when moving from liquids to purees and from baby cereals to chunkier foods, including a larger variety of foods. Eating is instinctive to begin with and continues to be so if not interfered with in any way (such as having to be tube fed for one reason or another, e.g. early surgery on a cleft palate). It is a learned behaviour and children can learn not to eat as well as to eat.

Normal Development of Feeding Patterns		
Age	Food	Activity
Up to 6 months old	Drinking breast milk or formula	Sucking
From 4-6 months	Milk, formula, cereals, purees	Suck, begin cup drinking
Up to 7 months	As above also teething biscuits	Suck, drink from cup, spoon
Up to 12 months	Include chopped finger food	Spoon (use upper lip)
Up to 15 months	Fine chopped food included	Cup, spoon, begin to lick lips
Up to 24 months	Adult food cut up	No waste when cup drinking

Problem Feeding

Problem feeding of any sort is a red flag issue telling us that something is wrong and should be addressed without delay. It is possible for some parents to think of their children, mistakenly, as just picky eaters and for the problem to go undetected. While it is not unusual for a toddler to go through a picky phase and give no cause for concern, it does not necessarily mean he has a food aversion. However, if the feeding issues remain for any length of time, it is important to have them investigated as there may be an underlying cause, such as a food allergy, toothache, digestive tract disorder or medical issue, rather than just his preference for some foods. Where children are avoiding touch, or are acting in a Tactile Defensive manner, they are frequently fussy eaters as the sensation of touch on skin on the inside of the mouth is the same as touch on the skin around the outside of the mouth and face. They may be over sensitive to all but soft textureless foods. Feeding problems in general may have an effect upon or lead to any one of a number of issues including health, malnutrition, dehydration, under-development, academic performance, self-esteem and family and interpersonal relations, so it is better to identify and treat these early on.

The introduction of new foods can lead to a feeding disorder. This is called food neophobia, or fear of new foods. Such children are fine so long as you give them the sort or types of food they like or are used to, but when they are presented with something a little out of the ordinary, as may happen when away on holiday, the child simply refuses to touch, taste or handle the food. Even when encouraged by the parent to, "Just try the food," the child may cry or act up.

It is natural for young children to be wary of new foods or what looks like new food. The child may eat, or be more inclined to eat, what he sees others in his family eating. Again, if he sees others enjoying what to him is a new food, in a pleasant, light atmosphere around the table, he is more likely to be favourably disposed towards it and eventually accept it into his diet.

Parents who are fussy eaters themselves should not be surprised if their child turns out to be the same. Using food as a bribe or reward can have a negative effect upon a child's eating habits, as can punishment for not complying with a parent's request. For example, "If you don't eat it you will get no dessert," or, "You won't get to see your favourite DVD unless you eat this." It is also important not to discuss your child's poor eating habits in front of him or around the table at meal times, as this may only make matters worse. You are more likely to get a positive outcome if you don't force or judge his reaction. It is better to present him with the food he is having difficulty with a dozen or so times for a greater chance of success. If you are still worried about the lack of vitamins in his diet you could possibly give them to him, having consulted a doctor first, as a food supplement.

Behavioural issues can give rise to feeding problems. It may be that the child is using food to gain attention, particularly if there is a younger sibling who seems to him to be getting all the attention. Children quickly find out that if they throw their food down or behave badly, then they will attract the adult's attention. It is a small step from getting attention to finding out that they can control the adult by refusing to eat any or just a limited amount of food. The child may find the anxious parent trying to coax or attempting to persuade him to eat with promises of, "I'll give you something nice if you will just try a little." A further step, following on from getting attention and controlling the parent, is that the child finds he can use food as a a weapon. In practice this translates into statements such as, "If you don't let me watch TV or let me stay up late, I won't eat my dinner." These are all behavioural problems and can be accompanied in extreme cases by hitting, biting, kicking or vomiting, all to get others to do what the child wants.

Sensory Issues in Feeding: Possible Origins

The next issue to consider is children who are over or under responders regarding feeding issues. There is more prolific research and a greater tendency for children to be hypersensitive (over responsive) children as opposed to being hyposensitive (underresponsive) and this is even more noticeable when it comes to feeding disorders. This may be so because over responsiveness is more easily recognised. Such children are more likely to cause a fuss if they are given the food they do or do not want and so draw the parent's attention to the disorder. Unless you are more observant, the under-responsive child, because he is more passive, can almost go unnoticed since, although somewhat selective, he will eat food without the same degree of protest. Where the over responder will usually want bland, soft colourless foods such as yogurt, bread, chicken and chips, the under responder will want to eat crunchy foods such as crisps, apples, dry cereal and crusty bread.

The origin of sensory feeding disorder is not clear. Some think that its roots are of a genetic nature, others attribute it to uncomfortable painful reflux, and still others link it to an uninhibited Moro reflex. This can cause children to be over responsive to anything that is too bright, too loud, too smelly or too tactile. This should not be too surprising since the sensations of touch which we feel on the surface of the inside of our mouths are as intense, or even more so, than those felt on the outside of our bodies.

Another area of thought attributes this difficulty to infants who have been tube fed for a period of time due to illness. The feeding problems arise from the child being deprived of positive sensory input to the mouth, having little or no experience of sucking or swallowing, or having forgotten just how to use these skills. Since tubing in the mouth can be an unpleasant experience, he may avoid using the mouth to explore and learn as other children do. The child may tend to protect and guard the mouth area because of this, which in turn can lead to lack of experience of food textures and tastes at a critical learning phase.

Whatever the cause, be it genetic, medical or neurological, parents should not take responsibility for creating the problem, blame themselves for the way they dealt with it, nor should they blame themselves for either the way in which they handled their lack of knowledge of the problem or failing to get professional help. The issues involved are neuronal, extremely complex and difficult to diagnose. It is more important, in this instance, to find solutions rather than a cause or apportion blame. Persist with encouraging change and try different types of blow/suck toys, e.g. straws and whistles and work indirectly at improving oral motor skills. The overall goal should be to develop the use of the mouth, in all its areas, in ways that are enjoyable for the child.

Sensory Issues Case Studies: Over/ Under Responsive Children with Feeding Disorder

In the chapter on Sensory Processing mention was made of over/ under responsive children and how they may behave in general. The remainder of this chapter now focuses on these two types as they relate to feeding disorders.

Over responsive or hypersensitive children are extra sensitive in one or more of the five senses (seven if we include the vestibular and proprioceptive systems). Here are two examples from the case files to illustrate just how diverse this can be and and how it can also include olfactory (sense of smell) disorder.

A 7 year old came into the room for an assessment wearing a "hoodie" that was pulled down to his eyes at the top, and over his nose at the bottom. Only his eyes were visible at the front. He found it very difficult just to enter the room, even with the windows and doors open, because of the smell. With his mother's encouragement, he did persevere for a while but there was no doubt that it was a real challenge for him to do so. Neither we nor his mother smelt anything out of the ordinary. Later it was discovered that cleaners had been in the room two days previously to clean the tables and that they had used spray cleaners. The smell was virtually undetectable to us, but overpowering for the child. Before he left the room he asked his mother for his cellophane-wrapped buns (Mr Kiplings) which he immediately put to his nose and sniffed deeply. He then came over and said, "Here, you can have a sniff too!" He obviously wanted me, whom he thought had similar difficulties, to share in his strategy for overcoming olfactory sensitivity.

On another occasion a child was referred to the clinic because he had a feeding disorder. He would only eat "Kingsmill" white bread. His parents took him on holiday to a part of the country where this brand was unavailable. When their supply of this particular variety ran out they quickly found out that, as far as their child was concerned, there was no substitute. In the end they had to bring him home to get further supplies, thereby ending their holiday.

These two incidents highlight just how selective some children, and indeed adults, can be over what they will allow to enter their mouths either because of the taste, texture, colour or smell of the food, or because of the extent to which environmental factors can have an impact upon them.

So, given the situation that your child is not feeding as well as you think he should, what do you do? You have ruled out all medical conditions, new food phobias, behavioural issues and you strongly suspect a sensory problem is the cause. Some questions which you might ask yourself are in three categories as follows:

Category 1: When did I first notice it? Was it in the early feeding stages when he had difficulty accepting the feel of the nipple in his mouth? Was it the actual smell of the breast? Was it when transitioning from milk to puree foods, from puree to solid foods or coming off a feeding tube and couldn't suck or swallow? Was he sensory in the region of the mouth?

Category 2: Which foods, liquids or smells does he or doesn't he like? It may be necessary to compile a list of these to include taste (sweet, sour, salty, spicy), texture (crunchy, soft, smooth, grainy, lumpy), smell (he is over/under sensitive or in avoidance of smells such as spicy, flowery or strong odours like cleaning fluids) or colour (green, white, light/dark brown, orange, red).

Category 3: What other reactions am I seeing? He gags, chokes or spits out certain foods or liquids. He only wants food at a certain temperature. He craves some foods. He complains that the smell, either in the environment or coming from the food, is hurting his nose, giving him a headache, causing breathing problems, making him gasp. He has limited food intakes. He prefers to drink water. He dislikes his teeth being brushed, or his face or mouth touched. He has difficulty transitioning from one task to another.

Included below is a table to enable you to highlight answers to these questions and therefore build up a picture of your child's feeding habits. This may in turn help you decide whether or not the issue is sensory in nature.

		Texture	Tastes	Smell	Colour	Reactions
Foods	Like					
	Dislike					
Liquids	Like					
	Dislike					
Smells	Like					
	Dislike					

Hyposensitive or under responsive children may appear quiet, watchful, withdrawn and lack desire to explore the environment. They may not even register hunger. Such children require high intensity sensory input to waken them up so to speak. Their preference is for strong tasting, intense flavours as well as sweet, sour, salty and spicy tastes. They tend to be messy eaters having food all over their faces without being aware of it. Also, they have difficulty feeling food in their mouths so they are inclined to stuff their mouths with food, take large bites at a time, and not chew food thoroughly.

Often they drool excessively. When not eating food, they always seem to have something in their mouths to chew on such as shirt sleeves, bits of string, rubber bands or the ends of pens and pencils. Furthermore, they frequently smell non - food items, also having a persistent need to chew to get more oral stimulation.

While hyposensitive children may not display all of these traits, there will, however, be a predisposition towards them. Observing and noting their behaviour at various times of the day will assist you in reaching a conclusion as to whether or not your child has a hyposensitive response to feeding.

Aspects of Intervention for Sensory Feeding Disorder

Possible solutions

Before addressing ways to help children with sensory feeding issues, it is important to set out some matters of a general nature for consideration.

1. **Feeding of younger children should be parent led because the parent knows the results of undernourishment which the child may not realise.**
2. **The child should be made aware that it is better to eat than not to eat. At the same time the child's sensory needs must be acknowledged and honoured.**
3. **Behaviour and boundaries can be negotiated, but they need to be achievable.**

A child can have too much information about sensory feeding issues and may try to exploit the situation so that it can easily become a behavioural concern. At the end of the day, the child is still a child and may behave as a child to take advantage of the situation.

Mealtimes, which are heightened sensory experiences, come with the expectation of eating and drinking and over-aroused children may want to protect themselves from the sensory experiences encountered at this time. If you try putting yourself in your child's shoes, you will get a better understanding of what he is experiencing.

As explained in the section on "Sensory Processing Understood," the same approach can be used to get children into a calm, alert state prior to feeding. Initially reading a book, singing rhythmically to the child or playing with small reinforcement toys may well distract the focus of the child to make eating more fun.

The overaroused child requires high intensity sensory input given by activities such as running, jumping and bouncing which will help to reduce sensory defensiveness, improve tolerances and support regulation. Using the Wilbarger Brushing technique with joint compressions is also a technique that has been successful for some of our families prior to meal times.

The under aroused child also needs sensory regulating activities, but their purpose is to arouse rather than calm. He may also require oral stimulation before meals to "wake up" his mouth. Stimulation of the areas surrounding the mouth is done in the following order:

1. The face with the cheeks
2 Jaw
3. Lips
4. Teeth and gums
5. The insides of the cheeks
6. The tip, middle and sides of the tongue
7. The roof of the mouth.

Stimulation of the outside of the mouth can be done with a wet cloth. For the inside, use a soft toothbrush. Do it slowly, and in a playful manner.

Mealtimes should be an enjoyable family occasion. Children who are continually in the alert mode need the right atmosphere so that eating is stress-free, pleasant and fun, but not play. There should be lots of reciprocal talking and eye contact in a happy, relaxed atmosphere without the forcing of food or threats about not eating. Comfort, safety and security are important at this time as is the eating environment. Smells, noises, lighting and activity around the table should not interfere with the eating experience.

Allow children to explore their food through their tactile senses, tasting and feeling before eating. The first step may involve the child just touching the food with his hands. Next, he touches it with his lips. Finally, the child chooses to bite the food. It may take some time to get to this stage. It is sometimes helpful to present the food on two differently sized plates - the larger for the preferred foods and the smaller for the non-preferred foods. The amount of food on the non-preferred plate can then be gradually increased. Keep the mealtime as routine as possible with few changes, ensuring that it lasts no more than half an hour. Ask other adults to refrain from commenting on the food, whether eaten or not eaten and also, when the child does eat some food, not to give praise, as this only draws everyone's attention to the child. If you are taking children to a new location for eating food, be sure to prepare them for it by showing pictures of the venue, if possible, and talking about what to expect in terms of lighting, seating, tables and waitresses.

The problem with "grazing" or frequent snacking between meals is that if children are allowed to do this, they have eaten so much food between meals that they have no appetite for food. Then, when mealtime comes round, all the preparations which you have made for them to explore food options may be wasted. It may be possible to restrict, in some way, the amount or type of food available or encourage the drinking of water but, as in so many of the issues surrounding food, you may have to "play it by ear." Only wipe the mouths of under aroused children, not over- aroused. It is best to use easily crunched food such as Rice Krispies and not hard, crunchy food.

A parent reported that she tried to vary the crunchiness of the food with softer options week about, but she found out that if she kept her child on hard crunchy food for a longer period of time it was difficult to get him to vary it.

For children who are orally tactile defensive the "oral motor swipe" can be effective. This is a technique devised by Patricia Wilbarger, noted also for her "Brushing Programme". This involves running a finger around the inside of the mouth behind the teeth once and then pressing down gently three times on the lower front teeth.

One mother reported her child as being sick and gagging frequently. Driving from home to the therapy centre, a distance of about thirty miles, she had to stop five times because her child was sick. The child could be sick up to twenty times a day. She learnt the technique and within a week the frequency of sickness dropped dramatically.

The chaining of foods is another approach that may help widen the scope of "acceptable" foods. This is a child orientated approach which builds on the child's successful eating experiences. First, a list is made of food tastes, textures and temperatures to detect patterns of food which the child will accept. Then look at foods which may be used for transitioning to "new" foods. The "new" foods are similar to the ones he is familiar with, and are used to create food chains which will help broaden his list of tolerated foods. Say, for example, if a child likes juicy, green apples it may be possible to introduce him to a pear. If a child likes mashed potatoes, cauliflower could be added, and if he likes fizzy water, fruit juice could be added to fizzy mineral water. The general rule is to expand the flavour before expanding the texture. It is also possible to mask flavours by adding sauces to fruit, vegetables or cereals. For example, mix vegetables and meat with BBQ sauce, or add honey to steamed vegetables.

Kerry's Story: A Case Study

Kerry is a seven-year-old who was referred by her parents because of concerns over "eating issues."

She was six and a half pounds weight at birth and was delivered in the 37th week. At two years of age she had no speech/touch/swallowing problems, although she did have several bouts of tonsillitis. At 3 to 4 years she was seen, because of suspected sensory issues, by an O.T. and a dietician who reported that they found no issues they could deal with.

At the time of assessment she was eating blended main meals, had a limited food choice and, in addition, was sensitive to smells and noises. She hated the sun shining in her eyes, the feel of certain textures of clothing and the sensation of travelling by car on hilly roads. Kerry would not blow her nose nor put her face in the water while swimming. Her eyesight and hearing were reported as being normal. She did have problems with concentration and attention and always wanted to know what was happening next. She also liked creative arts and could hold conversations with anyone.

Kerry has a sweet tooth, and would eat chocolate continuously if allowed. She prefers drier types of food such as dry toast or rice cakes and favours eating with a spoon. In addition, she is embarrassed eating pureed foods or what she calls "babyish" foods, but says, "I just don't know how to eat not babyish foods."

From her mother's report and from looking at the results of a Sensory Profile, it would appear that she has over reaction to sensory issues in the following areas: touch, taste, smell, visual and auditory sensations. Her mother also said that she first noticed the feeding difficulties when Kerry started weaning. Indeed she was fussy when moving from pureed foods to solids. With regard to tastes, Kerry likes sweet or salty foods. She will eat crunchy or smooth foods and foods at a warm temperature. Kerry likes spicy or flowery smells but has a heightened reaction to the smell of bananas, crisps or chips. Her mother was not aware of a dislike of any particular colours of food but tended to think that Kerry preferred light colours. Kerry will gag or choke when presented with foods she doesn't like. She likes toothbrushing and does not mind her face or mouth being touched.

For Kerry's mother the main issues were:

1. Giving her child a greater selection of food in her packed lunch (At present she will take dry bread or crackers, a smoothie and Frubies.)
2. Kerry has difficulty eating in the dining hall in school with the other children because of the smells she encounters.
3. When Kerry goes to other children's birthday parties, she is very restricted in what she will eat, and so can feel rather isolated and embarrassed as a result of not being able to join in the eating of food.

As part of a trial, Kerry was presented with a McDonald's cheeseburger and chips. The food was cut up into small portions and given to her. She was prepared to try everything. When she lifted the chips, she explained that she did not like chips, but she did put them to her nose and lips and then set them aside. She examined the piece of burger and bap, talked about it, and put it against her lips six times but it was obvious that she was in avoidance mode. It appeared she had made up her mind whether or not to accept the food before she had even tasted it. The one success was that she found a new type of wheaten cracker that she liked which she had never tried before.

The overall impression given is that Kerry's sensory issues have become behavioural and she has learned how to manipulate the situation. Feeding is one of the greatest concerns that will hold the parents to ransom. This state of affairs may not be recognised by the latter. Both parents appear to have adopted a passive role. The reason for this may be that Kerry's parents found it difficult to conceive and she was a much desired baby when she eventually arrived. They may have been fearful of doing anything that might have suggested to the child that she was not loved. There is always the danger that in the parents' desire to be the child's buddy, the role of the parent in disciplining is either overlooked or neglected. Kerry has an inherent fear of food. If her parents are constantly endorsing that fear they are, in fact, feeding it and consequently encouraging it to spiral out of control. What her parents must do is to adopt the parenting role by taking control and enforcing eating "rules and boundaries" where Kerry's choice of eating is taken out of her hands. They need to positively support Kerry and become proactive in encouraging a dramatic, immediate change in food presentation (no more blended food), and increasing greater tolerance of food through food chaining. This pragmatic approach needs to allow for parental support and encouragement. Mealtimes will take much longer, but the concern for an underweight child with a reduced food intake, who may become malnourished, is foremost in the parent's mind.

To date Kerry is no longer on blended foods, but is motivated to persist with this "new" regime. On her own admission to her mother Kerry said, "Part of my brain just doesn't want to eat this food." This has been a highly personal and difficult challenge for the family and the parents feel that, because of the child's age, it is a circumstance they find difficult to share with anyone. Kerry has since made significant progress by increasing her range of food intake, addressing her now recognised "fear" of eating new foods, and understanding that she can no longer avoid eating at the table by playing with her food. She is now mature enough to realise that eating is an extremely sociable event. Her greatest desire was to be able to eat a scone when dining out with her grandfather. This has now in part been achieved.

Key Points from Chapter 11

- Any suspected feeding disorder should be investigated promptly since it may indicate a serious health issue
- A feeding disorder may indicate a physiological disorder or neurological dysfunction
- The origins of feeding disorders may be: genetic in nature, a result of reflux, stem from an uninhibited Moro reflex, or attributable to tactile over sensitivity, tube feeding or oral DCD
- Food should not be used as a bribe or a reward
- Feeding problems may stem from behavioural issues
- Food chaining may help transitioning to "new" foods

Chapter 12

Sensory Sleeping Problems

The Big Idea

Sleep is a natural cycle

Regulation disorders affect sleep

The Academic Viewpoint

Many children with sensory processing difficulties (and their parents!) do not sleep well. Exhausted children do not think, behave, and maximise their learning potential, besides, being tired makes it even harder to deal with sensory challenges. Persistent sleep disturbances result in higher levels of stress hormones, irregular biorhythms, decreased attention and cognitive skills, and heightened overall arousal because the body compensates in order to combat sleepiness. Children with sensory problems may lack adequate rest for many reasons. (Sensory Smarts. Sweet Dreams)

Red Flag Issues

- Poor mother/infant bonding
- Difficult to calm
- Hard to get into a routine
- No awareness of day and night
- Poor regulation from birth
- Reluctance to switch off
- Wants into parent's bed most nights
- Will not go to sleep alone

Green for Go

- Calms easily when comforted
- Develops good routines quickly
- Acknowledges when tired
- Can amuse self in cot or bed for a time

Regulation Disorders Affecting Sleep

Sleeping disorders affect not only the child, but also the parents and can extend over a considerable period of time during which the parents become worn out with little respite in view. These children rarely sleep throughout the entire night without interruption, and to the parents, it often appears that, "the harder you try the worse it gets." When a child wakes up during the night because of a nightmare or fear of being on his own, he will seek comfort and reassurance in bed with his parents. On occasions like these, being firm and wanting to be consistent in your approach to the problem does not always work. Your sleep has been broken and it usually takes some time to calm the child down. This scenario usually occurs at a time when you have an early start next day.

Premature babies, children on the Autistic Spectrum, and those with sensory issues seem to be the children who suffer the greatest sleep problems. From the outset, as with feeding problems, psychological reasons and medical issues, such as ear infections, gastrointestinal problems, reflux, teething and sleep apnoea need to be ruled out. Following this you may decide to look for other reasons.

Before reviewing what these might be, first consider the normal pattern of behaviour which you may use as a base line for comparison purposes. The child goes to bed and follows a routine, perhaps of a parent reading a story, saying a prayer, tucking the child in, dimming or switching out the light and closing the bedroom door. The child falls asleep and if he wakens up, self-calms and then goes back to sleep on his own.

Should this not be the case, you may begin by looking at the child's sleeping pattern over the period of a few days. This review should be age appropriate because younger children require more sleep and naps through the day than older children. A sleeping schedule of the normal evening events for the family, as a means of appraisal, would include the sleeping arrangements for the household, the child's bedtime, the bedtime of others in the family, environmental issues including room temperature, the dimness of the light, use of blackout curtains, the bedroom door left open or closed and finally, the things that appear to disturb the child's sleeping pattern. These might include the door bell ringing, the telephone ringing, the child feeling hungry, toilets flushing, TV being on loud or the sound of heavy vehicles passing nearby.

Having reviewed all of these possible causes for disturbance in the sleeping schedule, including the environmental concerns, it is then possible to go on to finding out if the sensory systems support or hamper the child's ability to fall asleep and stay sleeping, and furthermore, to discover whether or not these systems help modulation and self-regulation.

As with the visual, auditory and tactile systems, children with sensory difficulties fall into two main categories: the HYPER and the HYPO. The hypersensitive babies have difficulty regulating, are very unsettled and generally do not soothe to touch. They will not tolerate being rocked; they wake up very easily, even to the quietest of sounds and do not suck their thumb or fingers to self-soothe. They do not establish a good sleep/wake pattern. If babies can't self-soothe they become fussy and irritable. The hyposensitive children, on the other hand, tend to seek out sensory input. They like to be tightly swaddled, bounced up and down on a therapy ball, patted firmly on the back and given deep massage. The use of a Sensory Profile will help determine the best soothing strategies to assist each sensory system and to promote modulation.

Sleeping is often a major problem for Autistic children. This is not to say that if your child has problems with sleeping that he is Autistic. One reason given for this is a serotonin imbalance which may be remedied by giving melatonin or clonidine, but medical advice should always be sought before proceeding along this path.

Other Options to Consider:

- Use calming down activities in the evening such as rocking back and forth, head to toe or side to side
- Use The Brushing Programme (described later) with joint compression

- Put the child in the crib while drowsy, but before he has fallen asleep
- Bathe and feed the child one hour before bedtime
- Avoid active socialisation before bedtime as this can increase separation anxiety
- Assist the child's efforts at self-calming by providing a teddy, tucking in the blankets or providing a "dummy" for sucking
- Ensure the bedding and pyjamas are sensory compatible
- Provide white noise or classical music such as Baby Mozart
- Play games during the day which will assist separation at bedtime such as Hide and Seek
- Understand that some children want to play at night because they find the daytime too stimulating
- Bathe in Epsom salts
- Use a weighted blanket for deep pressure
- Place the mattress on the floor for gravitationally insecure children

Having taken all of these matters into account and if you are determined to give some particular method a try, you could try this approach. When the child wakes up in the middle of the night, comes into your bedroom and wants to get into bed beside you, get up out of bed immediately, take him by the hand and return him back to his own bed without saying anything or making eye contact. Place him in his own bed and say, "Sleep." You may have to do this several times in the one night and it may take up to two weeks before the child will sleep right throughout the night in his own bed, but if it accomplishes the task it is worthwhile.

Some children object strongly to you leaving the room and may want you to stay. If this is the case, try staying a short distance from the bed until the child settles and over a period of time gradually increase the distance between you and him until you are able to reach the door, and finally get outside the door. To assist you with this process you may allow the child to keep "mummy's teddy" in bed with him as part of the process of addressing the attachment issue, but you should always ask for your teddy to be returned next morning so that he realises that the teddy is not his, but yours, and that he is just borrowing it at night.

Some success has been noted with older children using the "Sleep n Sync" programme. These are audio tapes which take advantage of the brain's capacity to function while asleep. They cover the issues of dealing with anger, becoming more flexible and help in easing transition. (These are available on www.amazon.com/digitalmusic)

Key Points from Chapter 12

- Sleeping disorders may be long-term in duration and can have a distressing effect on parents.
- There are many reasons for sleeping disorders including sensory issues, psychological, medical and environmental problems.
- An appropriate sleep pattern review may help to highlight the issues.
- Hyper and hyposensitive children will have different problems which may be better understood using a "Sensory Profile".
- There are many alternatives to consider which may help improve sleep quality.

Chapter 13

Vision

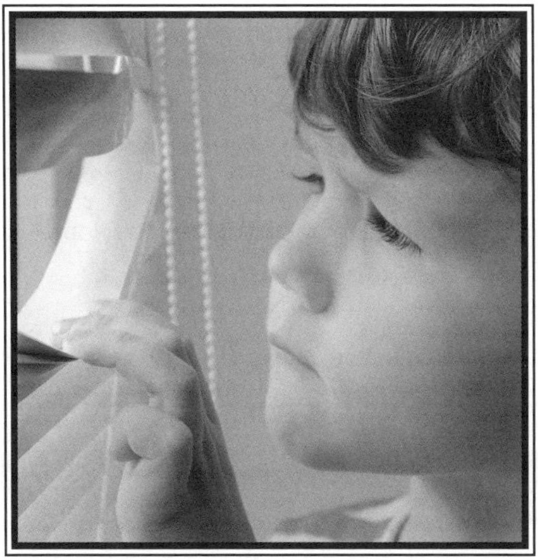

The Big Idea

This refers to visual perception and the processing of visual information found in the environment

Visual Perception is the ability to use vision to adapt to the environment. To do this we must integrate what is seen visually with cognitive concepts of space and object manipulation, timing and trajections.

Visual Perception involves visual memory, visual cognition, visual scanning and pattern recognition

If a child lacks visual scanning they do not develop visual attention

To learn easily you must be able to visualise verbal information

The Academic Viewpoint

A visual processing disorder can cause difficulty in seeing the difference between two similar letters, shapes, or objects, or noticing the similarities and differences between certain colours, shapes and patterns. Although visual processing disorder is not named as learning disability, it can explain why a child may have trouble with learning and performance. (National Centre for Learning Disabilities)

Red Flag Issues

- Cannot identify similarities and differences in geometrical shapes
- Has poor hand/eye coordination
- Poor at reading and copying from the whiteboard

Green for Go

- Good discrimination of numbers and letters
- Vision and touch work well together
- Is fluent in reading and has good comprehension skills
- Has good hand/eye control

Early Assessment

One day you get a note sent home from school, probably while your child is in Year 1 or Year 2, informing you that the School Nurse is going to pay a visit to the school to check up on hearing, eyesight and overall development. You may be invited to attend, but more probably not. These visits are important but, as far as vision is concerned, are of a rather restricted nature because of time constraints and the amount of training the nurse would be required to have in this area. The visual checks will look at colour blindness and acuity, or the ability for each eye to see clearly. When the checks have been carried out you will probably hear nothing more unless concerns have been identified.

It would be beneficial if early visual screening included assessment of other possible issues such as tracking, convergence, accommodation, directional awareness, visualisation, muscle imbalance, issues associated with pattern glare and, finally, the presence of retained primitive reflexes. (These issues will be discussed later in the chapter.) However, such checks would take considerably longer and require additional training for the nurse. A child with any one of these concerns will have difficulty with visual perception in school which, in turn, will undoubtedly lead to major delays in education. Should your child be falling behind because of these difficulties, it is important to get his vision checked out by an optometrist, possibly a behavioural optometrist, who will carry out a wider range of tests than those used by the school nurse. Another important point to remember is that, even though your child may be classified as having 20/20 vision, this merely applies to the clarity of vision in each eye and does not rule out other visual anomalies.

The eye has been described as the window that connects the world to the brain. A behavioural definition of vision would describe how we derive meaning and direct action by processing information we receive through the eyes. Indeed, the information which we get through the eyes tells us about what is going on in our environment - about the size, shape, speed, colour of an object. For example, is it coming or going, is it near or far away and is it in 2 or 3 dimensions? Reading, writing, spelling and arithmetic are all highly dependent upon vision. These form the core of the work that is carried out in school, so in this context, it is important to ensure that the eyes are functioning correctly.

From a very early age a child can see clearly up to about 20 centimetres. He begins to make sense of what he sees by using vision in conjunction with other sensory systems through the VOR (vestibulo-ocular reflex) to interpret and give what is seen meaning. This system stabilizes images on the retina, even if the head is moving, and it is driven by the vestibular apparatus in the ear. Since the head moves constantly, the VOR is very important. Should the vestibular system of semi-circular canals in the ear be damaged or not functioning properly, vision may be blurred or distorted. This is mentioned now because it is one of the reasons why some children have difficulty with motor skills (especially in games and P.E.) both gross and fine, including reading (this difficulty being a possible cause of Dyslexia).

The Visual Learner

Many of the children referred to the clinic have an overdependence on vision, and insufficient or limited attention is given by them to messages coming to the brain through other senses and other systems such as the vestibular, the proprioceptive, tactile or auditory systems. (Only 5% of the visual processing occurs in the eye itself, whilst the other 95% is associated with touch, hearing and proprioception.) When asked to carry out a simple motor task such as, "Sit on the bolster swing as if it were a horse," the child may look at his mother for guidance as though saying, "What do I do?" In this instance he may have motor planning difficulties, body awareness issues, ideation difficulties (discussed below) or auditory processing problems (see chapter 14). The visual learner, once he has been shown what to do, will then be able to carry out the task much more easily than by following verbal instruction alone. In other words, a child who focuses strongly on visual skills may be compensating for shortcomings in integrating the multi senses necessary for the learning process. These are children who need to see what other children around them are doing before they can commence activities.

Integrating Vision with Other Senses

Efficient learners use a strategy of integrating vision with auditory and tactile skills to provide the brain with as much information as possible. Children who are unable to integrate these sensory processes are at a great disadvantage when it comes to getting the most out of learning. Vision, when integrated with touch, assists perceptual skills such as recognition of size, shape and orientation of objects. Blind people compensate for loss of vision with increased tactile awareness. Learning is made more effective when both vision and touch work in harmony. Early learners should touch and manipulate numbers and letters to help imprint the images in their heads making learning a perceptual experience.

Many activities in the classroom require children to be able to multitask, i.e. to see, listen and do at the same time. Children who are visual learners depend a great deal on being able to learn by observation. This reliance on the visual system may go unnoticed in the early years of schooling when much teaching is of a visual nature. If, possibly by reason of auditory processing difficulty, they are dependent on visual cues, then the difficulty becomes more noticeable in Year 4 when much more of the learning is focused on the ability to listen well rather than visually observe. This ability to integrate the systems is essential for executive functioning, i.e. for paying attention, remembering, keeping track of more than one thing at a time and connecting past experiences with present action to plan, organise and complete tasks of all kinds.

Seeing in Pictures to Assist Memory

Observing a demonstration of how something is carried out is essential for children who have “ideation difficulties.” In other words they cannot get the idea of the required action. Visual skills do not stand alone. It is as important to integrate vision with touch, as well as to integrate vision with auditory skills. The children who are unable to integrate these sensory systems are at a great disadvantage for processing information. These are the children in the classroom who appear to lack attention and concentration. In literacy where children are responding to text, be it written or oral, they are expected to be able to understand what is being said, make inferences from the story, and respond to the text with empathy.

Nearly always, when children are referred with comprehension or attention difficulties related to literacy, they have auditory processing problems. This translates into the child struggling with processing the words which he is hearing, having never learned the strategy of thinking about the words in pictures. This strategy is referred to as visualising/verbalising.

If someone were to say to you, "The tall lady in the red dress is standing on the street corner," and you were asked an hour later what was said, you would realise that the ability to recollect a mental image or picture was a more efficient strategy for remembering than recalling the words spoken. Many children do not possess this ability and their processing skills are greatly disadvantaged.

Similarly, when assessing children with difficulties in maths skills, it is noticeable that they lack the ability to "see" the processes involved. Indeed, it is essential to visualise and manipulate auditory information relating to maths in respect of distance, direction and spatial awareness. The language of maths needs to convey the image of what is required with the correct meaning. Children who struggle with maths must be able to "see" the basic processes of addition, subtraction, estimation etc.

One leg standing with vision occluded will quickly determine the extent of a child's dependence on vision to inform his body awareness. He may be able to stand on one leg with the help of visual cues gained from stable objects in the room, but once the child is blindfolded, this difficulty will become apparent because he is not used to processing information gained through muscles, tendons, joints (proprioception) and the vestibular system to assist his balance.

In the classroom, a child with APD (auditory processing difficulty) may look at what others at his table are doing to inform him as to what to do when given some verbal instructions. If a child is a visual learner, i.e. he is heavily dependent on vision for learning, then this deficit has great implications not only for the child, but also for the teacher in terms of teaching style. Visually-orientated teaching will make the process of learning and understanding so much easier for the child than verbal explanations alone would. It will probably be more rewarding for the teacher as well, resulting in greater satisfaction from teaching and greatly improved outcomes for the child.

While some children pay too little attention to additional sensory stimuli, others pay too much attention. If a child has a Moro reflex which has not been inhibited, he may have great difficulty paying attention because he finds the lights too bright or the background (wall displays) too distracting. Tinted glasses may help in the former instance, while placing the desk in a visually "quiet" area may help in the latter.

There are six muscles attached to the top, bottom and sides of each eye, an internal muscle for focussing and one for opening and closing the pupil. This gives a total of sixteen eye muscles of which four are internal and twelve are external. It is a complex process to use all sixteen in conjunction with each other. A child is said to have good ocular motor control when he can use these muscles to focus both eyes on an object to produce a sharp image, whether near or far (called accommodation), turn the eyes in to focus on an object (convergence), is able to stabilize an image so that he can hold his gaze on the object for, say ten seconds (fixation), and also mobilise the eye to give good coordination for tracking the object when it moves in any direction. These were the processes mentioned at the beginning of the chapter.

Difficulties in these areas may be associated with uninhibited reflexes. The inability to focus with both eyes on an object (convergence) is associated with the TLR (tonic labyrinthine reflex). A retained TLR will mean that the child will have difficulty judging space and distance because head movements will alter muscle tone and balance and therefore the child will not have secure points of reference. Inability to see near or far (accommodation) is associated with the STNR (symmetrical tonic neck reflex) because an STNR is inhibited by crawling, and children who have not crawled initially have prolonged difficulty focussing on anything closer than arm's length. Tracking difficulties are associated with the ATNR (asymmetrical tonic neck reflex). The child with a retained ATNR will have difficulty crossing a midline position with his hands and the eyes will have a similar difficulty. Finally, a retained Moro reflex will have an impact on a child's fixation ability. It is important to check whether or not these reflexes are present and if so, perform the exercises which will help to inhibit them.

These visual motor skills use visual information to carry out an activity or transfer it to other systems that need it. Visual perception is the link between what the eye sees and the relationship with other senses. These skills match output with input. For example, John is riding his bicycle along the road when someone walks out in front of him causing him to brake quickly and stop to avoid a collision. This simple scenario illustrates the link between the eyes and the various systems. His eyes, vestibular and proprioceptive systems are all working together as he pedals along (eye/hand coordination, proprioception) maintaining his balance (vestibular). Sudden movement is observed which makes him react quickly (sensory motor) causing him to brake (proprioception) and put his foot down when stopped (vestibular and proprioception) to prevent himself from falling off. This event illustrates the visual-motor output being matched to visual input to make the situation meaningful, enabling a correct interpretation of the event and causing other sensory systems to kick in.

In the classroom situation, a child with visual-motor difficulties may see an object, but because of an inability to process or transfer this information, it bears no relationship to where he is walking. The result is, that he may bump into a desk or trip over an object on the floor, or fail to recognise differences in the floor surface, for example in PE when moving from the floor to an agility mat. He appears to operate in two separate worlds – the visual and the motor with information not being transferred from one to the other. Children with these difficulties may try to skip PE, stay in the toilet during PE, stay on the sidelines during games or pretend to be hurt. All of these are avoidance strategies.

Another visual-motor problem is difficulty with eye-tracking or what is called ocular motor pursuit. Tracking is used when reading or writing, following objects through space and keeping attention fixed on a task. When doing these activities children who have this difficulty have to relocate their place continually, often losing it when doing some of these activities. They may skip lines when they are reading, move the head and not the eyes to track, have difficulty catching a ball and reverse letters, figures and words. In addition, they may have saccadic eye movements, i.e. the eye appears to jump back to a central position while tracking on the horizontal and/or vertical axis. Again this causes a difficulty because of the eye having to relocate continually to the correct place.

Visual motor ability is the foundation for the development of perceptual skills. These include **spatial relations, form constancy, figure ground** and **visual closure, visual discrimination, visual memory** and **visual sequential memory**. Difficulties with understanding what is observed are commonly found in children with coordination problems. They have trouble organising, remembering and recognising images and symbols for reading, writing and mathematics.

Spatial relations capacity concerns the ability to see two or more objects in relation to each other and sequence or order letters as in spelling. **Form constancy** is about knowing that the object is still there even though it is covered. **Figure ground** is the skill to see or pick out an object in a distracting background. **Visual closure** relates to the ability to recognise a letter or shape even though it looks as though parts of it have been rubbed out. **Visual discrimination** is the capability of recognising similarities and differences in letters and shapes, e.g. b/d and p/q. **Visual memory** is the facility to recall a previous visual experience as in remembering words as a mental picture thereby assisting visual recall. For example asking oneself does it look right? Finally, **Visual sequential memory** is the ability to recall the sequence of objects without using sound/symbol support for the sequence.

The Normal Development of Vision from Birth to Eight Years of Age

Normally, checks on your child's eyesight will be carried out as follows: examination at birth for signs of abnormalities, 6-8 weeks check by GP, a test at 3 years carried out by optometrist and a 5 years check in school by school nurse. A child's vision should develop as outlined below:

- 6 weeks: follows a face with eyes and has steady fixation
- 2-3 months: reaches for things he sees
- 3-5 months: looks at objects more closely, blinks at threatening stimuli
- 6-12 months: focuses on objects near/far, shows interest in pictures, scribbles
- 2 years: acuity normal, optical skills smooth
- 7-8 years: development complete

There are some physical signs that may indicate possible eye problems which parents should be on the lookout for in the preschool child such as sitting close to the TV, holding a book close to the eyes, short attention span, squinting, tilting the head, frequent rubbing of eyes, sensitivity to light, difficulty with ball skills, blinking, and avoiding puzzles and colouring.

Symptoms of a School Age Child with Visual Difficulties

- Is slow to read
- Daydreams or has a dazed look as a result of relaxing the child's eyes because of muscle imbalance
- Has poor posture while reading
- Has difficulty with ball games
- Describes letters as blurred or jumping

- Reads/writes with face close to the page
- Is easily distracted
- Reads with one eye covered
- Has poor concentration
- Engages in prolonged use of finger as a pointer
- Rubs eyes
- Squints
- Tilts head
- Is sensitive to light
- Complains of headaches, eye pain
- Skips lines
- Loses the place
- Misses or substitutes words
- Has poor tracking skills
- Eyes jump back to midline
- Takes too long to do homework
- Has difficulty copying from one place to the other
- Has difficulty seeing/remembering what is seen
- Becomes stressed or tires easily when doing visually demanding tasks
- Has difficulty matching what is seen with what is known or with what is already understood
- Bumps into objects, trips forward, falls backward frequently
- Has inaccurate eye/hand or eye/body movement

There is a great need to give such children the understanding that they have a physical difficulty, for sometimes they may think that they themselves are the problem or that they are wrong or stupid. It seems to them that they are the only ones in the class who are not "getting it." The danger is that such a child may withdraw, learn not to take a chance, and get caught up in a self preserving response. Each time the child makes a mistake his self confidence, self-worth and self- esteem all diminish. Few children with visual dysfunction have a true sense of self worth.

The visual processes involved in the activity of reading are the final areas for consideration. What we ultimately desire in the reading process is to eliminate the voice reading in the head and move directly from the printed page to visual imagery.

When a child makes visual contact with a page of writing he needs to be able to locate the first word (fixation), align both eyes on the word (binocularity), see it clearly (accommodation), move along the line of print (tracking) and process sequentially. The next stage is to process the symbols of visual language either as phonetic decoding or decoding using visual memory. The final stage is to comprehend what is written down and use, by means of imagery, the information for a specific purpose by recalling the details required.

Key Points from Chapter 13

- Having 20/20 vision does not necessarily mean that a child has no problems with vision.
- Vision is used in conjunction with the other sensory systems by means of the VOR (vistibulo-ocular reflex).
- Efficient learners make proficient use of the auditory and tactile systems in conjunction with the visual system.
- The ability to form mental pictures will greatly improve sequencing and memory.
- Learning, primarily by use of vision, has implications for both pupil and teacher.
- Ocular motor control involves the ability of the eyes to focus, converge, fix and track an object. Retained reflexes will have a big impact on these.

- Perceptual skills are affected by visual motor ability.
- There are many indicators of visual difficulties.
- Visual problems have a great bearing on self-esteem.

Chapter 14

Auditory Processing

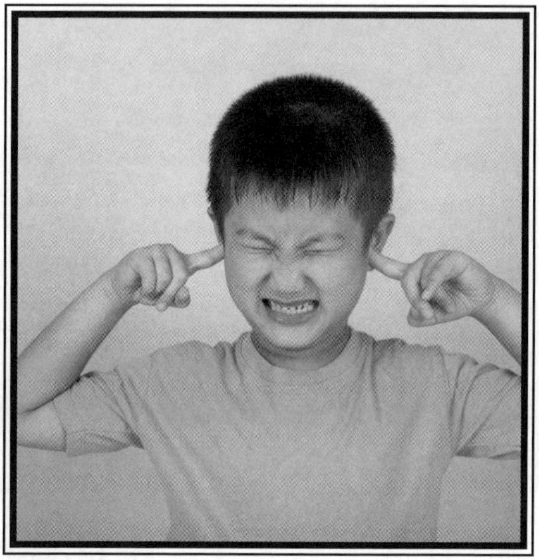

The Big Idea

Auditory processing disorder is not a problem with hearing, but with processing what is heard.

The Academic Viewpoint

An "auditory processing disorder" is a hearing or listening problem caused by the brain not processing sounds in the normal way.

It may affect your ability to:

- **pinpoint a sound**
- **tell which sound comes before another**
- **distinguish similar sounds from one another (such as "seventy" and "seventeen")**
- **enjoy music**

It may be difficult to understand speech when there is background noise, if more than one person is speaking at a time, if the person is speaking quickly, or if the sound quality is poor (if it's over a loudspeaker or in an echoey room, for example). Instructions can also be difficult to remember. (NHS Choices)

Red Flag Issues

- Difficulty following verbal instructions or totally gets the wrong idea from processing only some of the words spoken
- Puts hands over ears
- Requests instructions to be repeated
- Does not visualise verbal information
- Ear infections going undetected for a time in the first three years of life
- Mispronounces some words repeatedly
- Needs to see the picture when being read to
- Is distracted by 'white noise'

Green for Go

- Appropriate expected reaction to sound
- Well organised to follow instructions
- Good understanding of what is read and said

Leslie's Story:

A Case Study in APD (Auditory Processing Disorder)

Leslie is in P2. He appears to be a confident, sociable, friendly and articulate child. He was quite happy in the therapy room environment and readily engaged in the therapist's requests. His mother expressed concerns about his behaviour in school (orange lighted on several occasions by the teacher for his behaviour) and about difficulty in completing his homework. Leslie hates homework and it seems, both to himself and to his mother, to take for ever to complete. At the end of the therapy session he overheard comments about exercises he could do for "homework". He immediately picked up on this and expressed his dislike of anything that involved homework. He was fine, however, when told that it did not involve any type of bookwork nor anything that resembled school activities or writing.

In class he gets distracted easily, finds it difficult to remain in his seat, shouts out, apparently does not listen, has difficulty following instructions, is over talkative, takes a long time to write and he has difficulties with spelling.

At home he often does not respond when spoken to. It seems as if he does not hear when spoken to and sometimes his mother has to touch him or give him a visual cue to attract his attention. He likes the volume on the TV to be louder than normal.

As a child, he learned to walk quickly and would be described as an "on the go" child with a need to fidget. He had "glue ear" as a baby which cleared up by the time he was five years old.

During the assessment session he continually tried to second guess verbal instructions, coming up with his own ideas and suggestions before the instructions were completed.

Among other tests during the session, he was given the Scan C test which is a standardised test for Auditory Processing Disorder (APD). In this test a child is asked to repeat aloud certain words which he hears through headphones. For example, "Say after me the word house. Say after me the word dog." He hears words in his left ear in one section of the test and some in his right in another part. Some words are given with noise in the background such as would be the case in the classroom. From this test it was obvious that Leslie had a right ear advantage in addition to difficulty hearing in a noisy environment.

Apart from this standardised test, there were many clues in Leslie's behaviour strongly suggesting that he was suffering from Auditory Processing Disorder (APD).

It is important to understand, at the outset, that APD is not a hearing problem, but a processing problem and it is essential to make a clear distinction between these. The child, however, needs to be able to hear before he can process what has been heard. This anecdote illustrates this difference. During an assessment session, a girl aged four was playing with a child's tea set. The therapist said to the child, "Give Amanda a cup of tea." I was sitting nearby taking notes on what the child was doing. She got up and came over and presented me with a cup of tea. What precisely had the child processed from the therapist's instruction to cause her to do this? What she heard was, "Give a man a cup of tea," not, "A man da." Another child reported instantly to her mother that her teacher was "going to Belfast on a 'horse' tomorrow." What the teacher had said was "she was going to Belfast on a course."

Consider first the subject of hearing, including the tests that are carried out initially to ensure a child can hear properly, and also the way hearing develops as he grows. Furthermore, observe what is involved in auditory processing and problems that may occur if all the systems are not functioning as they should.

Shortly after birth children are given a hearing check. The first test is an AOE, an automated otoacustic emissions test, which takes only a few minutes and can be carried out while the baby is asleep. Should this test prove inconclusive, another test can be given that is the AABR, or automated auditory brainstem response. This test uses three sensors positioned at the back of the head and a pair of soft headphones placed over the baby's ears. A computer analyses how well the baby responds to soft clicks relayed through the headphones. A further hearing check will be given in primary school.

Auditory Development 0-4 years

Included here is a developmental hearing checklist (adapted from kidshealth.org) which will give some indication as to what behaviour may be considered normal during the first four years of life.

0-3 months

- Reacts to loud sounds
- Calms down and smiles when spoken to by mother
- Recognises your voice
- Stops/starts feeding in response to sound
- Coos and makes pleasure sounds
- Cries in different ways for different needs

4-6 months

- Follows sounds with eyes
- Responds to change in tone of voice
- Pays attention to music
- Babbles (ppp, bbb, mmm)
- Laughs
- Babbles when excited or unhappy
- Makes gurgling noises when alone

7-12 months

- Plays peek-a-boo
- Turns and looks in the direction of sound
- Listens when spoken to
- Understands common words like cup, juice etc.
- Responds to requests... come here, want more?
- Babbles using long and short groups of sounds, e.g. ta ta, up up up

- Babbles to get and keep attention
- Communicates with gestures, e.g. waving/holding up arms
- Imitates different speech sounds
- Has one or two words by first birthday

1-2 years

- Knows a few parts of the body and points to them when asked
- Follows simple sentences, e.g. roll the ball
- Enjoys simple stories, songs and rhymes
- Points to pictures when named in a book
- Acquires new words regularly
- Uses a few one/two word questions
- Puts two words together, e.g. more juice…where's kitty?
- Uses many different consonant sounds at the beginning of words

2-3 years

- Has a word for almost anything
- Uses 2/3word phrases to talk about and ask for something
- Uses "k, g, f, t, d, n" sounds
- Speaks in a way that is understood by the family
- Names objects to ask for them

3-4 years

- Hears you when you call from another room
- Hears TV at the same sound level as others
- Asks questions: Who? What? Where? Why?
- Talks about activity in preschool
- Uses sentences with 4 or more words
- Speaks easily without having to repeat syllables

Auditory Processing Disorder

In school, as well as eye checks, children in Year 1 or Year 2 will be given a hearing check. The point is that this screening check assesses only how well a child hears in ideal conditions as opposed to how well he processes and makes sense of sound, including spoken language in everyday situations. Auditory processing is about the ability to interpret, store and access information and to recognise subtle variations between different sounds and timing in speech. A child with APD may only process a part of what is heard correctly and miss the rest or perceive a totally incorrect idea of what has been said. The brain, in any event, will try to make sense of what has been heard.

Returning to Leslie, the more obvious signs that he has APD include being easily distracted, finding it difficult to follow instructions, shouting out, second guessing instructions, appearing not to hear when spoken to, liking the TV volume loud, having difficulty with spelling, being an "on the go" child who fidgets and finds it difficult to sit still, tiring easily and finally, having an early history of "glue ear" or ear infection which may not have been detected for a while.

Before giving a comprehensive list of signs and symptoms of APD, we need to consider something of the anatomy and physiology of the ear and the physics connected with the process of hearing and listening. This will enable us to gain a good insight into the perceptual difficulties of children with APD and also the possible causes.

The human ear forms in utero between 4-8 weeks in the pregnancy. Myelination of the auditory fibres (rather like the plastic coating on electric wires) happens between 24-28 weeks and from this time sound perception begins to develop slowly. The ear will be mainly tuned in to the internal sounds heard in utero, but the foetus may respond to external sounds as well. After birth, the baby's ears still contain fluid which clears after a few days and then he can hear a wide range of sounds. During the first three years of life, the child has the potential to learn his own, or any other language, and because each language has its own distinctive frequencies, he will learn to tune in to these.

Sound cannot travel through a vacuum. It needs some medium, such as air, water or bone, to carry it to the ear. The sound waves are funnelled into the external ear canal and strike the eardrum which, in turn, is set in motion causing the middle ear bones to move. These vibrations displace fluid in the ear (cochlea) causing hairs within it to move. The position of the hairs and the intensity of the movement indicate the nature of the sound. This information is sent via the auditory nerve to the brain for interpretation. Sound entering the right ear thus passes to the language centre in the left hemisphere of the brain, while sounds entering the left ear have a slightly longer journey of a few milliseconds before they reach the language centre in the right hemisphere of the brain. This slight delay may cause a child who has a dominant left ear to have difficulty processing instructions. A dominant right ear is more efficient than the left for receiving the sounds of language.

Sound is composed of vibration, motion and energy. It can vary from high to low pitch and from loud to soft. Pitch, or frequency as it is more accurately termed, varies in the human auditory range from 20 hertz (low frequency) to 20 000 hertz (high frequency). Dogs can hear much higher frequencies than humans, but not as low ones, and bats can hear higher still. The ability to distinguish sounds for language requires good hearing in the 125–8000 hertz range.

Incidentally, as we get older, the ability to hear the higher frequencies diminishes.

Previously mentioned was the importance of the first three years of life in developing skills for learning language. A child has to learn to focus on, or tune in to, some frequencies and filter out other unnecessary sounds. Some children are seriously disadvantaged in the early years because they develop nose, throat and ear infections, such as 'glue ear'. These infections can cause temporary loss of hearing at a crucial stage and can go unnoticed for some time.

The loudness, or volume of a sound, is measured in decibels (dB). A volume of 20 dB is considered normal for hearing. In a noisy classroom the volume may rise to 40 dB. A child who needs a volume of 40 – 60 dB to hear is considered to have a moderate hearing loss, and over 60 dB, a severe hearing loss. However, a child whose hearing falls in the 20 – 40 dB range may have difficulty in differentiating similar sounds like 'b' and 'p', 'th' and 'f', 'ch' and 'sh', which are in the higher frequencies in the English language. This is particularly so if there is any hearing loss within this range.

Leslie, as we noted earlier, had many signs of APD. There are many more which are listed below. These will give greater insight into the difficulties children such as Leslie, and indeed many adults, face. Often when explaining these indicators to parents, they say, "Oh I can easily identify with some of those," or, "I have always had those difficulties but I thought that was just me." Some strategies that may prove useful when dealing with this disorder in the classroom are included. Finally, strategies which you and your child may use to limit auditory processing challenges are added.

Signs and Symptoms of Auditory Processing Difficulty

- Delayed or no response to oral instructions or questions
- Gives routine response such as "yes" to everything that is said to them
- Talks loudly
- Has difficulty in telling the direction from which a parent is calling him
- Is unusually sensitive to noise
- Complains about noise
- Likes the TV to be louder than normal
- Has a tendency to confuse similar sounding words
- Confuses or forgets multiple directions if given in one sentence
- Regularly misunderstands oral instructions or questions or asks for extra information
- Says, "Huh?" or, "What?" frequently
- Often needs clarification or repetition of information
- Has difficulty understanding what is said to them when there is background noise
- Is uncomfortable in places with a lot of noise or poor acoustics
- Has poor auditory attention
- Is over talkative
- Is easily distracted, has a short attention span, seems to daydream a lot
- May have problems with phonics or discriminating speech sounds
- Has difficulty perceiving high frequency sounds such as: t, f, s, k, p, th, sh
- May have poor expressive or receptive language

- May have spelling, reading and other academic problems
- Finds abstract information may be difficult to follow
- Mental maths problems may cause difficulty
- May have reduced auditory memory
- May have behavioural problems
- Behaviour and performance may improve in quieter settings
- May have delayed language development
- Has difficulty sequencing the sounds of words
- Has inconsistent responses to the same auditory stimuli
- Has difficulty expressing desires, often blames others for not understanding
- May be disorganised and forgetful
- May find it difficult to follow and take part in conversations
- Has difficulty organising and integrating thoughts
- Tires easily
- Cannot sit still

The five main areas which affect children both at home and in school are:

- **Auditory Figure-Ground Problems:** when a child cannot pay attention if there's noise in the background. Noisy, low-structured classrooms can be very frustrating.
- **Auditory Memory Problems:** when a child has difficulty remembering information such as directions, lists, or study materials. It can be immediate ("I can't remember it now") and/or delayed ("I can't remember it when I need it for later").
- **Auditory Discrimination Problems:** when a child has difficulty hearing the difference between words or sounds that are similar, e.g. coat/boat or ch/sh). This can affect

following directions, and reading, spelling, and writing skills, among others.

- **Auditory Attention Problems:** when a child cannot stay focused on listening long enough to complete a task or requirement (such as listening to a talk in school). Children with APD often have trouble maintaining attention, although health, motivation, and attitude also can play a role.
- **Auditory Cohesion Problems:** when higher-level listening tasks are difficult. Auditory cohesion skills include drawing inferences from conversations, understanding riddles, or comprehending verbal maths problems. These require heightened auditory processing and language levels. They develop best when all the other skills (levels 1 to 4 above) are intact. (1995-2015 Nemours Foundation/ Kidshealth.org Reprinted with permission)

In a classroom situation, if you are faced with a child whom you suspect has, or who has already been diagnosed with APD, what steps might you take to alleviate the circumstances? Some of the strategies mentioned here are also applicable in the home.

Classroom Strategies for APD

- Ensure the class is quiet before you begin speaking
- Obtain the child's attention before you speak to him possibly by means of a private cue such as raising a hand or tapping on the desk
- Speak slowly and clearly
- Rephrase information rather than repeating it
- Seat the child at the front of the class with dominant ear towards the teacher

- Allow the child to move to a quiet area for independent work or reading
- Always provide written instructions on the board when speaking and also additional instructions on paper for the child
- Use concrete materials or pictorial representations where possible especially for maths
- Try to explain the purpose of the task - the whole concept if possible
- Present instructions in small steps
- Be precise
- Make sure the child knows what to do
- Write key vocabulary on the board
- Do not give homework out quickly at the end of the class when some are packing up to leave and it is noisier
- Allow the child more time to respond to a question
- Ensure a quiet working environment
- Give the child more frequent breaks as it takes more effort to pay attention
- In group debates, only one person speaks at a time, while others listen
- A homework timetable or home/school book allows both parents and teachers to share information

Children who have **auditory sensitivities**, termed auditory defensiveness, fall into the APD category. This term is used to describe children who find it difficult to listen in a noisy environment such as a classroom with background noise going on most of the time. The cause for this may possibly be traced back to an uninhibited Moro or Startle reflex which was discussed earlier. Children, in the early stages of life, may be startled by sudden changes in movement, temperature, brightness of light, pain and, for the purposes of this discussion, noise. Children with this uninhibited reflex hear all the sounds in an environment which others are able to filter out, such as a fan on the computer, the noise made by a fridge or traffic passing by outside. These sounds become irritating, distracting and even overwhelming, consequently increasing the child's anxiety level. Their reflexive coping strategy is to try to block out the sound by putting their hands over their ears. If this does not work they don't know how to deal with the situation. They may get cross or try to leave the noisy environment. Such children can be difficult to manage, especially if teachers are unaware that this is a difficulty peculiar to them. They never think of telling anyone how they are feeling so they just live with this "disorder". It is unlikely that the child will grow out of this difficulty. Indeed, some parents inform us, when they understand more about APD, that they have some of these difficulties themselves.

Most of us, when working in a noisy environment, have the ability to tune in, or out, various sounds entering the ear. At the base of the back of the neck lies the brainstem which is about the size of your thumb. At the core of the brain stem lies a part called the "reticular formation". Part of its function is to help a person decide how much attention to give to a sound or sensory input. It acts like traffic lights for all processing. Some sounds are stopped whilst some are allowed through. Noises, such as an alarm bell or siren, are alerting, while others, such as soft music or water trickling in a stream, are calming. The reticular formation can be trained to ignore certain sounds or to react to others. If we hear a monotonous sound such as a boring sermon, we can tune out the noise for a time and then tune in again when the closing hymn is announced. This ability to tune in or out is also dependent on how well rested or tired we are. If we are tired, our ability to process auditory sensations will be greatly reduced.

Therapies

So far within this chapter, the discussion has focused on the difference between hearing and processing, i.e. what is involved in actually hearing a sound and then what is involved in the processing of sound and making sense of it. In addition, the signs and symptoms of APD were noted. The question now arises as to what may be done to help or remedy these difficulties.

All except one of the current therapies in this area are based around the work of a French E.N.T. surgeon named Alfred Tomatis MD. There are at least six interventions: The Listening Programme, The Tomatis Method, Auditory Integration Training (AIT), Samonas Sound Therapy, Johansen Individualised Auditory Stimulus (IAS) and Musica Medica. Tomatis' idea was that music based sound stimulation can improve auditory processing. The Johansen (IAS) is based on the work of Christian A. Volf. From these six therapies The Listening Programme (TLP) will be described as an example, including other benefits which may be derived from using it.

TLP Level 1 consists of ten CD's of psycho-acoustically modified, "classic-like" music which is safe to use. Its purpose is to create measurable changes in the brain. It has been found by many to be an effective treatment method that gently trains the auditory system to process sound accurately for improved listening, learning, attention and communication. People of all ages, who are in need of auditory retraining, claim to have benefited from using the programme. Each CD, or album, is of 60 minutes duration and is comprised of four 15 minute segments. Each segment is divided into three 5 minute tracks. The first track of a segment is A, followed by B and then C. Track A is accommodation which supports listeners as they adjust to filtered sounds, Track B provides the greatest intensity of filtered sound with audio bursting, and track C helps organise the experience and return listeners to a natural listening environment.

Typically, the listening is done on five days of the week with the remaining two days taken off for integration. Daily listening sessions with headphones (the open type) usually last for 30 minutes and may be carried out either as one single 30 - minute session, or two 15 - minute sessions. Younger children may begin with as little as sessions of two minutes duration. Other activities may be carried out simultaneously such as art, crafts, colouring or playing with Lego, but activities which include extraneous noise, such as watching TV, should be avoided.

Areas of change which have been noted, following the use of TLP Level 1, are attention and concentration, listening and auditory processing, speech and language, memory, communication, social skills, self-esteem, relaxation, reading, sensory processing, self-regulation, balance and coordination, organisational and planning skills, and creative and spatial processing. Curthoys' (2010) work points to direct activation of the vestibular receptors by means of air conducted sound.

According to Tomatis (1999), different frequencies are associated with different functions. The lower frequencies have a calming and relaxing effect, while the higher frequencies alert, charge and energise. Furthermore, lower frequencies (0-750 Hz) impact on balance, rhythm, coordination, muscle tone, body awareness, sense of direction, laterality, right/left discrimination and eye tracking. On the other hand, mid range frequencies (750 - 4000Hz) impact on memory, concentration, attention, speech, language interpretation and vocal control while the higher frequencies (4000+ Hz) facilitate imitation, ideas, ideals, improved speaking voice and social skills.

While some studies and research have been carried out as to the effectiveness of TLP, it is difficult to pin down evidence that states that all of the above mentioned changes are seen in every child, and indeed this should not be expected because of the complex nature of the changes. Anecdotal evidence from parents of children who have used TLP is very convincing as to its efficacy.

Key Points from Chapter 14

- The focus of APD is on the processing of sound as opposed to the hearing of sound
- The first three years of life are crucial for language development
- The checklist of signs and symptoms will help you recognise a processing issue
- There are 5 main areas in which problems occur
- The teacher may employ strategies which will make it easier for the child with APD to cope in the classroom
- Auditory defensiveness is a condition in which children find it difficult to modulate sound
- The Listening Programme is a therapy which has been found to bring about change in more areas than auditory processing

Chapter 15

The Tactile System

The Big Idea

You can cope with both touching others and being touched

You can incorporate touch into learning

The Academic Viewpoint

The tactile system is the largest sensory system and plays a major part in determining human physical, mental, and emotional behaviour. Touch sensations flow into the brain to tell us that something is touching us and play an important role in body awareness and movement. (Hopscotch Therapy)

The tactile sense or sense of touch is a huge sensory system that gives us information needed for visual perception, motor planning, body awareness, academic learning, social skills and emotional security. (Therapy Space Bristol)

Red Flag Issues

- Over/under responsive to pain
- Excessively fussy about clothing/fabrics
- Seeking/avoiding touch
- Avoids messy play
- Dislikes hair washing or cutting
- Avoids others in personal space
- Over reacts to touch
- Overreacts to pain or minor injury
- Has diminished reaction to pain or injury
- Dislikes showers, bathing and personal grooming

Green for Go

- Adequate reaction to pain/temperature
- Acceptance of uniform and other clothing
- Tolerance of others in personal space
- Enjoys messy play
- Accepts personal grooming, showers and bathing

Everyone needs to be touched and needs to use touch in order to learn and explore the environment. Our tactile system precedes the auditory and visual senses as a means of learning, and yet its impact appears to be the least understood or thought about. We are not too surprised if a child needs a pair of glasses to assist his vision, or has difficulty with hearing and needs an aid, but the consequences of tactile dysfunction are rarely considered. An observant parent will be on the lookout for their child either having, or developing, visual or auditory difficulties and see that he is helped as quickly as possible. Indeed, the Health Service, as already pointed out, has a system in place to diagnose and treat such problems in the early years. However, when it comes to children with tactile issues, these seem to cause less concern to others. This is possibly because they are seen less frequently, or because we do not give due consideration to the skin, the largest tactile organ of the body, and its ability to give and receive tactile information. Nevertheless, this system is of great importance.

The only possible exception to this area being given less attention is in the incidence of tactile deprivation (this was the case in Romanian orphanages) where infants have been left unattended for hours on end. Research (1999 reported in The Why Files) showed that these children, because they did not receive sufficient stimulation, had a disorganised tactile system, were underweight, found it difficult to handle stress, scored lower in cognitive tests, and were tactile defensive which is a disorder of the tactile nervous system. In this instance, we can easily accept that touch, or the lack of it, can be an issue.

Studies have shown that children, who have had tactile input from parents, can, nevertheless, be born with tactile defensiveness which can go undiagnosed for years. Tactile defensiveness may be described as emotional responses which are out of proportion to, or are an extreme reaction to, the kinds of touch that most people would be familiar with, e.g. hugging, cuddling, stroking, massaging and tickling. This condition can cause parents great distress because they feel that their child is rejecting them. Fortunately, there is now a greater understanding of this disorder among a range of professionals and they are able to advise and reassure these parents about the dysfunction. As an aside, research (NHS networks, 2010) has demonstrated that premature children who are massaged for fifteen minutes per day gain weight more quickly than those who do not receive this tactile input.

Development of the Tactile System

First we shall consider how the tactile system develops, before looking at what can go wrong and then reflect on how help can be given to these children.

A foetus, as early as eight weeks old, may begin to show signs of responding to touch. Touch is followed by the development of the vestibular system, then that of smell, taste, hearing and vision, in that order. The sensation of touch first develops around the mouth and then spreads from head to toe, including the palms of the hand and the soles of the feet, until the whole body responds to touch. As the mother moves about, the child receives tactile stimulation in the form of temperature, pain and touch. The mother's movement has a deep pressure, massage-like action on the foetus, which has a calming effect. By 20 weeks there are tactile receptors all over the body, and by 24 weeks a touch to the palm will elicit a weak grasping response which becomes stronger by 26 weeks. The baby may hold on to anything his hand can grasp, such as the umbilical cord. In utero, the baby may soothe, calm or comfort himself by bringing the hands to the mouth or face, and at 26 weeks he can get his thumb into his mouth. This has a very calming effect.

In the early stages of pregnancy, touch is a defensive mechanism which is discriminative in nature, but by the time of birth it is associated with feeding, comfort, security and later with exploration of the environment. At birth, the baby's brain is able to register heat, cold, pain, pressure and body position. The most sensitive areas of his body are the lips, genitals and hands. This remains the case throughout life. The young child explores his environment through touch in these areas, particularly the mouth area.

Receptors in the tactile system are divided into two types: discriminative and protective. The protective receptors are found around the hair follicles and may respond to waves of air moving across the surface of the body. It is by this means that we establish where the body ends and space begins. The discriminative receptors come into play when we interact with an object. These are active when we deliberately touch something and passive when something touches us, including our clothes and the furniture we sit on. The protective receptors are in operation until we are touched and then the discriminative receptors take over. However, if the protective system is over active and the child is touched, he will withdraw from touch and be unable to use his discriminative skills.

Touch Sensitivity (over responders)

Most of the information received through the skin, in a normally functioning system, never actually requires a response as it is processed as non-threatening. This is because the system ignores stimulation of a routine nature such as the feeling of clothing on the body or sitting in a chair, and these feelings are not required for us to function in the environment. This is called sensory modulation of touch. It is about the brain's ability to regulate incoming information, use what is relevant and disregard the irrelevant. This ability to modulate tactile information proves to be a source of difficulty for some children. Some overreact to touch while others underreact. Children who overreact to being touched avoid physical contact, including all types of sport in which physical contact plays an important role. They even dislike the idea of physical contact so much that they may shy away when someone comes near them, particularly if they cannot predict how that person will react to them. (This may be a reason why these children prefer to play with adults whose behaviour is more predictable than that of small children.) When someone comes near such a child with the threat of touch, the brainstem will override logic and he will go into fright/flight/fight mode. These children can also overreact to flies, bugs and other flying insects whose movements are unpredictable, displaying an irrational avoidance of these. They may also have a fear of dogs, as these too can be unpredictable in their movements.

Over responders may hate any or all of the following: haircutting, hair washing, showering, nail cutting, tags on clothes or getting their hands in paint or gooey stuff. They may be stubborn about the clothes they wear and fussy about the detergent used for laundering their clothes. They may eat only certain foods, depending on the colour or texture. Also associated with over reaction is low pain threshold, causing them to overreact to tiny cuts and grazes and injections. Strangely enough, they may not even notice deep bruises.

Touch: Under Responders

Children who are under responsive to touch sensations have a high threshold to pain. They love contact sports, fighting and roughhousing. In addition, they may not even feel touch, unless it is firm, and they seem to be unaware of scrapes and bruises or obstacles that get in their way. Be advised and do not take them into a china shop! These children are compulsive "touchers". They do not mean to be annoying, but use touch to define where they are, their position in space, distance from objects and muscle tone. They are sensation cravers and feel the need to be stimulated. Furthermore, they like to be hugged tightly, crawl between or under heavy objects, bang the head against the wall, bite their hands, wave or shake their hands, chew or suck things, wear tight or heavy clothes. The also love the deep pressure caused by lots of blankets on the bed.

The following two case studies help to illustrate both of these conditions.

Case Study: Ryan's Story Tactile Hypersensitivity

Ryan is a four - year - old who is over sensitive to touch. He came to the clinic with his grandmother, who is also his carer, because she was completely distraught. This was as a result of being presented with a very negative picture of her grandson by the class teacher, who was continually complaining about his behaviour.

Ryan was increasingly disruptive in class. He refused to follow the teacher's instructions or observe rules and boundaries within the class. He would not sit still for any length of time. He got up and did as he pleased. He fought with the teacher when she directed him to something that displeased him. Ryan would also push other children or kick out at them, especially when asked to line up, and would even act like this with his teacher. As a result, he was on a restricted day. Ryan complained that his teacher and CA spoke too loudly and he objected strongly when they touched him. (It is seldom the case that sensory issues appear in isolation. In this instance tactile difficulties appeared with auditory processing difficulties.) Often he was taken to the principal's office because of concerns for other children's safety. Very soon he learned that he preferred the principal's office to the classroom environment and would behave in a way that ensured that he was frequently brought there.

Behaviour at home was more manageable. His grandmother had not considered him to have any perceptual difficulties, but as the school year progressed, pressure was placed increasingly upon her to consider transferring him to a special school. The relationship between her and the school became increasingly strained and this was the actual reason for the grandmother's referral.

At the clinic Ryan presented as a chatty, sociable, active four - year - old. He was observed to be an "on the go" child who wanted to explore everything in the room. Consequently, he would go to a piece of equipment, look at it briefly, and then move on. The one item which he really liked was Thomas the Tank Engine, and indeed, he played with this for quite a long time. From the outset, he did not want to be led or directed, but wanted to initiate and act out his own ideas on the equipment available. When the therapist intervened tentatively, Ryan became verbally challenging and defensive. He would then leave that piece of equipment and seek an activity he felt confident doing. In particular, he favoured throwing, catching and playing with balls. It was obvious that he was extremely creative in generating ideas involving others in his play, but was totally resistant to the therapist involving him in something she wished him to try. Ryan had very good use of language, but was used to focusing on his desires and getting his own way.

What soon became evident was his reaction to being touched. Even a light touch brought howls of disapproval. However, on occasions when he wanted to go on a piece of equipment and was having difficulty getting on by himself, he would allow the therapist to hold him when helping him get on. Ryan was very robust in his use of equipment such as playing with the large therapy ball, which he bounced, threw, or kicked with great force. On the other hand, when he bumped or banged into an object, whether or not it was his own fault, he lay down and cried and rubbed the place that was hurting. He had difficulties with boundaries being set for him and would rather do just what he wanted to do. Another issue for him was transitioning from one activity to another. He needed to be led, not pushed.

School considered him to be a slow learner, but it soon became apparent that he had very good perceptual skills, exceeding all the requirements of an assessment for a five - year - old. He quickly grasped the idea of sequencing, although he found handwriting skills challenging. When motivated, Ryan wanted to demonstrate his ability, but he got frustrated at times and became defiant. The reason for this is that he is very aware of his own limitations and engages in avoidance behaviour which is very controlling. He seeks to engage you in his ideas rather than for him to comply with yours. (This behaviour is typical of children with motor planning and ideation difficulties.)

A sensory profile identified a definite difficulty with processing touch. Ryan has a low threshold for touch and avoids unpredicted or invasive touch. He has an inability to regulate himself when touched or threatened with touch. His reaction is to hit out and become defensive or to avoid the situation by withdrawing from others. He is a solitary child in the playground and prefers to play by himself where there is no danger of anyone touching him. When he did elect to play with his peers, he was continually in trouble for being too rough and hitting out.

It is easy to understand the teacher's "take" on this child. He is badly behaved. He pushes and hits out at other children, without any apparent reason, when standing in line or when they come close to him. He has difficulty with boundaries and class rules, shouts out when the teacher or CA touches him, is always on the go, running from one place to another without settling to any one activity. Moreover, he gets frustrated easily and is defiant, even with the teacher, and is seen as being aggressive and uncooperative.

Ryan's behaviour stems from sensory needs and, as such, he is a sensory driven child who finds it difficult to self-regulate. This will be observable in his attention and concentration, his ability to attach meaning to language, and his interactions with others. The reality is that in order for him to listen and focus, his sensory needs must first be met.

Norah's Story: A Case Study of a Tactile Hyposensitive Child

Five - year - old Norah was referred by her mother, due to her inattention, distractibility and lack of awareness of the structure within the classroom.

It soon transpired that she is under responsive to touch. She has no idea of personal space and appears clumsy because she bumps into objects and trips over even the smallest obstacle lying on the floor, such as a small toy. Furthermore, she has difficulty manipulating small objects and her eye/foot coordination is poor. Norah continually pulls at her clothing as this increases proprioceptive input and gives her greater body awareness. In effect she is a sensation craver, running from one piece of equipment to another, without spending time at any. She wants to touch everything and loves tight hugs. She is totally disorganised and does not realise when she has hurt herself. In school, she will go to the toilet to run her hands in the cold water because she enjoys the cold sensation. Norah is over focused on the visual system and under focused on the others, including the proprioceptive system. The lack of input from this system results in poor body awareness and poor feedback, especially when moving, which contributes to her dyspraxic-like tendencies. This child is a passive under-responder.

Assessing Tactile Sensitivities

When it comes to evaluating the tactile system, several approaches may be used either individually or together. Frequently time constraint means that you have to be selective as to the methodology. The main methods of testing involve observation, discussions with parents, grandparents and carers, and finally, formal testing.

Ideally, observation of the child should take place over a period of time and be done in such a manner that the child is not aware of what is happening. The child should therefore be unable to predict what you are looking for. The main things to look for are the tactile effects the child is either seeking or avoiding.

In addition to those indicators of tactile difficulties which were mentioned in the two case studies, there are others which may not at first be apparent to the casual observer.

Hypersensitive Indicators

The hypersensitive child may:

- be stubborn about which clothes to wear (prefers loose clothes and soft textures)
- be stubborn about the way to do things (everything has to be done his way)
- avoid washing, showering and hair cutting or combing and cutting nails
- be unable to show affection, so the mother finds it difficult to establish a warm relationship
- have poor judgment for speed, timing and distance (unsuccessful at sport, low motor confidence)
- overreact to cuts and grazes but does not notice bruises
- Avoids contact sports
- have difficulty concentrating on academic activities
- be distracted by normal tactile stimuli such as paints, paste and desks and chairs
- dislike drying with a towel
- have allergic skin reactions
- have poor temperature control (his body can heat up when doing even light activities)
- dislike being touched but may want to touch
- dislike messy play
- have fussy eating habits (selective about choice of food)
- be selective in choice or avoidance of toys
- require clothes to be laundered in a specific detergent
- insist on having clothes tags completely removed

Hyposensitive Indicators

Conversely the hyposensitive child may:

- be a daredevil
- have poor protective extension and control (loses balance easily and doesn't react to falling over)
- have no sense of danger; is a danger to himself and everyone around him
- be oblivious to injury to self and others
- be unable to read his own/others body language
- have a high threshold to pain
- love contact sports
- be a compulsive "toucher"
- be like a bull in a china shop
- be clumsy, tripping over small objects
- have a poor body scheme (internal awareness of body position and shape)
- sit half on/off a chair without noticing discomfort
- love to wear tight clothes
- have low muscle tone
- tire easily, poor or weak grasp
- hit or bite himself when frustrated
- enjoy vibration and movement which provides strong sensory feedback
- prefer spicy or very sweet foods
- seek messy experiences for long periods
- seldom realise when he drops something

From interviews with parents, information may be gathered about such things as eating habits, sleeping patterns, interactions with parents and other children, clothing choice and play habits. It should be noted that children rarely have difficulty with sensory modulation (the ability to filter out unimportant sensory information) in only one sensory system. These difficulties may appear in any of the following senses: the tactile, visual, auditory, gustatory (taste), olfactory (smell) or any combination of these. The above indicators may help to guide the interview process.

Tactile Response Testing

There are three types of testing that may be carried out which are as follows:

1. Localisation of touch
2. Object identification (stereognosis)
3. Tracing (graphesthesia)

These all come under the banner of tactile feedback, for in each test what is being looked at is the response to touch. They identify the child's ability to internalise and make sense of how he is touching, thereby giving him a perceptual image from a motor input. All perception is gained through touch and movement.

Localisation of Touch

Localisation of touch, as the name suggests, can help determine whether or not a child has the ability to localise touch and know which parts of the body have been touched. This test also shows which parts of his body are/are not sensitive to touch and whether the child feels uncomfortable with tactile stimulation. It is possible for a child to be able to identify touch on the upper part of the body but not the lower, and on one side of the body but not the other.

Children to be tested should be blindfolded and wear minimal clothing so that a variety of places may be touched unhindered by clothing. The child is touched with something like a cotton bud dipped in talcum powder and is then asked to place an index finger where he felt he was touched. This is done in a random way and details of the response are recorded. He should be within one to one and a half centimetres of the place.

If a child cannot localise touch, or has a reduced awareness of which part of the body was touched, this indicates both poor body concept and poor body schema. His body map is poor or non-existent. Such children have low sensitivity to pain or temperature and, as such, are at risk of injury. They may run outside on a cold day without a a coat on and may not even notice this. These children have poor knowledge of how parts of the body work together so any motor skill will prove difficult.

Object Identification

The second test is object identification (stereognosis) by size, shape and texture. This may be carried out with the child blindfolded. A familiar object, such as a key, brush or spoon, is placed in the child's hand for identification. Another method is to place the objects in a "feely" bag, getting the child to try to identify these by touch alone before removing them from the bag. Literate children may be asked to identify 3D letters and numbers in the bag. Children with this difficulty are missing out on touch as a vital tool in the process of learning. They are much more dependent on visual cues.

Tracing Test

The final test is a tracing test (graphesthesia). While the child is blindfolded, letters or numbers are drawn with a blunt object, like the end of a pen, on the back of his hand and he is then asked to identify them. The same may be done on the child's back. The hand or back is wiped over between "writing" each letter. Difficulty in letter recognition may indicate that such a child is hyposensitive to touch and in addition has perceptual difficulties.

Fundamental Principles for Therapy Intervention

Before discussing various intervention therapies, mention should be made of a few underlying principles which will increase the effectiveness of any work carried out with the child. It should be understood from the start that the child's response to tactile difficulties is not due to emotional or behavioural problems, but is the consequence of either an over or under aroused sense of touch. The best experiences for the child are nurtured in trust. A child must trust whoever is working with him and, where possible, activities should be child-directed, allowing him to follow his inner drive. Heavy work and vestibular stimulation help to modulate the tactile system and make the interventions more acceptable to the child. Care should be taken with new circumstances or situations in which the child feels threatened. It is best to establish rules before beginning work and these should remain consistent throughout.

When you see the child following the rules, praise him. Having said that, positive behaviour should be encouraged and rewarded using (a) reinforcers (something the child likes and enjoys such as swinging and jumping or a favourite activity) and (b) praise (using the child's name, describing to the child what you see him do and telling him how you feel about his actions). Reinforce verbal praise with positive touch, i.e. touch the child on the shoulder or forearm so that they will begin to associate touch with a positive experience. For the child who is always seeking attention through negative behaviour, pre-empt this with positive, verbal reinforcement. One strategy may be to approach the child, then touch his arm and say something like, "Well done, I see you have started." It is always best to avoid power struggles. This may be done by giving alternatives or by compromise. We all have a tendency to say "no," but it is possible to get around this difficulty by giving alternative choices instead. Should the sensory system be overloaded and if the child is receiving too much stimulation, consider such things as the noise level, brightness of lighting, the size of the space, the number of people in the room, and the temperature.

You may have noticed that as yet no distinction has been made between intervention therapies for under or over reactive tactile systems. The reason is, strangely enough, that most of the interventions are similar and vary only in degree, intensity and duration.

Intervention in the tactile system falls into two categories (1) the direct and (2) the indirect. When someone, other than the child, administers tactile activities, it is said to be direct. These may include massage, drying the body with a towel or rolling a therapy ball over his body. Activities are said to indirect when the child presses or touches his own body as in a blanket roll, a log roll, a forward roll, carrying a backpack, doing heavy work like push ups, carrying heavy weights and coming down stairs on arms (supervised). It is best to begin with indirect activities for children who are sensory defensive, and to commence work on the least sensitive areas of their bodies, usually the back of the arms or hands.

Brushing

Brushing, using a special brush (Therapressure brush), is an effective way of of desensitising someone with tactile difficulties.

This is a technique that is largely misunderstood and misrepresented as a treatment approach. In order to be fully equipped to use this intervention, the developer of this treatment approach (Wilbarger, 2002) recommends that only people fully trained by herself, or by one of these knowledgeable trainees, is sufficiently competent to carry out treatment using the brushing technique. On a personal note having done the training with Patricia Wilbarger this is an intervention applied frequently in our practice with very positive outcomes. Without this knowledge the technique may be replicated incorrectly, as seen on some Youtube sites.

Before brushing takes place, the child should be evaluated to determine if sensory defensiveness is present and how significant it is. Medical conditions should also be considered, e.g. if the child has psoriasis, open lesions or cuts, damage to limbs or joint pain. Also, psychological considerations to be taken into account include the state of arousal in the child's nervous system, i.e. how calm he is. All those involved with the child, i.e. family, friends, carers should be made aware of the purpose of the brushing, and the amount of time spent brushing in one session as well as the frequency of brushing.

Assuming all the above points are taken into consideration, brushing may commence by brushing firmly on bare skin including the hands, arms, back, feet and legs. Brush the tummy only if the child is constipated. This is followed by joint compression at the ankles, knees, hips, hands, elbows, shoulders and trunk. Brushing may also take place over the clothes but care must be taken to ensure that the clothes are held firmly so that tactile stimulation is not given by the movement of clothes. It is necessary to closely monitor the effects of this type of brushing on the child for the first few days so that it may be modified as to frequency and duration.

The advice based on the teaching of Patricia Wilbarger, is to brush firmly avoiding light touch. You do not need to brush for twenty minutes at a time or in a particular direction. The brush should be held horizontally so as to cover as much area of the skin as possible. Maintain contact with the person being brushed by placing one hand on the body while brushing with the other. Brushing will only take a few minutes, should be carried out about every two hours while the child is awake and be followed up with joint compression. Joint compression of the limb involves holding the arm/leg straight out. Take hold of the hand/foot in one hand and the elbow/knee in the other. Then, keeping the arm/leg straight, give a series of short gentle pushes of the limb into the shoulder/hip joint. The elbow, wrist, and knee joints can be given compression by placing a hand on either side of the joint and squeezing the hands together a few times. The finger joints are more easily compressed by squeezing between the finger and thumb. Brushing should always be followed up with joint compression. Use only the Therapressure Brush which is specially designed for the purpose and has a large number of bristles. It is readily available on the internet.

Key Points from Chapter 15

- Difficulties with the tactile system may easily be overlooked.
- An 8 - week - old foetus may show signs of responding to touch.
- There are two types of receptors in the tactile system, i.e. discriminative and protective.
- The brain is capable of disregarding predictable tactile information but children with sensory difficulties may either overreact or be unresponsive.
- You may test for, or observe, many indicators of these conditions.
- Interventions for both under/overreactive systems are similar and vary only in duration, intensity and degree.
- They may be either direct (administered by someone else, as in brushing), or indirect (administered by the child himself).
- Brushing of the body should always be followed up with joint compressions.

Chapter 16

Handwriting

The Big Idea

Handwriting is one of the most important aspects of school life involving 30-60% of class time.

It is the main way children can evidence their learning, and speed and legibility are essential to exam success.

Handwriting is not a visual skill but is essentially a motor skill requiring instruction, assisted teaching and motor confidence.

Children with early arm or hand function delay and poor upper body control will have difficulty with handwriting.

The Academic Viewpoint

The development of fast, fluent handwriting does not always occur automatically. Many children....do not possess the writing skills they need to cope with the demands of ...education. This may be due to developmental delay, specific learning difficulty or neurological impairment. Or it may be simply that they have been allowed to write in an inappropriate way ... .Whatever the cause, the activity of handwriting for these children requires an inordinate amount of mental and physical energy. As a result they become despondent and reluctant to write.
(Addy, 2004)

Red Flag Issues

- Poor upper body tone and control
- Difficulty with compressibility (strength through the pencil)
- Inability to hold a pencil in a dynamic tripod grasp (thumb and index finger secure and drive the pencil whilst it rests on the middle finger. The 4th and 5th fingers tuck into the palm whilst referred to as wheels remaining on the table allowing the child to see what they are writing)
- Starting letters and numbers from the bottom to the top
- Inconsistent sizing, spacing and a lack of height discrimination in handwriting
- Avoiding pencil skills and colouring in
- Sentences and story writing short
- Struggle to get written homework done

Green for Go

- Good core stability and shoulder strength
- Good in-hand manipulation
- No difficulty in the mastery of forming letters and numbers
- Enjoys writing stories with volume

One of the most important aspects of school life, and one which becomes increasingly significant (30-60% of activities in school are fine motor based) as a child progresses through school, is handwriting. With so much time spent at this activity it may be assumed that the actual process of writing would be given priority to enable children to be able to write quickly, fluently and legibly.

This is not always the case and many children who have difficulty in this area can easily become frustrated about the presentation of their work. It can also become a major cause of difficulty for those who teach them and for parents helping with homework, because of the child's avoidance of pencil work. Their writing may be slow, messy, laboured and illegible. This frustration, at least from the child's perspective, is translated as a sign of his failure, and before him is the visible evidence. This is often the cause of avoidance of pencil work. Very often, even as adults, adverse opinions are formed of individuals based upon handwriting alone.

Motor Skill

Handwriting is a motor skill that allows for expression of thoughts, feelings and communication with others. As Addy (2004) describes it, "Handwriting is... a complex psycho- motor skill that requires instruction, experience and practice... and is... the graphic result of motor, perceptual and cognitive processes…" (p.9) It is an activity which brings together, in one operation, much of what has already been discussed: dominance, core stability, midline awareness, bilateral awareness, perception, body awareness, reflexes, gross and fine motor skills, motor planning, eye/hand coordination, and visual and tactile perception. Some children have a deficit in one or more of these areas, so it must be even more difficult for them. Handwriting must be TAUGHT. The formation of each letter and number shape is different and before the child begins to form the letters and numbers he needs to recognise and match them visually and consistently. Making the shape with play doh or clay is an essential step, as this makes the letters and numbers three dimensional. Only then do children get a mental image of each letter and number enabling mental manipulation and visualising in space. This allows for spatial recognition, correct positioning and mental rotation of letter and number shapes. This is essential before beginning to draw the shape on paper.

Prior to commencing letter and number writing, some children have developed the idea of scribbling and making their mark on the page. This has to transition from an impulsive squiggle to a controlled, planned straight vertical line and circle. Some children get the idea of this quickly whilst others get the idea but lack the necessary motor control, motor planning and fine motor ability required. This results in frustration, a dislike of all aspects of tool control and a determined avoidance of pencil work. Handwriting becomes such a challenge as the child grows that they become adept at writing quickly, lacking self-correction and refusing to repeat work to perfect it.

It is important to be aware from the outset that the learning environment is crucial. A teacher or parent with a friendly voice, who can make handwriting an enjoyable, even exciting activity, and who encourages a child and helps him feel he is successful, is well on the way to providing an atmosphere which will prove to offer the best foundation.

If a child is coping well with handwriting, his self-esteem and self-confidence are greatly enhanced. Unfortunately the reverse is true. Poor handwriting is a cause of angst, not only for the child, but also for the teacher and the parent. Consider a teacher who is handed a piece of written work where the writing is heavy and black, where poor use of a rubber is evident, and where letters are sloping in all directions with little regard for size, shape, spacing or positioning on the line. When all this occurs after a handwriting lesson, then the teacher may well wonder what is going on. Has the child not been listening, or is he just untidy in his work and habits? Is he not trying hard enough, lacking concentration and attention, of low intelligence, not interested or motivated, perhaps even lazy?

On the child's part, having tried his best, he may feel worried, scared, stressed and in fear of having to repeat the exercise. Of course, any one of the above or even all of them may have been applicable to the child, but then the question must be asked, "Why?" To answer this question we must look at all the foundations which need to be in place before a child begins to write: physical, neurological (including reflexes), cognitive and the learning environment (including atmosphere). Readiness for writing, together with mastery of writing readiness skills, is important otherwise a child may develop bad writing habits that are difficult to correct and he may easily become discouraged. Obviously, the earlier a problem is observed, the easier it is to effect change in the younger child.

The Physical Foundations for Handwriting

The basic physical foundation for handwriting is core stability, which includes both trunk and shoulder stability. These, in turn, provide stability in the forearm, the wrist and the hand. All of this promotes the precise finger and thumb movements necessary for handwriting. The gross muscles in the trunk and shoulder provide strength, mobility and stability in the arms and shoulders to maintain the trunk in an upright sitting position so that the hands are free to move.

The first areas to consider are the trunk, shoulders, arms, wrist, and hand including the thumb, fingers, hand arches and webs to see the part each plays in the skills required for good handwriting and to ascertain what may be done to ensure effective operation of all these components. Then, other contributing factors for the production of legible, fluent handwriting need to be taken into account. These will include neurological processing and cognitive influences. Finally, the physical environment, readiness skills, and what signs to look for when children are experiencing difficulty in handwriting will be explored.

Core and Shoulder Stability

Poor core stability is rarely seen on its own and usually signifies poor muscle tone in general throughout the body. Even if the muscles of the hand are strengthened, the impact of poor shoulder and postural stability will be such that these will make for difficulties in fine motor function in the hand. Handwriting uses slow, controlled shoulder movements, so if the joint is not stable, it is impossible to achieve the control required.

To observe difficulties in the trunk area, look for a child who leans on his arms, body slumped over his work on the table and resting his head in his hands. In the shoulder girdle area look for joints which are not stable, lack of head and trunk extension, lack of refined movement such as over/under activity when reaching, internally rotated shoulders and winged scapulae when weight bearing on arms (the shoulder blades appear to sit up). The child may be unable to support his body weight through extended arms when on his tummy and find it challenging to do a wheelbarrow walk. These difficulties may also be observed in 4 point kneeling when a child finds it difficult to hold this position, wobbles, locks his elbow joints, turns his foot in for greater stability and braces his arms against his sides. The following exercises will help strengthen core and shoulder stability and, in addition, strengthen the arms.

- Sit-ups, trampoline jumping, prone extension over a therapy ball, contact sports, scooter board activities;

- arm circling with arms outstretched, push-ups, wall presses, sky writing, donkey kicks, writing lazy eights in the air, crab walking, tug-of-war, moving on monkey bars, animal walks, chair presses, wheel barrow walks, swimming, crawling around an obstacle course, writing on wallpaper hung vertically above eye level;
- rope pull on scooter board, using tongs for lifting objects from one container to another, bat and ball games, push/pull activities, playing catch with a weighted ball, taking weight on arms over a therapy ball, joint compressions (see brushing programme).

Wrist Stability

In order to optimise the use of the hand for fine movement, it is necessary to have wrist extension with fingers in opposition (known as the position of function), i.e. the hand cocked backwards from the forearm. This allows for better hand movements including thumb position, finger movements and hand arching. Children who are unable to do this often try to compensate by locking the wrist in the flexed position (hand bent forward, fingers facing the inside of the forearm) to get greater stability. The extensor muscles in the back of the wrist need to be strengthened to overcome this tendency. The following exercises will help steady the wrist in extension.

- Weight bearing on both hands with open palms, writing on elevated or sloping surfaces, wheelbarrow walks, crab walks, using therapy putty while extending the wrist.

Thumb in Opposition to Fingers

There are three muscles at the base of the thumb which are needed for stability and strength. These guide movement and help regulate pressure and dexterity when the thumb is working in opposition to the fingers and are assisted by wrist extension. Some children tend to pull the thumb against the index finger so that there is no web space (the open space between finger and thumb when they are in opposition). Holding the pencil in this grip will quickly tire the hand, cause the writing to be heavy and reduce the accuracy of positioning the marks on the paper. Children with this difficulty find it hard to pinch a ball of play doh into a pancake shape. Some exercises to develop thumb movement are:

- squeezing a ball or play doh, playing with finger puppets, bursting bubble wrap, placing pegs on a shoe box and taking them off, thumb painting, scrunching paper using the thumb, finger/thumb exercise, i.e. touching each finger in turn with the thumb.

Separation of the Two Sides of the Hand

When writing, it is important to separate the two sides of the hand. This is necessary because the little finger side of the hand (ulnar) is used to enable the hand to slide across the page, while the other side (radial), i.e. the thumb, index finger and middle fingers provide the precise movements for writing control. The ring and little finger should remain stationary, curled in the palm of the hand as when winding up a toy. Any extension of the little and ring finger indicates that this function is not working properly. The holding of a paperclip under these fingers while writing will facilitate the correct grip. Exercises that will improve this ability are:

- peg moving, scissor cutting, rolling small balls of putty with fingertips, placing stickers on a vertical page, snapping fingers, using squirt bottles.

Hand Arches

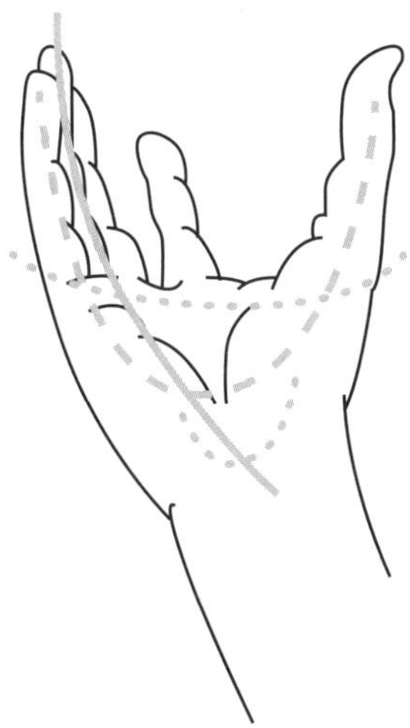

Basically there are three arches in the hand which, when working properly, make the hand a dynamic tool. These arches let the hand adapt itself to carrying out everyday tasks. They enable the hand to grasp differently shaped objects (long, round, big, small), direct the movement of the fingers and grade the power required for each grasp. Consequently, they provide all the skilled movements within the hand. The oblique arch is formed when the thumb and fingers come into opposition (see dashed line). There are two transverse arches - one at the base of the fingers and one at the wrist (dotted line). These are used for cupping the hand. A longitudinal arch is required for a raking action of the fingers (see solid line). The arches may be strengthened by doing the following exercises:

- rolling play doh on the table or between the hands, cutting tubes of play doh into small pieces with a knife, seeing how much rice you can hold in your hand, paper tearing for collages, using spray bottles, games involving tweezers, touching each finger in turn with the thumb.

All of the above activities are carried out for the strengthening of muscles and ensuring that each part of the body involved in handwriting is able to function correctly.

The Impact of Neurological Processing on Handwriting

Imagine a child sitting down to write and the thoughts that pass through his mind subconsciously, about the position of his body and his readiness to begin the writing process. Am I balanced in my seat? Can my head move to scan the page? Can I feel the pencil in my hand? Am I exerting the right amount of pressure on the pencil? Is my grip on the pencil comfortable? Can my wrist and hand travel smoothly across the page? Where is the exact location of my limbs? These are just a few of the multitude of thoughts, of which we are unaware, that occur as we write.

To allow these thoughts to pass back and forth to the brain from our sensory receptors, we need an effective sensory system. There are three main sensory receptors in use as we write. First are proprioceptors, which are found in the muscles, tendons and joints. These provide information about the position and movement of the body and limbs. Next are touch receptors, which are located in deep tissue providing information on changes in pressure and vibration through the skin. Lastly, the vestibular receptors in the inner ear register movement in the trunk and the hand and assist in keeping us in an upright, stable position which is crucial for performing tasks of a fine motor nature. Handwriting involves head and trunk movement as the head turns to scan the page. The vestibular receptors allow the posture to adjust as appropriate.

Kinaesthetic Considerations

Kinaesthetic awareness of the movement and positioning of the limbs, without having to see, is also required for exerting suitable pressure on the pencil. Practice of these movement patterns is built up and stored in the motor memory to be called upon when needed. In time, this motor memory becomes automatic, and so allows the attention to be focused on the more important aspect of composition of writing, rather than the motor task. Kinaesthetic feedback from the receptors matches the motor plan to the execution of the movement. If there is a deficit in feedback, it will be evident in a fist-like grip, limited mobility in the fingers and in heavy pressure on the paper, as the child attempts to redress the situation. In other words, the child has no efficient motor plan or motor memory (similar to that used in clutch control when driving). Each time the child commences handwriting it is like starting anew.

Bilateral and Midline Considerations

Handwriting requires the use of both sides of the body and both hands in a coordinated way. One hand stabilises the page when writing and feeds it to either right or left, depending on handedness, while the other moves across, depending on the range of stretch. The supporting hand then needs to readjust the page to maintain a comfortable writing position. This skill is noticeably absent in children who do not have good bilateral skills. (Bilateral coordination was discussed earlier in the section on midline awareness.) The ability to use both sides of the body is required in many activities including walking, running, scissor cutting and handwriting. This can only take place if there is good communication between both hemispheres of the brain.

Running alongside bilateral coordination is the ability to cross midline. This is the ability to be able to reach across the imaginary midline of the body, stretching from head to foot, with either hand to carry out activities. This capability is required as the hand moves across the page from left to right, crossing midline as it does so. It is similarly necessary as the eyes track the hand movements. Difficulty in crossing midline may be observed if the trunk is not able to rotate. Instead, the whole body moves in line with the hand as it transverses the page. Changing the pencil into different hands as one hand reaches midpoint, getting stuck in the middle, and difficulty drawing some letters such as "x" also indicate this problem. Asking a child to draw an open pair of scissors without handling or touching them will clearly confirm his inability to cross midline.

Visual Considerations

Handwriting is often thought of as a visual skill and, of course vision does play an important part, especially early on. **Visual discrimination** (the ability to recognise details of visual images such as size, shape, form, colour, position), **visual perception** (the capacity to give meaning to what is seen and use this information to recognise, recall and discriminate), and **visual sequential memory** (ability to recall visual information in sequence) all play an important part in organising, remembering and recognising visual symbols and letters. **Visual motor integration** (the eyes and hands working together in a smooth pattern involving visual perception and eye/hand coordination) is important in monitoring the writing. However, since handwriting is dependent on patterns of movement and the storage of these patterns in the motor memory, when it comes to speed and fluency, kinaesthetic feedback reduces reliance on visual input. The more automatic the movement, the less important vision becomes. Children with perceptual motor difficulties or children with DCD have inefficient receptors, producing unrefined motor control. This causes slow, heavy, clumsy and uncoordinated writing movements.

Tactile Considerations

Tactile issues may also have a bearing on handwriting, particularly in relation to discriminative touch. (Refer to chapter 15 on the tactile system.) The child who is unresponsive to touch may have poor internal body awareness and may not be aware of his sitting position, i.e. sitting with his bottom, half on, half off the chair without realising it. He also may tire easily. Some children are over reactive to touch and, as a result, they will dislike anyone touching them or invading their personal space. Those teaching handwriting need to be conscious of this, even when touching in a reassuring way. Such children should be seated beside another child, as opposed to facing each other, so as not to invade their personal space.

Auditory Considerations

Teachers should be aware of the problems that might arise when dealing with a child who has auditory processing difficulties. Such children may only be listening with their dominant ear and processing only a fraction of what is being said, particularly in a classroom environment where there is often a buzz of activity and background noise. To take account of these conditions, it is best to seat the child at the front of the class with the "good" ear towards the teacher, and give instructions slowly and visually, where possible.

Other Sensory Considerations: Retained Primitive Reflexes

In the chapter on primitive reflexes, five primitive reflexes were mentioned and the importance of these being inhibited at an early age was highlighted. Four of these five reflexes mentioned previously, if not inhibited, have an impact on the development of handwriting skills.

The Moro or Startle reflex in infants may be caused by the child being exposed to an unexpected stimulus such as bright light. The uninhibited reflex can result in hypersensitivity to strong light sources such as fluorescent tube-type lighting. The lighting in a room should be neither too bright nor too dim to compensate for such a child's aversion to intense lighting, which could impair his ability to work in that environment. Similarly, a teacher or parent should be aware of possible visual distractions in the background, such as highly coloured wall displays which can have an unsettling effect upon this type of child. Other effects of an uninhibited Moro reflex include poor balance and reduced stamina which are requirements for effective handwriting.

The Palmar or Grasping reflex, if uninhibited, can lead to a lack of awareness of the pressure required to grip the pencil. Also, because of the Babkin Response, this may lead to the tongue protruding between the teeth when concentrating on fine motor hand skills.

A retained ATNR can cause difficulties in balance, eye/hand coordination, hand dominance and eye tracking. It may also cause the use of excessive hand pressure on the pencil, bilateral difficulties and midline awareness. All of these have a bearing on the achievement of good handwriting. If retained, this reflex has an impact on the child's movement patterns by dividing the body into two parts, the left side and the right side and until integrated, can cause significant difficulty with dissociated body movements, e.g. in trunk rotation and bilateral and sequencing skills.

The STNR is normally inhibited by the age of eleven months. If retained, it affects handwriting skills because of the impact it has on eye/hand coordination, balance and bilateral skills, posture, muscle tone, concentration and attention, and the ability to sit still. This reflex divides the body at the waist. Whatever the top half does, the bottom half does the opposite. This is noticeable when a child flexes forward over a desk and needs to secure the lower half from extension by wrapping his legs around the chair legs.

Hand Dominance in Relation to Handwriting

It is common to find mixed hand dominance in young children as they are undecided as to which hand to use as the dominant one. Sometimes they will use one hand for one activity and another for a different activity. It is best to get this sorted out as soon as possible so that children do not become confused, have difficulty with midline awareness and present as being awkward or clumsy. Once the dominant side has been identified (possibly through a timed posting activity with each hand), parents and teachers should reinforce the dominant side verbally and through gross and fine motor tasks. A child who has learned that he has a stronger and weaker side, and chooses to use the stronger side, will be more spontaneous on the dominant side. Other ways to help identify the dominant hand, when confusion exists, are to observe which hand spontaneously reaches for the spoon, or to see which hand is used for finger feeding and which is used by the child to rub or scratch his nose. If the child is given two wooden spoons to hit one against the other from above, the dominant hand will always be holding the spoon on top.

A Review of the Major Issues

A synopsis of the issues already discussed is set out below. The length of the list indicates just how complex the skill of handwriting is and the variety of processes that it involves. The requirements for successful handwriting are as follows:

- adequate strength and tone in the shoulder, trunk and pelvic muscles;
- stability in the forearm and wrist;
- strength in the muscles of the hand for pencil manipulation
- the two sides of the hand are able to work together in a coordinated way to be able to sustain handwriting without tiring;
- the hand arches are well developed to allow the application of the right amount of strength to the fingers;
- proper web space is formed to maintain an efficient pencil grip;
- the child is able to form a dynamic tripod grip;
- in-hand manipulation skills are developed to achieve an appropriate pencil grasp;
- somatosensory perception is acquired to permit processing, integration and functional use of the senses to inform body awareness in space, proprioceptive and vestibular feedback to inform the correct pressure required, and movement and balance for a stable position;
- the ability to motor plan to conceive the idea, organise a plan of action and carry out the sequence required;
- cognitive skills attained include the ability to listen to and follow instructions, know where to start, understand the locatives (such as up/down/above/below/next to/on the

line), can pay attention, use memory for recall and not rush work;

- bilateral skills developed for reciprocal movements (one hand dominant, one hand supporting) and complementary movements (using both hands simultaneously but independently);
- have visual attention skills and not be over/under stimulated by visual input and be able to screen out peripheral visual information and can eye track;
- have good eye/hand coordination; be able to integrate visual perceptual information with hand movements to produce motor response, can space letters, can keep writing on lines and
- have visual spatial skills, i.e. can see relationships in letters as to: size, proportion, space, orientation, direction, accurate letter formation, and letter closure.

Teaching Tips for Handwriting and for Helping Children who are Struggling

Different countries adopt differing approaches to teaching handwriting. In Norway children learn cursive or joined writing initially and bypass print script. In the UK and Ireland the normal process for teaching handwriting initially is printed script. This print script is taught in capitals and lowercase letters. From an Occupational Therapist's perspective, basing practice on the work of Jan Olsen's handwriting programme, "Handwriting Without Tears", success has been achieved, even for very reluctant handwriters, by using her ideas. This programme involves multisensory and active hands-on strategies. As discussed earlier, engaging a multisensory approach to learning improves the child's generalising and spontaneous use of the skills learned.

This hand writing programme is based on teaching capital letters first and involves the use of hands-on material to build the letters from wooden pieces initially. The child then goes on to write these letters on a miniature notebook sized blackboard with a series of motor tasks to reinforce the motor plan for each letter. Left start capitals (L,E,F,H,T,I,D,B,P,K,RM,N,U,V,W,X,Y,Z) are taught first, followed by middle start capitals (A,C,O,Q,G,S,J).

The reason for this is that learning capital letters involves lifting the pencil and using a series of strokes, whereas lowercase letters are harder for some children to learn because they involve one continuous stroke, frequently changing direction.

It is best to teach the child to start at the top of the letter and work to the bottom on all strokes. Where a child struggles with pencil grip or holding the pencil in a dynamic pencil grasp or tripod grasp, experience has taught that shortening his pencil to approximately 4cm will ensure that he holds the pencil correctly.

Tripod Grip
1 - Tall finger (Side)
2 - Thumb (Pod)
3 - Pointing Finger (Tip)
All fingers are slightly bent

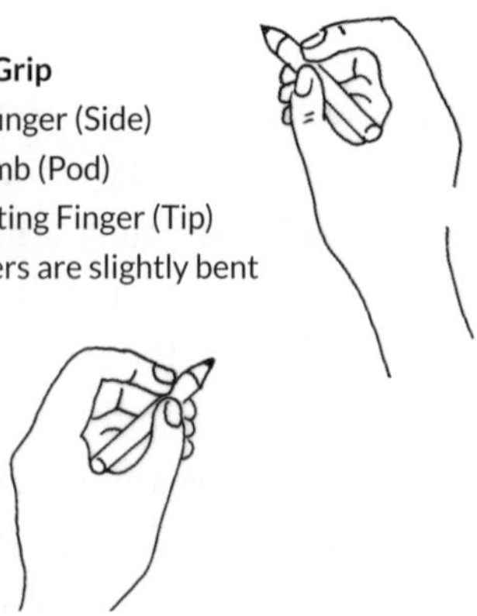

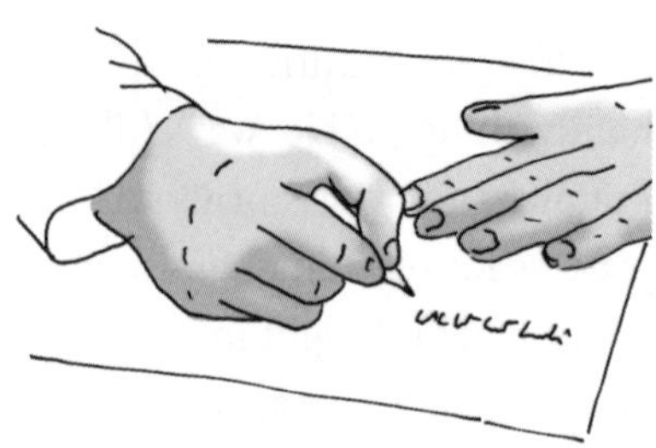

How to form a dynamic tripod grip

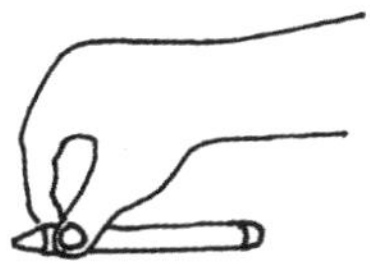

Place pencil on the table pointing away from you. Pinch pencil and pick it up. Pinch the pencil where you should hold it - on the point where the paint meets the wood.

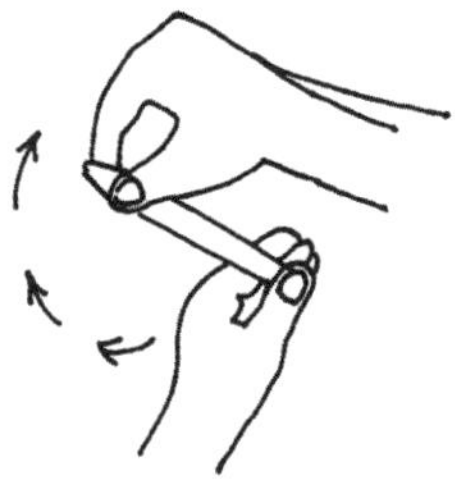

Hold the eraser and twirl it around.

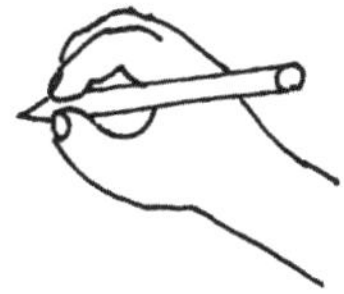

There you are!

Use crayons when the child is beginning to colour or print as a shorter, chubby, triangular crayon will allow the child's hand better feedback.

When teaching "b" and "d", letters which frequently cause confusion for children with motor challenges, teach "c" first and then another down stroke will make "d". So, first the "c" shape and next the "d". This allows for visual and motor learning. The letter "b" will then prove less confusing to learn and is more easily remembered.

When teaching lower case letters, start with c, o, s, v and w. These are the same as capitals only smaller.

Tracing or dot to dot copybook writing is not the best way for children to learn, because children become focused on looking for the dot or line direction and not the intrinsic motor feedback which permits the letter to be repeated without vision. Otherwise, they do not develop the motor plan but proceed to draw their letters rather than write them.

Observation of Children Writing

While these skills apply mainly to children just beginning to write and learn pencil skills, teachers should be on the lookout for these levels of abilities to be all in place. There may be older children who have slipped through the net and are experiencing difficulty in writing stories, reports etc., as opposed to handwriting. They are clever at disguising their struggles, but close observation will assist in uncovering them. Look for children who:

1. have good verbal but poor writing skills;
2. punctuate in a random manner;
3. have spelling errors such as reversals, omissions and phonic approximations;
4. talk to themselves while writing;
5. are slow to copy, lose the place on the page, and use their finger to follow the line;
6. write illegibly even when given extra time;
7. mix print with cursive style writing;
8. write with irregular shape and slants;
9. watch the hand that is writing;
10. have an unusual grip;
11. leave words unfinished or leave them out altogether;
12. have eyes which tend to blink or water;
13. do not seem to care, talk to neighbours and drop their pencils on the floor.

An example of a handwriting check can be found in the appendices.

Discussion of a Handwriting Check: Alisha, a Case Study

Below is a P4 girl's handwriting check. Alisha was told to write her name and the date at the top of the page. Then she was told to stay between the lines and draw a line from the mouse to the cheese. The next instruction was to copy the ten different patterns in the spaces below each one. Lastly, the next three parts of the check were to (a) write the numbers 1-10 on the line, (b) write the letters of the alphabet in lower case on the next line and finally (c) read and then copy out the sentence on the lines below.

The handwriting errors are apparent. What is not so obvious are the difficulties Alisha is experiencing. To begin with, note the handwriting faults.

- Reversals of 3, 5, 9.
- Differently sized figures and letters.
- Several letters not placed on the line and poorly spaced.
- A mix of small and capital letters.
- Poor closure on 8, 10, o, g, d.
- The letters q, y, p and j do not extend below the line.
- The fifth pattern is replicated as a series of c's.
- The letter z is written as the figure five reversed.
- The writing is heavy in some places and lighter in others.
- No differentiation of small and large letters.

Analysis of the Handwriting Errors

The writing in the first of the ten patterns to be copied was not of uniform size. Verbal instruction was not understood as Alisha, instead of writing the first pattern as directed in the space underneath impulsively continued the pattern on the same line, over writing into the next pattern. The second pattern was initially written on top of the model pattern, then below it but it dips at the end. The third pattern is written as M's, the fourth as W's and the fifth as a series of c's. In the sixth pattern there is no differentiation as to size. The next pattern was written as a horizontal line with a series of o's drawn beneath. The eighth and ninth have no differentiation as to size, and the child just could not copy the tenth pattern at all.

The reversals of letters and figures would indicate that this child has a problem with L/R awareness. She also has visual discrimination difficulties which are shown in an inability to copy patterns, reproduce letters on/below/above the line, keep letters the correct size and shape and space them accurately. The heavy writing in places would point to poor proprioception resulting in poor compressibility and tight grip. When writing the alphabet, several letters were squeezed in at the end, which suggests she has a spatial awareness difficulty. Failure to form the 8, 10, g and d properly indicates visual closure problems. Furthermore, Alisha could not form the final pattern at all and this shows she has issues with crossing midline. When she comes to a new pattern that causes her difficulty, she matches it to a shape with which she is familiar. The third, fourth and fifth patterns evidence a visual perception problem/motor planning difficulty.

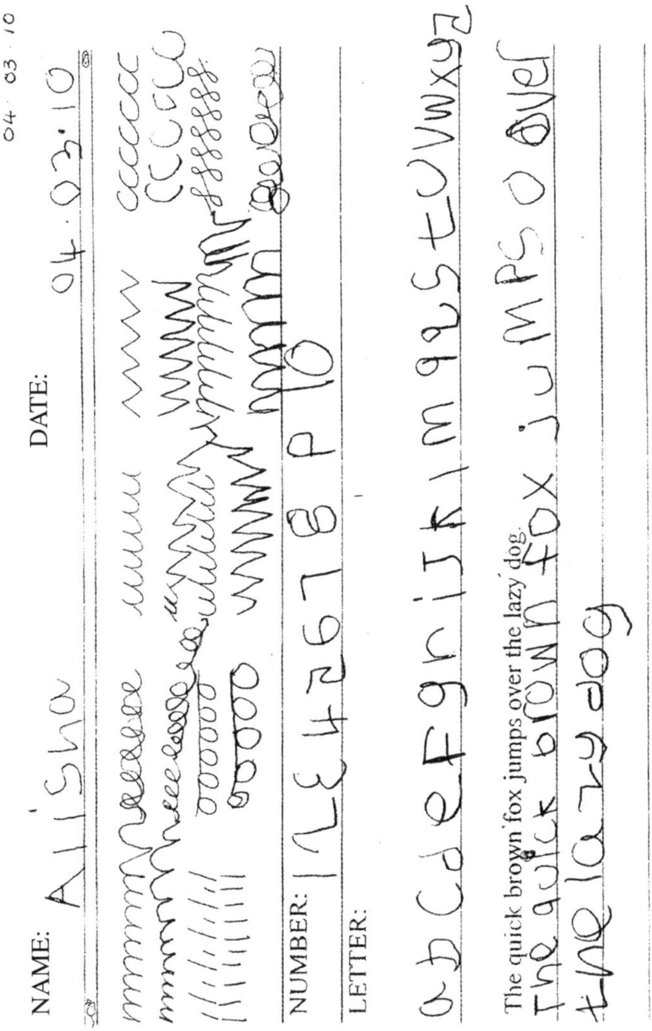
NAME: Allisha
DATE: 04.03.10
NUMBER:
LETTER:
The quick brown fox jumps over the lazy dog.

Key Points from Chapter 16

- Handwriting is a taught skill.
- Handwriting is a complex skill involving motor, perceptual and cognitive processes.
- A positive learning environment in the teaching of handwriting promotes confidence and self-esteem in the pupil.
- Handwriting is necessary to evidence knowledge, and when doing exams speed and fluency of handwriting is essential.
- Effective use of the trunk, shoulders, arms, wrist and hand is necessary in the promotion of good handwriting.
- The main sensory receptors in the proprioceptive, vestibular and tactile systems all play an important part in producing good handwriting.
- Other considerations of a kinaesthetic, bilateral, visual, tactile and auditory nature are essential for good handwriting, including possible retained reflexes and hand dominance.

Bibliography

Addy, L. (2004). Speed Up! A Kinaesthetic Programme to Develop Fluent Handwriting. Nottingham: L.D.A.

Ayres, A. J. (2005). Sensory Integration and the Child. USA:Western Psychological Services.

Ben-Sasson,A. et al.(2009). in Journal of Abnormal Child Psychology.

Bloom, B.S. (ed.) (1956). Taxonomy of Educational Objectives, Handbook I: The Cognitive Domain New York: David McKay Co.,

Brown, D. Dbl. Review (Jan-June 2007).

Cheatum, B. A. & Hammond, A. A Physical Activities for Improving Children's Learning and Behaviour. Human Kinetics USA.

Cool, S.J., (1987). Cited in, Brown, D. (2007).

Curthoys, I.S. (2010). A critical review of the neurophysiological evidence underlying clinical vestibular testing using sound, vibration and galvanic stimuli. : Clinical Neurophysiology, 121 (2): 132-144.

Delaney, T., (2008) The Sensory Processing Disorder Answer Book. USA: Sourcebooks, Inc.

Edwards, S. J., Buckland, D. J. & McCoy-Powlen, D. J. (2003). Developmental and Functional Hand Grasps. USA: Slack Inc.

Fisher, A.G., Murray, E.A., & Bundy, A.C. (eds). (1991). Sensory Integration: Theory and Practice. Philadelphia : F.A.Davis.

Fraker, C., Fishbein, M., Cox, S. & Walbert, L. (2007). Food Chaining: The Proven 6-Step Plan to Stop Picky Eating, Solve Feeding Problems, and Expand Your Child's Diet. USA: Da Capo Press, Perseus Books Group.

Gallahue,D. (1993). Developmental Physical Education for Today's Children. Dubuque, Wm. C. Brown Communications, Inc.,

Gilmore, Tim. (1999). "The Efficacy of the Tomatis Method for Children with Learning and Communication Disorders: A Meta-Analysis". International Journal of Listening, 13:12.

Goddard, S. (2002). Reflexes, Learning and Behaviour, A Window into the Child's Mind: A Non-Invasive Approach to Solving Learning and Behavior Problems. Oregon, USA: Fern Ridge Press: Oregon.

Hannaford, C. (2005). Smart Moves: Why Learning is not all in Your Head. Great River Books: Utah.

Kaufman,R.K. (2015). Autism Breakthrough: The grouind-breakingmethod that has helped families all over the world. USA: St. Martin's Press

Kurtz, L. (2008). Understanding Motor Skills in Children with Dyspraxia, ADHD, Autism, and other Learning Disabilities: A Guide to Improving Coordination. London and Philadelphia: Jessica Kingsley Publisher.

May-Benson, T. A. (2005). Development of a Test of Ideational Praxis. Unpublished dissertation manuscript. Phd, Boston University.

May-Benson,T.A., Teasdale,A., and Koomar,J. (2006) Prevalence of Sensory Behaviour in Children with SPD. The Spiral Foundation.

Miller, L. J. (2006). Sensational Kids. New York, USA: Penguin Group. USA.

Miller,L.J. et al.,(2012). Family & Relationships. BookBaby

Mucklow, N. (2009). The Sensory Team Handbook: Michael Grass House.

Robinson, E .et al.(2012). Teaching Practices that Promote Motor Skills in Early Childhood Settings. Early Childhood Education Journal.

Richardson, A. J. & Wilmer, J. (2001) Association between fatty acid symptoms and dyslexic and ADHD characteristics in normal college students. In British paper given at British Dyslexia Association International Conference, University of York, April 2001.

Stokes, B. (2002). Amazing Babies. Move Alive Media Inc.

Stordy, B. J. 'Dyslexia, attention deficit hyperactivity disorder, dyspraxia - do fatty acids help?" Dyslexia Review, Vol. 9(2), 1997, pp.1-3.

Stordy, B.J. (1997) Dyslexia, attention deficite hyperactivity disorder, dyspraxia - do fatty acids help? Dyslexia Review, 9 (2), 1-3.

Tools To Grow (Blog) www.toolstogrowot.com

Warshowsky, J. H. (2012). How Behavioural Optometry can unlock your Child's Potential: Identifying and Overcoming Blocks to Concentration, Self-Esteem and School Success with Vision Therapy. London: Jessica Kingsley Publisher.

Wilbarger, J. & Wilbarger, P. (2002). Wilbarger approach to treating sensory defensiveness and clinical application of the sensory diet Sections. In alternative and complementary programs for intervention, In Bundy, A.C., Murray, E.A., & Lane, S. (eds.) Sensory Integration: Theory and Practice, 2nd Ed. F.A. Davis, Philadelphia, PA.

Useful Websites

A list of useful websites and resources can
be found on our main website:

www.therapyfoundationsforeducation.co.uk/resources

A Programme of Motor Activities for Nursery, Ks 1 Children and Beyond, Employing Sensory Integration Principles

This programme has been devised for children of preschool, reception class and P1 age who have poor motor ability (possibly as a result of retained primitive reflexes) and who are not demonstrating general school readiness with the intention of detecting their difficulties and providing a means of helping them. It can easily be adapted for older children and has been used with children in years 1-7.

Many of the principles and ideas can be modified for older children in a more age appropriate way. The aim is to represent all the stages of motor development and reflex integration. As noted at the beginning of the book, motor ability and motor attention underpin both physical and cognitive development. The idea of this programme is, first of all, to get the children into a calm, alert state (modulation) so that learning may take place and the children derive the greatest benefit from the session.

There are children at all stages of education and in all educational settings who experience difficulty in learning. They have labels of various sorts: ADHD, ADD, and ASD, Dyslexia, Dyscalculia, and speech and language difficulty. Nevertheless, there are also children in mainstream education with no labels whatsoever who attend our clinic for assessment and treatment sessions. They are, however, not performing up to expectation, possibly because of poor application, concentration and attention. Such children find it difficult to sit still, listen to instructions, write and draw, and often appear disorganised and clumsy. They particularly dislike PE and games and often misbehave or find some other way to avoid these activities. They know that they have difficulty with sensory issues and it is easier for them to avoid movement challenges rather than risk failure or, worse still, being laughed at.

The first purpose of this programme is to help children modulate their levels of arousal, and then to identify and assess their motor difficulties. Finally, it will provide activities in a setting that will allow for motor development at the individual's own pace to improve motor skills, concentration and attention. These activities should be enjoyable. Each session begins with warm up activities and ends with a period of relaxation.

The programme takes into account **modulation, praxis and relaxation**.

Modulation

Sensory integration and modulation were discussed in Chapter 8. Sensory modulation activities come first in the programme because of the importance of children being calm and alert so as to make best sense of the incoming information arriving from various sources in their physical world. The child must be able to register the information before he can react to it. An under aroused child may appear disinterested, disorganised, withdrawn or dreamy and require active stimulation. On the other hand, a child over aroused by light, noise, touch or movement may not be able to cope with the lesson. They may have difficulty paying attention, concentrating, sitting still and they want to be "on the go" all the time. It is important to remember that both over and under aroused children may have low muscle tone, poor postural control, poor core stability and low endurance. As a result, they will tire easily. Bear in mind also that gross motor skills underpin fine motor skills and may also have an impact on the ability to pay attention. These children lack motor attention and move impulsively, informing motor awareness visually. Sensory modulation allows the central nervous system to regulate the child's attention and activity level. A well regulated child will automatically filter out irrelevant information to allow sensory modulation to happen.

Some General Considerations

- Proprioceptive input (Ch. 3) is the best way to help modulate behaviour. It is achieved through patterns of controlled, heavy work.
- If possible, give daily exercise (15mins.) without worrying too much about changing clothes.
- Provide plenty of free movement (both unilateral and bilateral) activities without too much concern about left or right or orientation.
- Choose activities in less challenging balance positions.
- Use general movement activities at the beginning of the session as a warm up activity and also just before the relaxation period at the end.
- Allow children to progress at their own pace with lots of encouragement and praise and without overcorrection or any criticism. The idea is that they are not in competition with others, but DO notice when they are able to perform a task which was previously causing difficulty. You may help them to get in the correct position or you may break the movement down into stages to make it easier to do.
- When giving instructions, be aware of children with auditory processing difficulty and demonstrate the movement either yourself or with a child you know can do it.

- Endeavour to develop control of movement impulsiveness by developing motor attention.
- Allow the children in the group to set the pace of the activities and do not be in a hurry to complete the programme.
- Always demonstrate the desired physical response or action and, when giving spatial directions, walk children through space, giving them a forward marker.
- When verbally directing "go over there", have a floor spot indicating "there".
- Have fun!

Included is a list of gross motor skills which may be used to supplement the list of activities provided.

Group 1
Walking, stepping, hopping, jumping, leaping, crawling, bounding, galloping, running and skipping,

Group 2
Bending, curling, turning, twisting, stretching, swaying, sliding, rolling, tumbling and swinging

Group 3
Lifting, pushing, pulling, hitting, punching, throwing, kicking, catching, shaking and striking

Group 4
Sitting, balancing, hanging and climbing

Praxis

The second element of the programme after modulation is praxis, or motor planning, of which postural control, bilateral and sequencing actions and body awareness are a part. The idea of praxis was discussed in Chapter 6. It encompasses **Ideation, Motor Planning** and **Execution** (the thought, the plan and the action).

Ideation is the conceiving of what to do - a cognitive activity involving generating and developing an idea, taking into account the environment and drawing upon previous experience. **Motor planning** is about figuring out how to do it, which parts of the body will be involved and which strategy will be used to carry it out including the sequence of actions required. The final part, **Execution,** is the actual accomplishment of the task. Motor planning can be improved by practising an action the child can already do and then, extending it by introducing a new component to the task or doing it in a variety of ways. For example, if the action is throwing a ball, variety may be introduced by changing the size or weight of the ball, increasing or decreasing the speed, or rolling it across the floor to make it easier to follow. (You may change the frequency, duration and intensity of the activity.) Just the right challenge will depend on the amount of sensory feedback (visual, auditory, tactile, proprioceptive and vestibular) the child is able to process on the day.

Postural Control

An important part of praxis is postural control. In the chapter on reflexes it was noted how the primitive or early reflexes are replaced by postural reflexes which encourage postural control of both static (still) and dynamic (moving) balance. The sequence in the normal development of a baby goes from lying on back (supine) to lying on tummy (prone), to rolling, to sitting, to various types of crawling, and finally to kneeling, to standing, and ultimately to walking. The programme takes this line of development into account and includes activities in each of these positions, which will encourage greater control.

Supine

Some children have difficulty planning how to lie on their backs on the floor. When in this position, check that they are comfortable. Let them stay in this position for a while before rolling onto their sides. While in the supine position, they are getting both tactile and proprioceptive input, as well as an opportunity to move their limbs independently and improve trunk stability and weight-bearing. In this position children should be able to maintain the entire body on the floor and slowly rock the body up/down using their heels maintaining alignment. This is an essential movement as it is a small focused move that controls the whole body. If some children cannot perform this movement, they can work on it until they can do it.

Prone

The prone position (on tummy) can prove hard work for some children due to poor core stability at pelvis and shoulder girdle and because they have always resisted adopting this position. If this is so, then they should simply work for short periods in this position. If the primitive reflexes have not been entirely inhibited there will be a tendency for the child to extend the hips and knees when he starts to move. Working in this position will encourage the integration of the primitive reflexes, promote weight-bearing through the arms and strengthen pelvic, shoulder girdle and neck muscles. In addition, by working with children in prone, they gain awareness of balance and symmetry, while providing proprioceptive and tactile input to assist the development of body awareness supporting anti-gravity postures. A small roll placed under the chest at armpit level will assist in keeping the younger child in this position. He may object to this at first, but it is worthwhile persevering.

Rolling

Rolling should be in a straight line, but some children find it difficult to find a starting position and stay flat. Often they will roll off the course and become dizzy after only a few rolls. (Please take this into account, otherwise you may have a sick child on your hands.) However, rolling helps inhibit primitive reflexes while also providing proprioceptive, vestibular and tactile input into body awareness.

Sitting

The next stage in the developmental sequence is sitting upright with feet extended. In this position there are opportunities for stabilising and rotating the trunk, allowing the arms to move and weight bear. This position provides opportunities to integrate primitive reflexes and receive input into body awareness through the vestibular, proprioceptive and tactile systems.

Crawling

While all stages of postural control are important, the crawling stage is vital to bilateral integration, especially when the limbs move in an alternate pattern, i.e. left leg, right hand and vice versa. Children may go through an initial stage of dropping the bottom onto the heels to rest and proceed as if bunny hopping, or perform amphibian-type crawling, i.e. moving both limbs together on the same side.

The reciprocal movement helps inhibit the primitive reflexes and encourages communication between the left and right hemispheres of the brain. In the crawling position, placing the pressure on the arms and hands helps strengthen them. It also provides an opportunity to develop balance and body awareness through tactile, vestibular and proprioceptive input. Where children have missed out on this essential stage, they can present with arms used in avoidance of people and objects and walk in a high guard position (arms held at shoulder height and flexed upwards) or swing their arms in absence of the rhythm of the legs when walking or running.

Kneeling

The difficulties faced in the kneeling position are finding balance and rotating the head and the body. The trunk needs to work independently of the lower limbs and the eyes must scan and track in the absence of head movements. However, overcoming these difficulties will assist stability and postural control in pre-standing positions. Should tall kneeling prove challenging for children, try, 4 point kneeling whilst moving up on the arms into a tall kneeling position.

Standing and Walking

It is important to emphasise that reaching the milestones mentioned previously is vital before beginning to stand and walk. All too often, parents are pleased to see their child walk early. This frequently means not spending enough time on the floor at early stages or even missing a stage completely. Do not be tempted to do this. Missing out or spending insufficient floor time at a stage can often lead to difficulties later on through:

1. not fully inhibiting the primitive reflexes;

2. missing out on early slow, rhythmical movements;
3. not achieving good core stability through strengthening the muscles in the pelvic and shoulder region;
4. poor bilateral integration. (The previous three problems result in walking with quick steps to maintain balance, walking with high guard, walking with a wide base, having floppy limbs and trunk, having difficulties with timing and motor planning, and behaving in an impulsive way in general);
5. poor trunk rotation.

Bilateral Integration and Midline Awareness

Having looked so far at modulation and various aspects of praxis, we turn now to bilateral integration and midline awareness. These issues were discussed in in chapter 4 and concern the ability to use both sides of the body or to use both hands as a pair as opposed to using either the left or right side without reference to each other. Bilateral integration means using all the twos - two eyes, ears, hands and feet - as pairs. Midline awareness is seen in reaching one hand right across the middle of the body and also in using both hands in smooth, reciprocal movements to carry out such tasks as tying shoe laces, using a knife and fork, using scissors for cutting out and holding a page steady with one hand while writing with the other. Difficulty in this area may be noticeable in these actions: jumping with two feet together, reciprocal crawling and ski walking.

Body Awareness

Much of what has already been discussed has an important bearing on body awareness. This was also previously discussed in Chapter 4. Mention was made of the many aspects of body awareness such as body image, identifying and naming body parts, body scheme, laterality, midline awareness, and directionality. In essence, body awareness is the mental image built up by the brain through the information it receives from various sources including the eyes, ears, skin and the vestibular and proprioceptive systems. It is knowing where the body is in space, i.e. the capacity to form a three dimensional picture of where the various parts of the body are in relation to each other or the environment without having to look to see where they are. In effect, it is an internal awareness and involves knowing the names of the various body parts and being able to name them or point them out on their own or on someone else's body. All aspects of praxis, including postural control and bilateral awareness, are involved, as are the prepositions used to indicate space: over, under, between, beside, against, in, on, below, above etc.

Relaxation

All sessions should end with a period of relaxation which will only take a few minutes. This should be done while the child is lying in either the prone or supine position in a quiet environment and remaining as still as possible. Some techniques which may be tried are deep breathing, visualising, thinking, and tensing and loosening muscles in various parts of the body. These will be explained in greater detail in the activity plans. The idea is to allow the children to experience the feeling of being at rest, being comfortable and peaceful. Following this period of relaxation the children should leave the room quietly in small groups. The website *www.moodcafe.co.uk*

provides additional relaxation exercises to those given at the end of each session. These are featured in the downloadable leaflet *Relax Like a Cat.*

Assessment

The following is a simple assessment designed for reception/P1 children. It consists of ten activities scored on a three point scale. The scoring is as follows:

- 1 point = has no difficulty;
- 2 points = has some difficulty;
- 3 points = can not do it at all.

The scoring is subjective and arrived at purely by observation. It may be carried out by parents, teachers or classroom assistants, with emphasis on ease of scoring while still giving the adult a quick guide as to which of the children is experiencing difficulty. A baseline assessment is suggested. It may be repeated ten to twelve weeks later for comparison and, if desired, after twenty and then thirty weeks. This could easily comprise a full year's work.

A score of ten suggests that the individual is experiencing no motor difficulty. The higher the score the greater the difficulty the child is facing. There are ten observations to be made which, hopefully, are achievable for busy staff, but that number may be increased if time and staffing allow. Three out of the ten observations are not directly linked to a physical movement but will give insight into the child's overall performance.

The first step is to observe the child's ability to transition from one activity to another (1 point = easy transitioning; 2 points = some difficulty; 3 points = great difficulty). This observation may be made in a variety of situations in order to give a general picture.

The next is the arousal level of the child. (1 point = just right, 2 points = some difficulty, 3 points over/under aroused)

The final observation concerns the length of time the child can stay relaxed in the supine position (1 point = 20 < 30 secs; 2 points = 10 < 20 secs; 3 points = 1 < 10 secs.). The longer they can stay relaxed the better.

The next seven activities seen in the grid below are:

1. heel/toe walking forward/backwards along a line or tape stuck on the floor;
2. crawling forwards/backwards on hands and knees using reciprocal movements;
3. rolling in a straight line for three complete rolls
4. crossing midline with hand to ears/knees;
5. One leg standing (left/right leg, then with eyes closed);
6. fingers/thumb touching (touch each finger in turn with thumb);
7. hop, jump sequencing repeated three times.

Score 1 point if the movement is carried out easily, evenly and smoothly; 2 points if he has some difficulty - can start but can not complete; 3 points if he can't do it at all but looks around to see what the others are doing. Ten activities are used in the assessment, but if time permits, others may be added, e.g. bear walking and hopping on one foot. Transitioning may be observed in various activities, locations, environments and positions. As you will have observed the higher the score, the greater the difficulty the child is experiencing.

ASSESSMENT GRID FOR MOTOR ACTIVITY OUTCOMES

Name	Date	Transitioning	Arousal Level	Relaxation	Heel /toe walking fwd & back	Crawling fwd & back	Rolling in a straight line	Cross midline ears/ knees	1 leg standing	Fingers/thumb touching	Hop/jump sequence	Baseline total	Retest after 10 weeks	Retest after 20 weeks	Retest after 30 weeks

The motor activities are based around three major considerations which are: **Body Awareness, Postural Control** and **Bilateral and Sequencing** actions. Each of these categories is sub-divided into seven sections which include activities in supine, prone, rolling, sitting, crawling, kneeling and standing or walking. This makes a total of 21 sessions. Each session will begin with modulation (heavy work) activities and end with relaxing, cooling down activities. At the end of each period, teacher observations and a list of the equipment required are listed. The equipment needed for each lesson has been kept to a minimum but may easily be supplemented as desired. When counting down the seconds, count from 5 or 10 back to 1.

SECTION ONE

Session 1: Body Awareness

Modulation

- Running on the spot (use the commands: Start, Freeze) X3
- Wall presses X5
- Animal walk like a bear (hands on ground, bottom in the air)
- Tug of war (with partner pulling arms)

Supine (flat on back)

- Lift head, look at toes (arms by side), then lower the head X5
- Turn head to L/R to look at neighbour X5
- Bend knees in/out, keep feet flat X5
- Curl into a ball holding knees (count to 5)
- Move out to lie like a star fish (arms/legs extended)
- With legs slightly apart and feet upright move feet like car wipers X5
- Make angels in the snow shape (arms and legs spread wide, head looking up)
- With arms crossed on chest and knees bent bring knees and arms together X5

Relaxation

- Lying on back, breathe in then hold (count to 5), then breathe out slowly (count to 5) Where children have difficulty place a soft toy on the tummy and watch it fall on blowing out and rise, breathing in
- Wiggle toes, pull toes towards face then hold (count to 5)
- Relax, lie quietly, (count backwards from 10 to 1)

Teacher looks for: ability to listen, to respond quickly to commands, lying still with body in alignment

Session 2: Body Awareness

Modulation

- Running around room (commands: start/freeze) X3
- Walk around room stamping with feet
- Sit facing partner feet to feet , pull partner's hands
- Commando crawling across floor
  While in prone (flat on tummy)
- Lie in a circle in prone, heads facing in to the centre, pass bean bags around circle hand to hand

Prone (flat on tummy)

- Lift head, (hold for 5), lift head and arms, (hold for 5), lift legs from pelvis (hold for 5).
- Lie in a circle in prone, heads facing in to the centre, pass bean bags around circle from hand to hand
- Commando crawl under, over around between obstacles, e.g. mat, chair, box, cones, hoops or or therapy noodles.
- Lift head, (hold for 5) lift head and arms, (hold for 5) lift legs from pelvis (hold for 5)

Relaxation

- Tighten, loosen tummy muscles (count to 5)
- Tighten, then loosen fists (count to 5)
- Wrinkle up face as if smelling a bad smell (count to 5)
- Lie still like a starfish on a rock (count from 10 down to 1)

Teacher looks for: ability to listen and respond quickly, ability to tense and relax, commando crawl, hold positions, lie flat and still and not engage with other children.

Equipment: beanbags, chairs, mats, boxes, cones etc. for obstacle course

Session 3: Body Awareness

Modulation

- Skip around room (commands: start/stop) X3
- Wall press (feet ½ m from wall, push against wall) X5
- Jumping jacks or star jumps X10
- Sitting back to back with partner, pushing in to each other
- Bunny hopping

Rolling

- Rolling from side to side, hands above head, 1 complete roll each way
- Roll to collect bean bag from box then back again X2

Floor movement

- In supine, move forward to get beanbag, pushing with legs
- In prone, move forward to get beanbag pulling on arms

Relaxation

- Push whole body into floor to make an impression in it (in prone)
- Stretch yourself as long as possible
- Curl up tight then uncurl and relax
- Lie still (count from 12 back to 1)

Teacher looks for: quality of movement, lying flat and still, rolling in a straight line

Equipment: beanbags, boxes to hold bean bags

Session 4: Body Awareness

Modulation

- Dancing round the room (commands: start/freeze like a statue) X3

In prone, assume Superman position (arms out to side, head and chest off the floor)

- Standing, perform, "Heads and shoulders knees and toes," song
- Play On the bank/in the river (commands to jump from one side of rope to other)

Sitting

- Sit on bottom with legs extended, shuffle forward, backward, sideways
- Sit in circle, legs extended towards centre, feet apart, pass ball around circle using 2 hands and rotating trunk
- In same position roll a ball to others calling out name
- Row your boat in 2s (feet together, hold hands, bodies move forward and back)

Relaxation

- Lie back and listen only to your breathing
- Tighten fists as tight as possible, then relax
- Think about a place you visited and liked e.g. beach, park, farm etc.
- Lie still, count from 12 down to 1

Teacher looks for: child listens to commands, acts quickly, quality of movement, holds position, lies still

Equipment: rope, ball

Session 5: Body Awareness

Modulation

- Jumping 2 feet together (commands: start/stop) X3
- Waddle like a duck
- Walk on tip toes
- Wall press X5

Crawling

- 4 point kneeling, (on hands and knees) use one hand to toss beanbag to partner and back again
- Repeat using the other hand
- 4 point kneeling, lift one leg straight out behind and waggle it, then the other
- In crawling position, push a bean bag forward with head
- Set out obstacle course, crawl around hoops, under chairs, over mats, between cones

Relaxation

- Lying on your back, imagine you are a big red balloon. Take a big breath to blow it up (feel your tummy rising) let the air hiss out, feel yourself get smaller and flatter X3
- Lie still and imagine you are enjoying yourself laughing and playing in a park with a friend or mum and dad
- Yawn and stretch, lie still (count backwards from 12 to 1)

Teacher looks for: quality of movement, holding position, listening to commands, lying still
Equipment: hoops, chairs, mats, cones etc. to make obstacle course

Session 6: Body Awareness

Modulation

- Bunny hopping X5
- Walking on heels with stiff legs
- Pushing/pulling partner's shoulders
- Do windmills with arms extended to the side, forward/backwards

Kneeling/high kneeling

- 4 point kneeling, rock slowly forwards and back on to heels X5
- Then slowly extend limbs individually (arms to front, legs to rear)
- Kneeling to standing position using first one leg then the other
- Throw beanbag to partner in tall kneeling
- Facing partner in tall kneeling, clap partner's hands (1 hand, 2 hands, crossing over) "A sailor went to sea, sea, sea etc." (hand clapping game)

Relaxation

- Lying on back, do deep breathing: breathe in, hold, breathe out, hold X2
- Wiggle toes
- Wrinkle face like when smelling a bad smell
- Hunch shoulders slowly (count to 5) then relax X2
- Think about what you could do to help others e.g. share toys, help put coat on, play with them, help them if they fall
- Relax, lie still (count backwards 12 to 1)

Teacher looks for: Quality of movement, listening to instructions, following instructions controlling impulsive speaking

Equipment: Beanbags

Session 7: Body Awareness

Modulation

- Jumping jacks or star jumps X10
- In the pond/on the bank game, (use a rope to separate)
- In supine: air cycling, raising and lowering leg (X5 each leg), knee hugging (count down from 5 to 1)
- Bear walking (hands on ground, bottom in air)
- In prone, arm wrestling with partner

Standing and Walking

- Walk frorward on heels/toes with stiff legs
- Repeat walk backwards
- Jump two feet together in straight lines, then side to side
- Hop on one foot/other foot X10
- Sing song standing in a circle "Heads and shoulders knees and toes." The second time through, miss out some words but do actions.

Relaxation

- Standing, shrink head into neck/elevate shoulders (count to 5)
- Tighten and loosen tummy muscles (count to 5)
- Lying supine arms by side, think of a colour you like that makes you feel comfortable and peaceful
- Relax, lie still (count from 12 down to 1)

Teacher looks for: Ability to respond correctly to commands, quality of movement, interaction with partner, lying still, the ability to hold position

SECTION TWO

Session 8: Postural Control

Modulation

- Running around leaping, commands: stop/go X3
- Walking like a crab commands: go/freeze X3
- Shuffle along on bottom, forwards/backwards
- Standing, move arms like windmills, forwards/backwards

Supine (on back)

- Touch floor with hand - first above head/beside hips, then crossing over to touch floor at side of head then beside hips
- Touch body parts; head/knees/shoulders/hips (encourage crossing midline)
- Lift legs in air, open/close, wide apart, pedal cycle (legs in air)
- Sitting, move arms in circles overhead together/separately
- Sitting, hold knees, rock side to side
- Hold toes, rock from side to side

Relaxation

- Lie on floor with hands by side try to make an impression in the floor with your whole body
- Breathe deeply, lie still like a starfish on a rock (count backwards from 15 to 1)

Teacher looks for: Listening to commands and quick response, quality of movement, ability to lie still, ability to cross midline

Session 9: Postural Control

Modulation

- Walk around taking giant steps, commands go/freeze X3
- Wall presses X10
- Lie in prone pull yourself along with arms
- Bunny hopping commands: go/freeze X3

Prone (all of next set of exercises done on tummy)

- Commando crawl (lie on tummy, use arms and legs to move) go round obstacle course moving in/over/under/between chairs, mats, cones, hoops, etc.
- Lift head and arms from waist (arms to front/to side) hold for count of 5 each time
- Move arms in circles at side forwards/backwards
- In a circle facing centre, legs behind, use both hands to pass a beanbag round the circle

Relaxation

- In prone, wiggle toes
- Tighten fists then relax X3
- Breathe in deeply – hold count to 5 breathe out X3
- Lie still, count backwards from 15 to 1

Teacher looks for: Listening, quality of movement, holding positions, responding quickly to commands, lying still
Equipment: Beanbags

Session 10: Postural Control

Modulation

- Run to beat of drum (slowly, fast, stop. In combinations)
- Walk around playing pretend instrument (big drum, flute, trombone, violin)
- In the pond/on the bank game using a rope to separate (commands: pond/bank)

Rolling

Be aware that some children may get dizzy more quickly than others. Allow them to sit and watch.

- Roll straight along a line on the floor
- Roll holding a beanbag in both hands above head to pass to a friend
- Set out obstacle course to roll over, under, between, around

Relaxation

- Curl up tight into in a ball then gradually uncurl
- Yawn and stretch in a long shape, a wide shape
- Lie quietly on back listening to breathing, count from 15 to 1

Teacher looks for: Moving to commands or drumbeat, quality of movement, listening, ability to lie still

Equipment: Beanbags, drum, items for obstacle course, rope

Session 11: Postural Control

Modulation

- Kangaroo hopping
- Walking with heavy stomping
- Hold partner's shoulders and try to push away
- Tug o war using skipping rope with partner

Sitting

- Sit in a circle with feet towards the centre, pass a large ball around using both hands
- As before, sit with legs apart, roll a ball to someone else, calling out the person's name
- In pairs sitting facing each other, play "Row, row, row your boat," using a hoop
- Shuffle forwards and backwards in long sitting
- Sitting, try to touch toes

Relaxation

- Stretch out fingers wide
- Curl up tight then stretch out long
- Lie quietly on back and think about how you could help others (give them a biscuit, play with them, push them on a swing). Then count backwards from 15 to 1.

Teacher looks for: Quality of movement, following instructions, lying still
Equipment: Skipping ropes, large ball, hoops

Session 12: Postural Control

Modulation

- Skipping around room commands: go/freeze X3
- Sitting holding a pole lengthwise (or rope) whilst being pulled by partner (change partners)
- Crawling like a crocodile, chase a partner who is also crawling

Crawling

- Crawling team game: put beanbag on back carry it round a cone and return to give to next person
- In crawling position form a circle facing inwards then throw beanbag to another in the circle
- Set up obstacle course to go over/under/around/through. Carry beanbag on back around the course without dropping it.

Relaxation

- Lying on back, tense all limbs then go floppy
- Imagine you are a big red balloon, breathe in to inflate count to to 5, hold for 3, then let the air hiss out
- Lie quietly, listen to yourself breathing in and out, count down from 15 to 1

Teacher looks for: Quality of movement, following instructions, interacting with a friend, lying still

Equipment: Wooden poles, ropes, beanbags, items for obstacle course e.g. chair, mat, hoops, cones.

Session 13: Postural Control

Modulation

- Jumping 2 feet together in a zig-zag pattern commands: start/freeze X3
- Wall presses X10
- Pull a partner along by legs then change partners
- Push partner's shoulders then change around

Kneeling

- Tall kneeling facing partner, do clapping game, "A sailor went to sea, sea, sea". 1/2 hands crossing over
- On knees, chase partner without falling over, change over
- Move on knees forwards/backwards to beat of drum (slow/fast/stop) try not to fall over
- 4 point kneeling, cat arches in/out with the back
- 4 point kneeling, move back/forward on to feet

Relaxation

- Yawn and stretch in wide shape hold for 5
- Wrinkle up face as if smelling a bad smell, hold for 5
- In supine wiggle toes back and forth
- Lie quietly, count backwards from 15 to 1

Teacher looks for: Crossing over midline movements, quality of movement, listening, lying still, and interaction with partner
Equipment: Drum

Session 14: Postural Control

Modulation

- Walk like a hen, holding ankles with hands
- Run around flapping arms commands: freeze/go X3
- Hold partner's hand for tug o war change over L/R
- Draw 2 tram lines on floor, hopping 2 feet together over the space

Standing and Walking

- Stand in a circle, sing "Hokey, Kokey" song with actions
- Walk on toes/heels with stiff legs
- Hold beanbag between feet and jump X5
- Walk backwards around an obstacle course
- Set out hoops over the floor placed close together, play "follow my leader" game. Leader can hop/jump/walk around course going from hoop to hoop. Change leader
- Standing in a circle facing inwards, pass ball 2 handed around the circle

Relaxation

- Reach up high, then curl up small X3
- Lie in supine, listen to soft music
- Lie quietly, count backwards from 15 to 1

Teacher looks for: Quality of movement, listening quietly, responding to directions, lying quietly, crossing midline
Equipment: Large ball, 2 skipping ropes to make lines, items for obstacle course, e.g. mats, cones, chairs, hoops, soft music CD

SECTION THREE

Session 15: Bilateral and Sequencing

Modulation

- Running round the room as if flying like a butterfly, then land on a flower, commands: fly/land X3
- Bear walking
- Row the boat with a partner using a hoop, both sitting
- Sitting, hug knees, partner tries to push you over then change over
- Jumping jacks or star jumps X5

Supine

- Angels in the snowgame. commands: lift one leg, lift other leg, lift one arm, lift other arm, lift one leg and one arm, lift other leg and arm
- Commando crawl in reciprocal pattern
- In supine, throw beanbag from hand to hand
- Lie in circle facing outwards pass beanbag around using only right/left hand

Relaxation

- Breathe in, count to 5, hold for 5, breathe out, count to 5
- Tighten, loosen tummy muscles
- Lie still like a starfish on a rock, count backwards from 20 down to 1
- From star fish curl into jellyfish. Whilst curling into your body breath out and when moving away from the body to starfish breath in. Repeat this from 5 times increasing the counts.

Teacher looks for: Listening, following instructions, quality of movement, holding position, lying still for a count from 20 down to 1
Equipment: Beanbags, hoops

Session 16: Bilateral and Sequencing

Modulation

- Bum shuffling using legs forwards, backwards, sideways
- “In the pond, on the bank,” game. Commands: pond/bank
- Penguin walking
- Wall presses X10
- Lying in supine, air cycling, raising and lowering 2 legs together X5
- Standing, windmills with arms to side circling forwards/ backwards

Prone

- Crawling like a caterpillar, commands: go/freeze X3
- In prone and in a circle, facing centre, pass beanbag around using any hand/left hand only/right hand only
- In prone, roll a ball from one hand to the other
- In prone, arm wrestling with a partner
- In prone, touch head, back, knee, foot with one hand then with the other hand

Relaxation

- In prone, stretch out long, count to 5; then curl up tight and count to 5
- Tighten one fist, relax, then other fist, relax
- Lie quietly listen to breathing count down down from 20 to 1

Teacher looks for: Quality of movement, responding to commands, crossing midline, placing hand on correct area, lying still for count of 20
Equipment: Beanbags, balls

Session 17: Bilateral and Sequencing

Modulation

- Commando crawling
- Crab walking
- Run around as if flying like a bee, with arms outstretched making a buzzing sound to light on a flower when told, commands: fly/ flower X3
- Lay out a skipping rope in a straight line, stand sideways feet together, jump from side to side

Rolling (rolling can cause dizziness, be on lookout for signs)

- Lie on back, hold a ball in hands above head, roll over to give ball to partner then roll back to your place, partner rolls to you to give you ball X3
- Lie along the edge of a blanket/towel, roll yourself up in towel, then unroll
- Rolling objects to develop coordination, sitting with feet forward, roll a ball diagonally back and forth to a partner on right side then the left side of you
- On own, dribble a ball along using feet, make sure the ball does not get too far ahead

Relaxation

- Stretch up tall to touch the sky, stretch wide like a house, curl up small like a mouse
- Hunch head into shoulders hold the position and count to 5, X3
- Lie still like a jellyfish on a beach count down from 20 to 1

Teacher looks for: Quality of movement, quick response to commands, ability to hold position, lying still for a 20 count
Equipment: Balls, towels or blankets

Session 18: Bilateral and Sequencing

Modulation

- Wall presses X10
- Bear walking
- Sequencing movements jump - jump x5, hop - hop x5, step - hop X5, jump-step X3, step - hop X3, jump - jump- clap - clap X3

Sitting

- Sitting in a circle facing centre play the *Simon Says* game, i.e. touch your head/foot/arm/leg/back
- Commands: put your hand ABOVE your head/shoulder/leg; BELOW your arm/leg/ear/mouth/nose; BEHIND your head/back; in FRONT of your shoulder/chest/head
- Sitting, roll a ball to hit a target, throw a beanbag into a box
- Sing the song, "Tommy thumb, Tommy thumb, where are you? Here I am, here I am, How do you do?" Repeat for, "Peter pointer, Mr Tall, Ruby Ring, Baby Small."

Relaxation

- Tighten tummy muscles hold 5, loosen muscles hold for 5 X3
- Yawn and stretch out like a cat X2
- Lie still like a cat asleep count down 20 to 1

Teacher looks for: Quality of movement, ability to sequence movements, ability to point to body parts, lying still for a count of 1 to 20.

Equipment: Balls, targets, containers, beanbags

Session 19: Bilateral and Sequencing

Modulation

- Galloping, commands: stop/go X3
- Move like a crocodile, chase a partner who is crawling
- 1 foot hopping, change feet
- Jumping 2 feet together: forwards/ backwards/hands to side/ hands in air
- Shoulder pushing with a partner
- Advance slowly and quietly towards a partner from behind aiming to pounce on them before they notice you

Crawling

- Follow my leader game, crawling along a twisting chalk line on the floor/objects laid out on floor
- Treasure hunt, crawling to find hidden objects
- Crawling fast like a mouse, slowly like an elephant
- Crawl through a tunnel made by a row of chairs. At end of tunnel throw a beanbag into a bucket crossing over the body's midline

Relaxation

- Breathe in, hold for count of 5, breathe out, hold for count of 5, repeat X5
- Shrink head into shoulders X3
- Lie like a jellyfish on a beach, count down from 20 to 1
- Do 10 starfish to jellyfish routines, with focused breathing out when moving in, and focused breathing in when moving out

Teacher looks for: Balance in movement, following instructions, quality of movement, crossing midline, lying still
Equipment: Beanbags, chairs, objects for treasure hunt, buckets/ containers

Session 20: Bilateral and Sequencing

Modulation

- Jumping jacks or star jumps X10
- Elephant walk, slow and heavy, waving trunk in figure of eight
- In 4 point kneeling position, rock forward on arms then, back on heels X5
- Standing behind partner, try to push partner away; then change around swapping roles.
- Skipping using a large hoop X10

Kneeling and Half Kneeling

- Move from kneeling position to standing on opposite leg (one leg standing)
- Throwing and catching beanbag with partner while assuming a half kneeling position
- Doing row your boat activity with partner, using a hoop in half kneeling position
- Clapping games with partner when in tall kneeling position, crossing over midline, "A sailor went to sea, sea, sea" game
- In 4 point kneeling, stretch out one arm, then the other, also one leg, then the other.

Relaxation

- Open hands wide, close fists tight X3
- Lie on back, press head on to ground, then shoulders, then back, then bottom, then legs, then feet
- Lie still and listen to your breathing in and out, count down 20 to 1

Teacher looks for: Quality of movement, holding position steady, crossing midline, lying still.
Equipment: Beanbags, hoops

Session 21: Bilateral and Sequencing

Modulation

- Skipping around objects on the floor, no rope involved
- Skipping in a circle, change direction on command: change X4
- Running on the spot on tip toes, commands: go/stop X3
- Running with hands on head/behind back/on hips/ in air, commands: freeze/go X3
- Hop to target on 1 foot, stop, stand on 1 leg for count of 5, then back on other leg

Standing and Walking

- Set out obstacle course, walk around the course playing follow my leader
- On your own, walk around obstacle course backwards
- Walk to drum beat slow, medium, fast
- Stand in pairs back to back, pass ball over head then between legs
- Walk with beanbag balanced on head

Relaxation

- Stretch up tall, curl up small X3
- Sit wiggling toes, pull toes towards face, hold for count of 5
- Screw up face like smelling a bad smell, hold for count of 3
- Lie quietly like a cat sleeping, count down from 20 to 1

Teacher looks for: Balance, quality of movement, responding to commands, lying still
Equipment: Items for obstacle course, drum, beanbags, balls

Sequence of Development Charts

Hand Function and Fine Motor Skills

- Swipes object.
- Reaches and holds objects.
- Claps hands.
- Grasps an object placed in hand.
- Uses both hands to reach for an object.
- Child holds a small object in each hand for a short time.
- Reaches for an object with one arm.
- Grasps an object with one hand and transfers to the other hand.
- Bangs object off the table or hard surface during play.
- Grasps, explores and manipulates a toy with wrist movement.
- Reaches for and grasps object with extended elbow.
- Reaches and grasps an object with thumb, index and middle fingers without the use of the palm.
- Bangs cubes together if held in either hand.
- Removes pegs from a pegboard.
- Takes objects out of a container.
- Releases objects voluntarily.
- Imitates marks on paper holding a crayon.
- Pokes with index finger.
- Uses both hands freely for play.
- Puts objects into a container.
- Places one block on top of another.
- Puts 3 or more objects into a container – encouragement. may be needed to complete the task.
- Builds tower using 2 blocks.
- Turns container upside down to get object out.

- Uses both hands freely – one holds, the other works.
- Places round peg in pegboard.
- Attempts to remove shapes from form board.
- Imitates marks with crayon.
- Starts to string beads.
- Builds tower using 5 blocks.
- Imitates 3 block train.
- Strings beads.
- Holds pencil for pencil work.

Learning Sequence for Skilful Play

- Child follows a rapidly moving object with eyes until it rolls out of sight.
- Looks for family members or pets when named.
- Looks for hidden sound.
- Imitates gestures in play – mother does something several times – see if child can copy.
- Looks at pictures when named and pointed to.
- Finds hidden object under cloth.
- Drops objects repeatedly.
- Knows what "No" means.
- Removes round piece from form board.
- Takes stacking rings apart.
- Posts simple shapes in a box by trial and error.
- Stacks rings.
- Nests beakers.
- Pulls string to obtain toy.
- Selects simple known objects.
- Identifies some body parts by pointing and touching.
- Recognises and points to 4 animal pictures.
- Points to item of clothing on request – socks and shoes, etc.

- Explores cabinets and drawers.
- Matches sounds to animals.
- Enjoys and anticipates nursery rhymes.
- Remembers where objects belong.
- Sorts colours; piles of red/yellow.
- Matches reds/yellows.
- Completes 4 piece matching colour toy.
- Completes stacking cups and stacks and grades them.
- Can manage peg men colour matching activity.

A Handwriting Check

The Handwriting Check is carried out to assess a child's perceptual motor skills. The first part of the check is copying basic shapes and identifies a child's ability to cross midline. In the next section the child is asked to copy more complex patterns. This will further identify impulsivity, the ability to self-correct, rhythm in writing, spatial awareness and midline crossing.

The child is then asked to write the numbers 1 -10 and the alphabet a-z in lower case. This will help identify consistency of size, shape and spacing, also if there is a mix of upper and lower case, and whether or not the writing is carried out top/down or bottom/up. All writing should be carried out top/down with the majority of letters having a left side start.

The final three parts will identify the child's ability to near/far copy and the speed, accuracy and layout of writing a dictated text. This section is suitable for year 3 onwards and the level of difficulty may be graded for older children.

Name:
Copy: 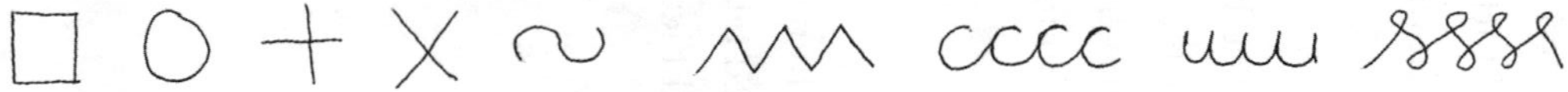
Numbers (1 to 10)
Letters (Lower case a-z)
Near copying (6 - 12 words , 8 - 12cm)
Far copying (12 words , 2 - 2.5 meters)
Dictation (9 - 12 words , record time)

Developmental Building Blocks

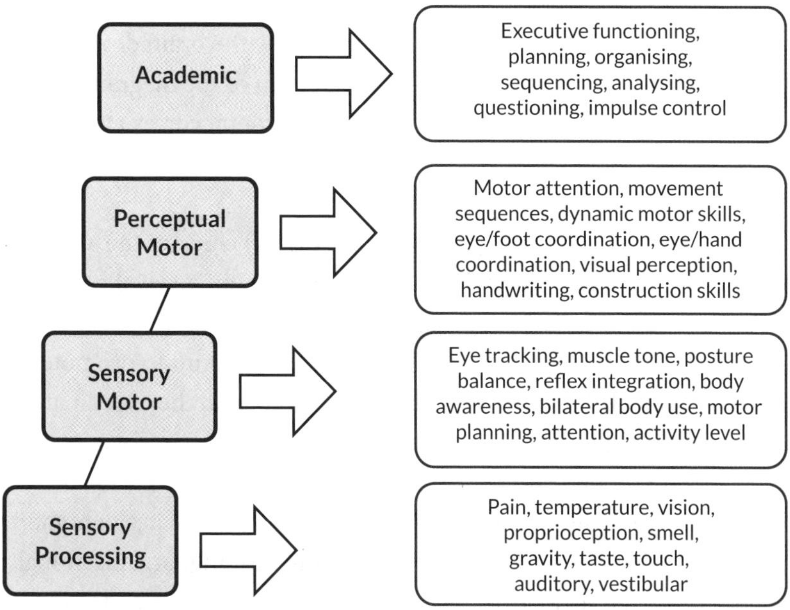

Approaches to Treatment

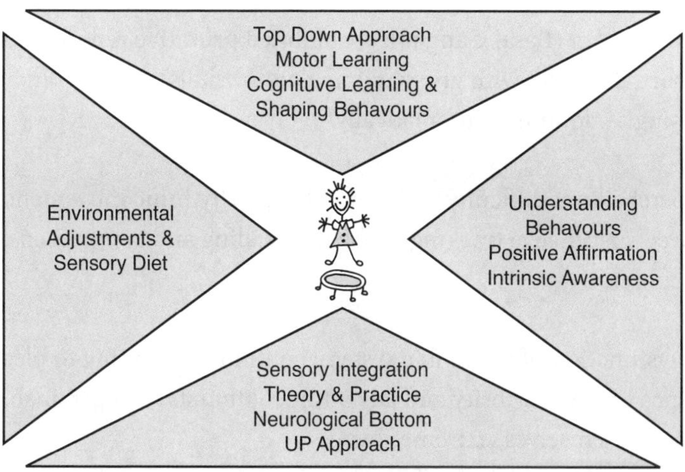

Developmental Building Blocks

The Building Blocks diagram illustrates how the brain develops from brainstem (and cerebellum) at the bottom of the diagram through the midbrain (limbic system) to the frontal cortex at the top of the chart.

The base of the diagram (sensory processing) conveys the ability of a new born baby. This includes early primitive or survival reflexes and self regulation. The next stage of development is integrating the sensory system through movement and the cerebellum to promote impulse control. This involves the limbic system and the coordination of sensory input with emotion. Motor attention and sequenced movement with bilateral coordination and perceptual skills are in the next stage of development. All of this then accumulates in higher order cognitive skills including executive functioning, organisational skills, emotional regulation and academic achievement seen in children by about the age of 6.

Signs of Dysfunction in these Areas

Brain stem (Basal Ganglia): uninhibited primitive reflexes, dislike of sport, difficulty with gross and fine motor skills, difficulty in learning to do things automatically.

Cerebellum: difficulty with smooth easy rhythmic movements, delayed speech, eye tracking problems, reading and comprehension difficulties.

Dysfunction of the limbic system: continually wanting to please, absence of play curiosity and adventure, outbursts of anger, inability to assert themselves, extreme shyness.

Only when the neural connections are sufficiently developed between the limbic and prefrontal cortex are we able to integrate information about external events with our inner emotions, drives, experiences and memories and react appropriately, coordinating thoughts and feelings.

The integration of the cerebellum promotes the linking up of the different areas of the brain and ultimately makes connections between doing and thinking.

Where there is difficulty with higher order cognitive skills, any identified problems must be consequential to poor integration at lower levels of development and specifically to the integration of the primitive reflexes. For example, difficulty organising and sequencing must be traced back to sensory motor difficulties and a difficulty between thinking and doing.

Approaches to Treatment

When a child presents with a specific problem, such as poor handwriting or an inability to tie shoelaces, the therapist/teacher has a choice regarding the approaches used for intervention. The Top Down approach illustrated at the top of the picture is based on motor learning and having the child practise the deficient skill, thereby dealing with the presenting problem and not the cause. A Bottom Up approach views the child holistically and sources the root of the problem. This is a neurological approach which explores the early stages of development, including integration and emergence of the reflexes and bilateral skill development.

In both approaches, environmental considerations and positive affirmation of the child are fundamental to positive outcomes.